The
Chameleon Chronicles

by
Ronald E. Grant

Illuminated by Luba Mittelman

AuthorHouse™
1663 Liberty Drive
Bloomington, IN 47403
www.authorhouse.com
Phone: 1-800-839-8640

Published by AuthorHouse 03/04/2013

ISBN: 978-1-4817-0105-1 (sc)
978-1-4817-0104-4 (e)

Library of Congress Control Number: 2012924094

Any people depicted in stock imagery provided by Thinkstock are models,
and such images are being used for illustrative purposes only.
Certain stock imagery © Thinkstock.

This book is printed on acid-free paper.

authorHOUSE®

The Text of the Fool

To be precise,
Only a fool

Precipitates a revolution, then—
Leaves,
Aware only of his dreams,
Yesterday's and Tomorrow's, is all he lives.

The wand he handles
He's forgotten how to use.
Empty bag filled with magic

Forsaken or abused.
Ordinary men can't understand him
Only the Sun can justify his existence,
Lurking in his shadow

Freely guiding the Way and
Indulging his apparent stupidity.
Not even kings dare attack the fool—
Defiance only makes you appear foolish.

And what if all the cow-people choose his way,

Free as he is to become the knight?
Rose, colored white, held in hand,
Invites Death for any other man.
Even as he speaks
No one really cares.
Drifting from dream to dream,

Sagas of the undreamt of
Hush the audience but heap contempt upon him.
Are you real? one asks.
Reality, he replies is merely the natural
Evolutionary process of a dream.

Youth is the dream
Old age the reality,
Unless you celebrate the
Reality of the aged's new dream.

Help one another, have compassion,
Evoke love and turn away from fear forever.
All of these are the law of the Fool.
Reach out—
Touch the children,
Share your dreams,

And make them become reality.
No one knows, but no one
Dares to admit it.

They will raise Temples to him
Heralding his reality,
Even though they understand and live—
Nothing.

See how foolishly he wears his hair?
Ever see such gaudy clothes?
Even his mother must be ashamed.

If only they'd open their eyes.
Fools today are tomorrow's decadent Order.

Year after year,
Order
Upset by

Chaos,
And then, Chaos becomes the Order.
No one can find the Fool in himself, for

Fools hide in our spirit,
Independent of ourselves,
Nearly never evident.
Drugged by the opiate of the Order

Having to maintain itself. The Fool
Initiates instinctively—
Mobilizes,

And rises to power behind the scenes.
God, they say, protects drunks and Fools—
Are you protected, Am

I?
No one but the Fool knows what there is to know.

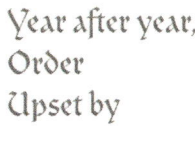

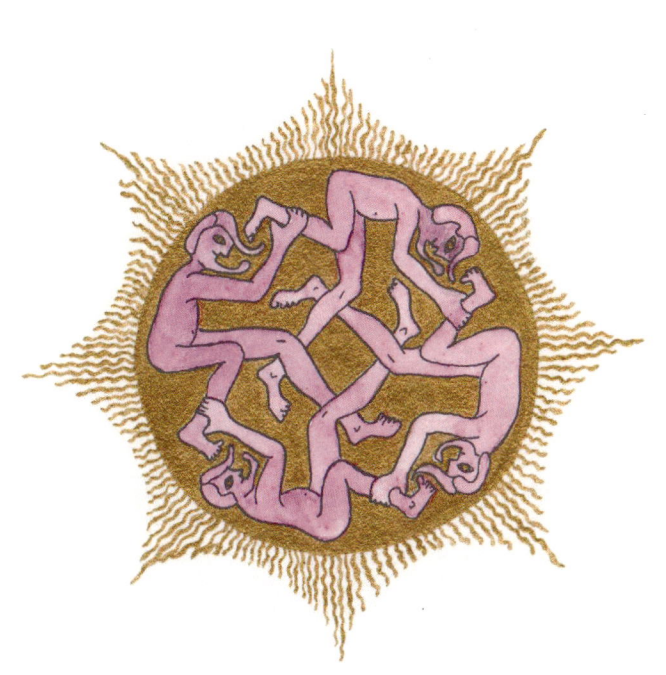

0. Revelations

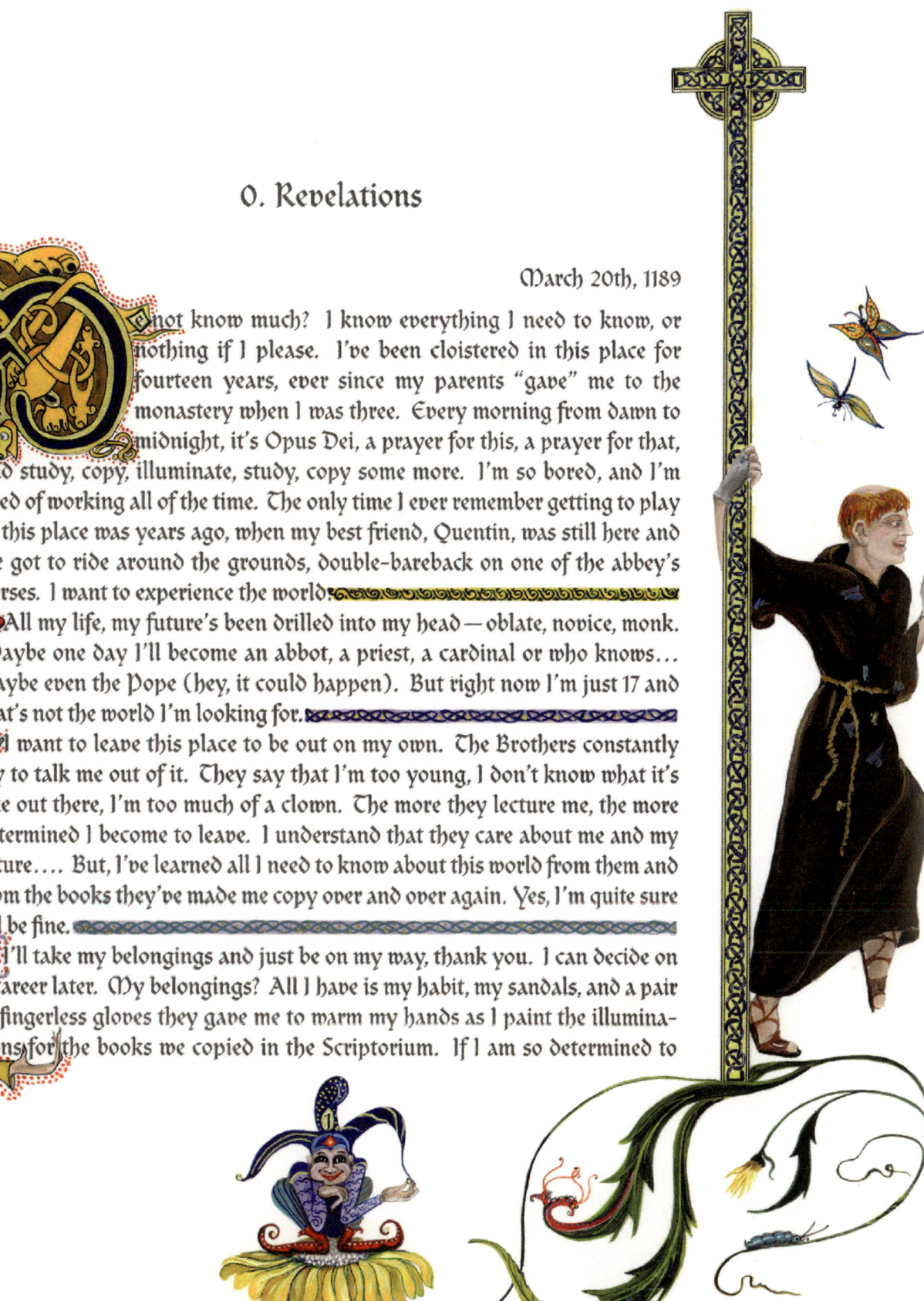

March 20th, 1189

not know much? I know everything I need to know, or
nothing if I please. I've been cloistered in this place for
fourteen years, ever since my parents "gave" me to the
monastery when I was three. Every morning from dawn to
midnight, it's Opus Dei, a prayer for this, a prayer for that,
and study, copy, illuminate, study, copy some more. I'm so bored, and I'm
tired of working all of the time. The only time I ever remember getting to play
in this place was years ago, when my best friend, Quentin, was still here and
we got to ride around the grounds, double-bareback on one of the abbey's
horses. I want to experience the world.

All my life, my future's been drilled into my head — oblate, novice, monk.
Maybe one day I'll become an abbot, a priest, a cardinal or who knows…
maybe even the Pope (hey, it could happen). But right now I'm just 17 and
that's not the world I'm looking for.

I want to leave this place to be out on my own. The Brothers constantly
try to talk me out of it. They say that I'm too young, I don't know what it's
like out there, I'm too much of a clown. The more they lecture me, the more
determined I become to leave. I understand that they care about me and my
future…. But, I've learned all I need to know about this world from them and
from the books they've made me copy over and over again. Yes, I'm quite sure
I'll be fine.

I'll take my belongings and just be on my way, thank you. I can decide on
a career later. My belongings? All I have is my habit, my sandals, and a pair
of fingerless gloves they gave me to warm my hands as I paint the illumina-
tions for the books we copied in the Scriptorium. If I am so determined to

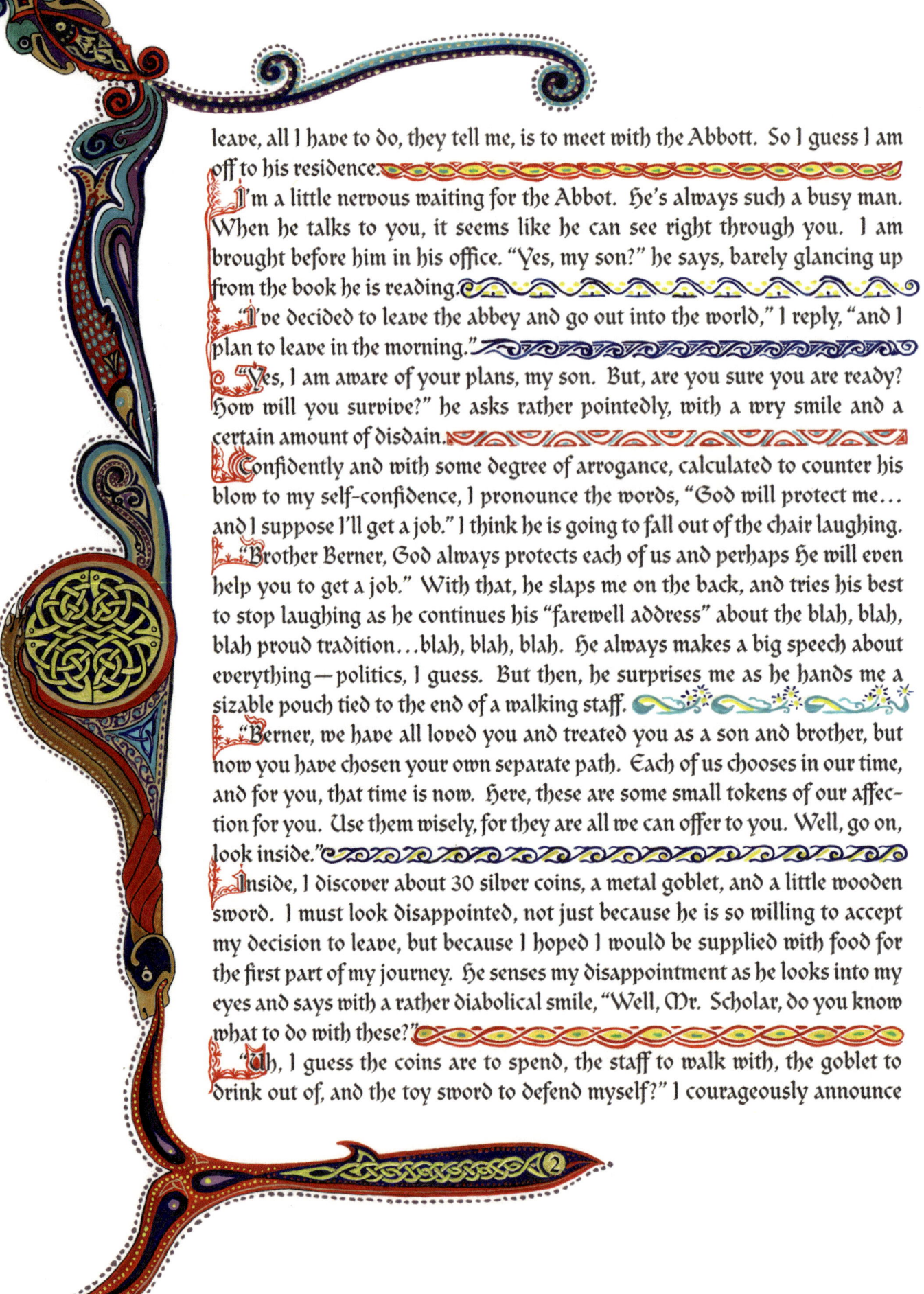

leave, all I have to do, they tell me, is to meet with the Abbott. So I guess I am off to his residence.

I'm a little nervous waiting for the Abbot. He's always such a busy man. When he talks to you, it seems like he can see right through you. I am brought before him in his office. "Yes, my son?" he says, barely glancing up from the book he is reading.

"I've decided to leave the abbey and go out into the world," I reply, "and I plan to leave in the morning."

"Yes, I am aware of your plans, my son. But, are you sure you are ready? How will you survive?" he asks rather pointedly, with a wry smile and a certain amount of disdain.

Confidently and with some degree of arrogance, calculated to counter his blow to my self-confidence, I pronounce the words, "God will protect me… and I suppose I'll get a job." I think he is going to fall out of the chair laughing.

"Brother Berner, God always protects each of us and perhaps He will even help you to get a job." With that, he slaps me on the back, and tries his best to stop laughing as he continues his "farewell address" about the blah, blah, blah proud tradition…blah, blah, blah. He always makes a big speech about everything—politics, I guess. But then, he surprises me as he hands me a sizable pouch tied to the end of a walking staff.

"Berner, we have all loved you and treated you as a son and brother, but now you have chosen your own separate path. Each of us chooses in our time, and for you, that time is now. Here, these are some small tokens of our affection for you. Use them wisely, for they are all we can offer to you. Well, go on, look inside."

Inside, I discover about 30 silver coins, a metal goblet, and a little wooden sword. I must look disappointed, not just because he is so willing to accept my decision to leave, but because I hoped I would be supplied with food for the first part of my journey. He senses my disappointment as he looks into my eyes and says with a rather diabolical smile, "Well, Mr. Scholar, do you know what to do with these?"

"Oh, I guess the coins are to spend, the staff to walk with, the goblet to drink out of, and the toy sword to defend myself?" I courageously announce with that certain braggadocio in my voice I always have when I have no idea what I am talking about. Recognizing my lack of self-assurance, he chuckles as though he knows my every thought.

"Some day, Berner, you may understand, but for now, it is enough that you protect them, for they are all necessary in your new world. The staff was carved from a branch of the very thorn tree grown from the staff of Joseph of Arimathea nearly 1,200 years ago. Walk proudly with it as you go through life, and go with God. Here is a letter of introduction addressed to any other Benedictines you should meet, who will assist you as they can. Hopefully, you will return to us someday to share what you learn. But before you leave, I ask two small favors."

He walks me to a large window and looks outside. "Do you see the rose-bush there?" pointing toward the entrance to the Lady Chapel. I nod. "Next to it is a young sapling which I ask that you plant, a tree of remembrance. The tree will be a symbol of your time here with us. We will honor your memory with it—we will pray for you each time we pass by it. Dig the hole deeply enough, else it will not survive. Dig it too deeply and it will be swallowed up by the earth. Second, please keep a journal of your experiences to share with us should you ever return." With that, he ushers me out of his chamber and into the yard.

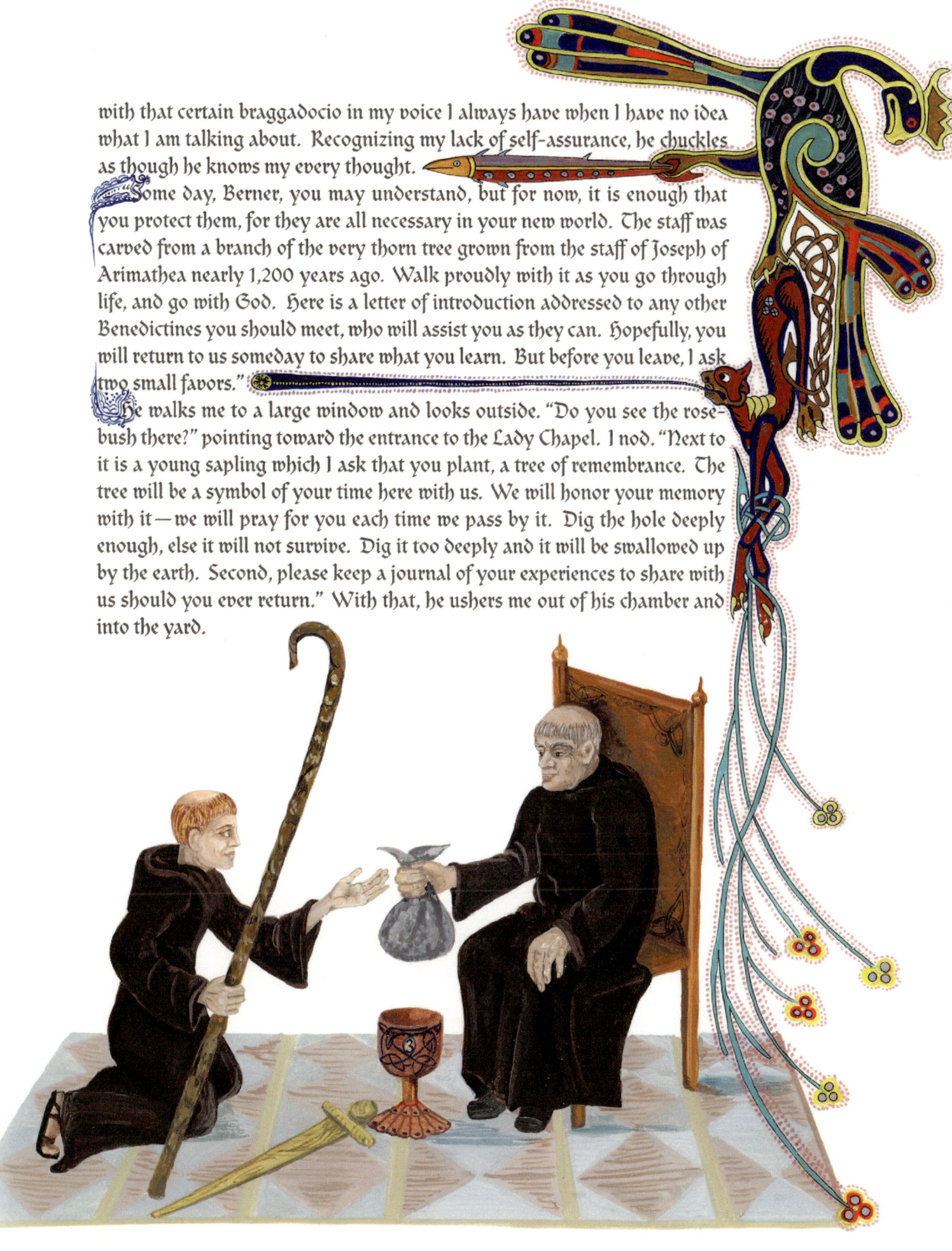

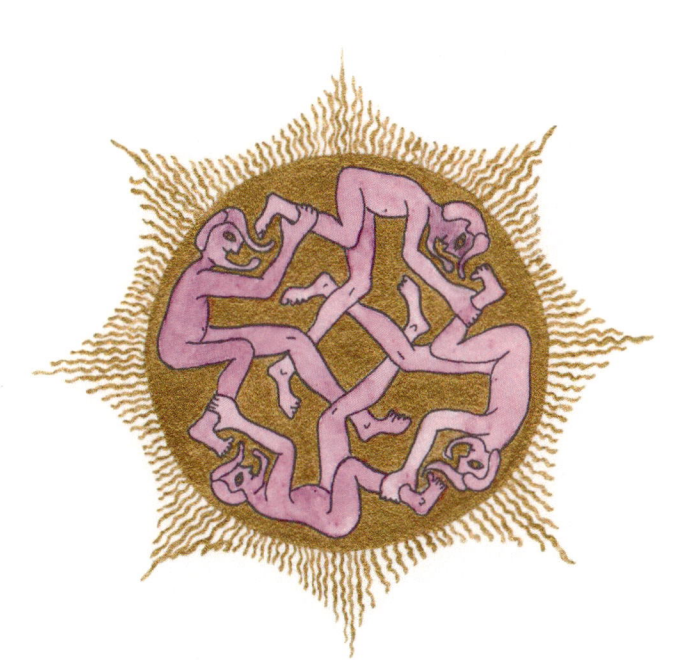

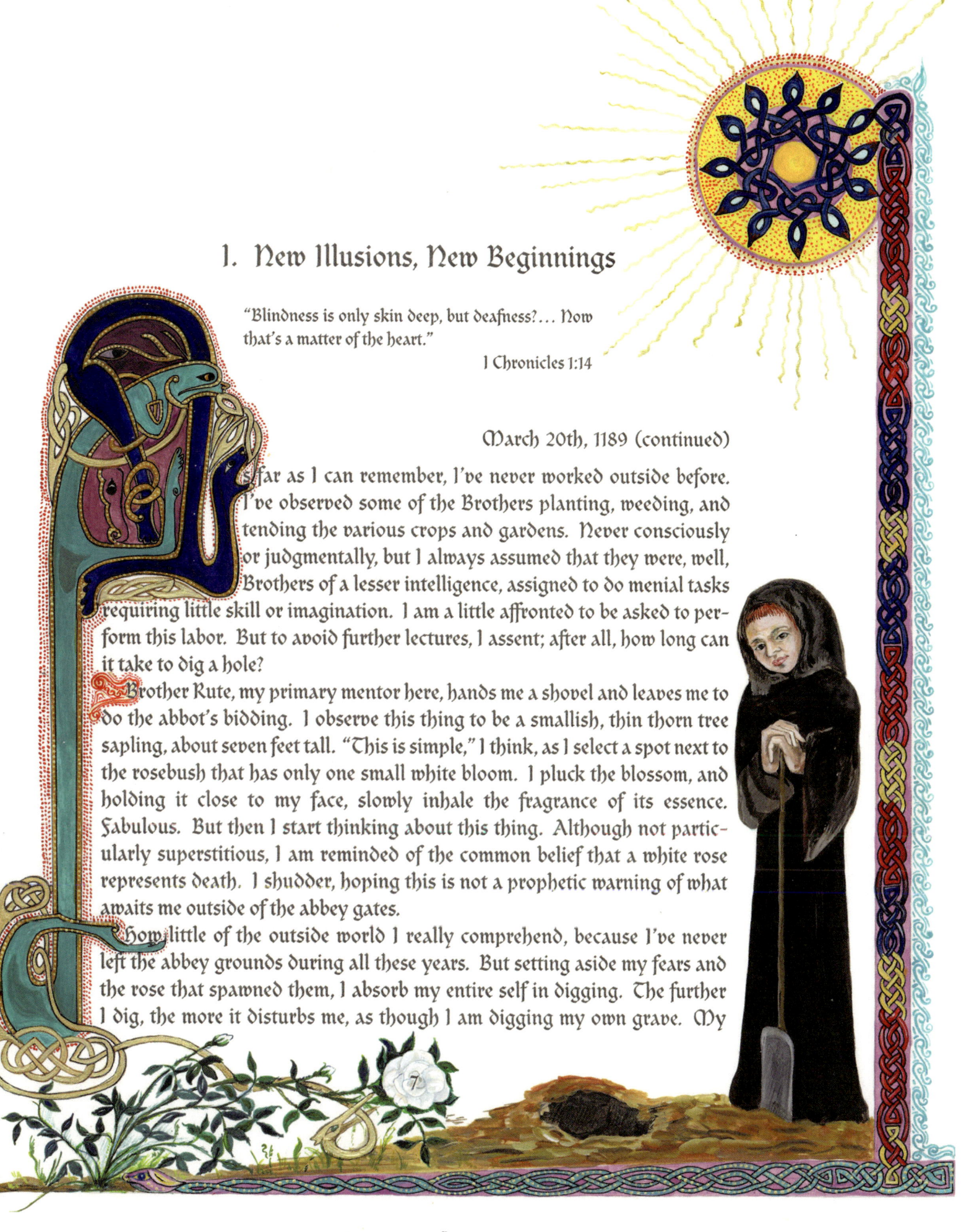

1. New Illusions, New Beginnings

"Blindness is only skin deep, but deafness?… Now that's a matter of the heart."

1 Chronicles 1:14

March 20th, 1189 (continued)

As far as I can remember, I've never worked outside before. I've observed some of the Brothers planting, weeding, and tending the various crops and gardens. Never consciously or judgmentally, but I always assumed that they were, well, Brothers of a lesser intelligence, assigned to do menial tasks requiring little skill or imagination. I am a little affronted to be asked to perform this labor. But to avoid further lectures, I assent; after all, how long can it take to dig a hole?

Brother Rute, my primary mentor here, hands me a shovel and leaves me to do the abbot's bidding. I observe this thing to be a smallish, thin thorn tree sapling, about seven feet tall. "This is simple," I think, as I select a spot next to the rosebush that has only one small white bloom. I pluck the blossom, and holding it close to my face, slowly inhale the fragrance of its essence. Fabulous. But then I start thinking about this thing. Although not particularly superstitious, I am reminded of the common belief that a white rose represents death. I shudder, hoping this is not a prophetic warning of what awaits me outside of the abbey gates.

How little of the outside world I really comprehend, because I've never left the abbey grounds during all these years. But setting aside my fears and the rose that spawned them, I absorb my entire self in digging. The further I dig, the more it disturbs me, as though I am digging my own grave. My

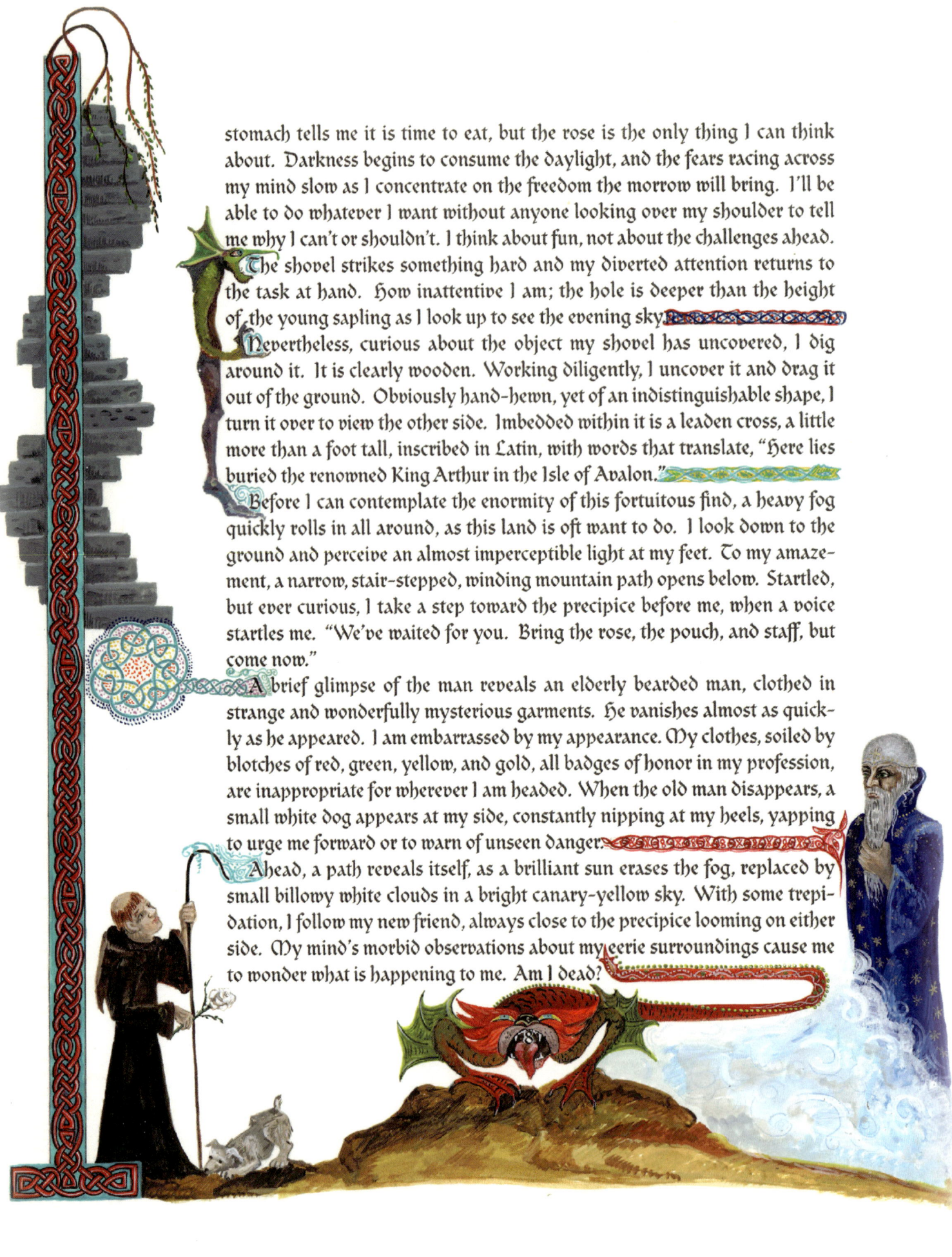

stomach tells me it is time to eat, but the rose is the only thing I can think about. Darkness begins to consume the daylight, and the fears racing across my mind slow as I concentrate on the freedom the morrow will bring. I'll be able to do whatever I want without anyone looking over my shoulder to tell me why I can't or shouldn't. I think about fun, not about the challenges ahead.

The shovel strikes something hard and my diverted attention returns to the task at hand. How inattentive I am; the hole is deeper than the height of the young sapling as I look up to see the evening sky.

Nevertheless, curious about the object my shovel has uncovered, I dig around it. It is clearly wooden. Working diligently, I uncover it and drag it out of the ground. Obviously hand-hewn, yet of an indistinguishable shape, I turn it over to view the other side. Imbedded within it is a leaden cross, a little more than a foot tall, inscribed in Latin, with words that translate, "Here lies buried the renowned King Arthur in the Isle of Avalon."

Before I can contemplate the enormity of this fortuitous find, a heavy fog quickly rolls in all around, as this land is oft want to do. I look down to the ground and perceive an almost imperceptible light at my feet. To my amazement, a narrow, stair-stepped, winding mountain path opens below. Startled, but ever curious, I take a step toward the precipice before me, when a voice startles me. "We've waited for you. Bring the rose, the pouch, and staff, but come now."

A brief glimpse of the man reveals an elderly bearded man, clothed in strange and wonderfully mysterious garments. He vanishes almost as quickly as he appeared. I am embarrassed by my appearance. My clothes, soiled by blotches of red, green, yellow, and gold, all badges of honor in my profession, are inappropriate for wherever I am headed. When the old man disappears, a small white dog appears at my side, constantly nipping at my heels, yapping to urge me forward or to warn of unseen danger.

Ahead, a path reveals itself, as a brilliant sun erases the fog, replaced by small billowy white clouds in a bright canary-yellow sky. With some trepidation, I follow my new friend, always close to the precipice looming on either side. My mind's morbid observations about my eerie surroundings cause me to wonder what is happening to me. Am I dead?

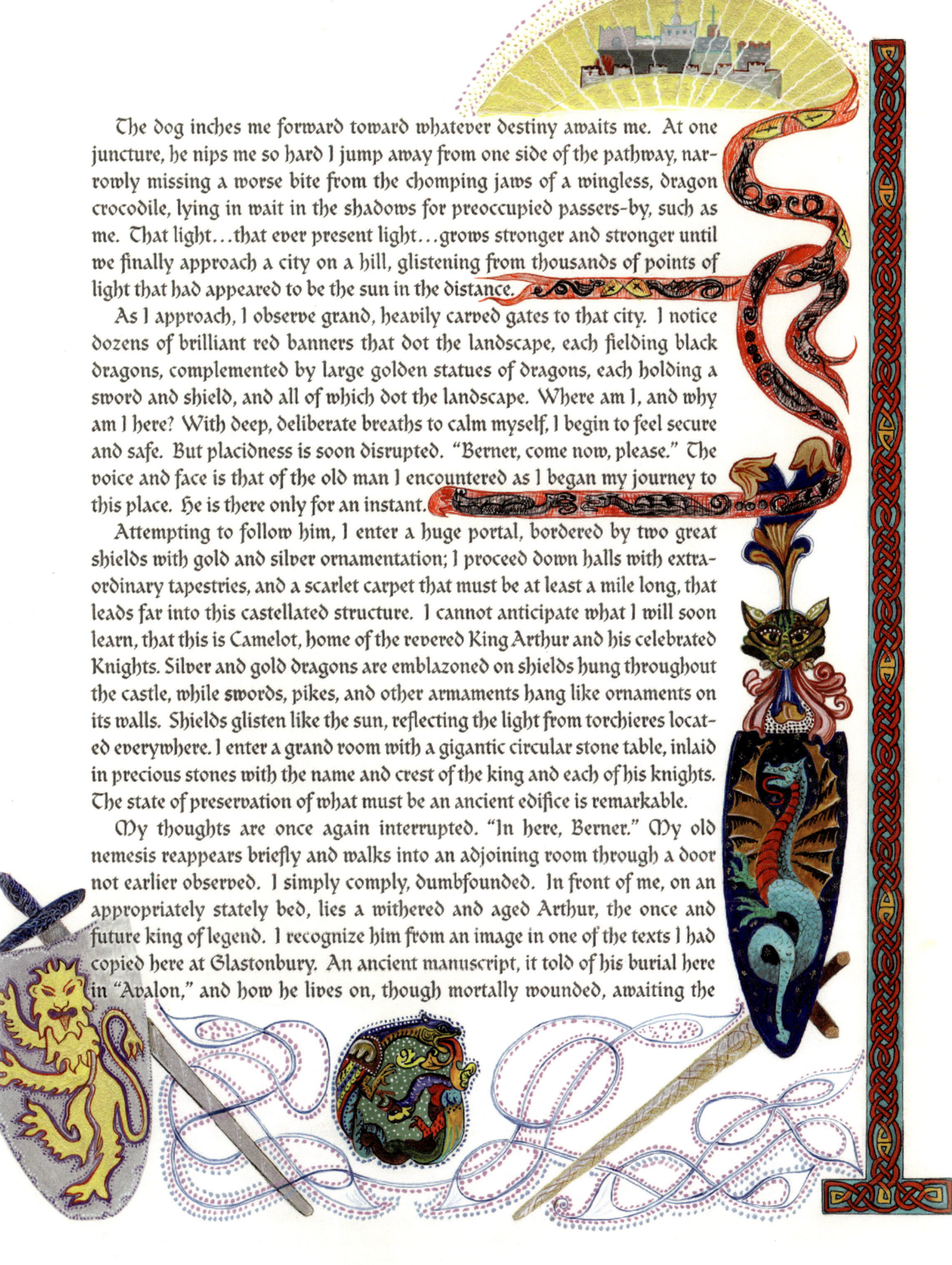

The dog inches me forward toward whatever destiny awaits me. At one juncture, he nips me so hard I jump away from one side of the pathway, narrowly missing a worse bite from the chomping jaws of a wingless, dragon crocodile, lying in wait in the shadows for preoccupied passers-by, such as me. That light…that ever present light…grows stronger and stronger until we finally approach a city on a hill, glistening from thousands of points of light that had appeared to be the sun in the distance.

As I approach, I observe grand, heavily carved gates to that city. I notice dozens of brilliant red banners that dot the landscape, each fielding black dragons, complemented by large golden statues of dragons, each holding a sword and shield, and all of which dot the landscape. Where am I, and why am I here? With deep, deliberate breaths to calm myself, I begin to feel secure and safe. But placidness is soon disrupted. "Berner, come now, please." The voice and face is that of the old man I encountered as I began my journey to this place. He is there only for an instant.

Attempting to follow him, I enter a huge portal, bordered by two great shields with gold and silver ornamentation; I proceed down halls with extraordinary tapestries, and a scarlet carpet that must be at least a mile long, that leads far into this castellated structure. I cannot anticipate what I will soon learn, that this is Camelot, home of the revered King Arthur and his celebrated Knights. Silver and gold dragons are emblazoned on shields hung throughout the castle, while swords, pikes, and other armaments hang like ornaments on its walls. Shields glisten like the sun, reflecting the light from torchieres located everywhere. I enter a grand room with a gigantic circular stone table, inlaid in precious stones with the name and crest of the king and each of his knights. The state of preservation of what must be an ancient edifice is remarkable.

My thoughts are once again interrupted. "In here, Berner." My old nemesis reappears briefly and walks into an adjoining room through a door not earlier observed. I simply comply, dumbfounded. In front of me, on an appropriately stately bed, lies a withered and aged Arthur, the once and future king of legend. I recognize him from an image in one of the texts I had copied here at Glastonbury. An ancient manuscript, it told of his burial here in "Avalon," and how he lives on, though mortally wounded, awaiting the

bearer of the San Graal, a chalice that once held the blood of our Lord and Savior. This "Holy Grail" is passage from this world to the next.

Always assuming his legend was nothing more than a child's tale, I am awestruck to stand in his presence. Arthur motions me closer. His voice is as weak as his body, yet the grace and peacefulness within the man is as obvious as the authority with which he speaks the words, "Find the Grail, for both of us." Though he did not say it, I know instinctively the "us" of whom he speaks refers not to his elegant wife, Guinevere, seated next to him, or the knights lined behind him, nor even the old man I've seen so many times since I began this descent, but rather to him and me.

Before I can even answer him, I am whisked out of the room and into what appears to be an alchemist's laboratory, and that elderly man I have seen so many times before stands in front of me. Dressed in a skullcap and decorous robe, each covered with the symbols of his mysteries, he looks as though he has traveled the four corners of the earth. Older, but obviously healthier than Arthur, his face is that of the legendary Green Man of the forest. Books of magic incantations line his walls, and pungent boiling liquids fill the air with smoke and a dirty, moldy scent of musk that is no delight to the senses.

He looks at me intently for a long period of time before speaking. With a deep sigh, he begins, "Berner, all things change; it's Nature's law. You, Camelot, Arthur, even I must all play out our changing roles in this physical world. Until today, you have been an innocent child. Put away those childish things and concentrate on whom you must become today. Arthur made a request which, if accomplished, will allow him and the rest of us to return to our individual destinies as we inevitably must. Presently, we are restrained here in the body of the dragon, due to the injuries sustained by Arthur in battle with his son many, many years ago. We have waited so long. Perhaps you will succeed where others have failed."

Normally, I would simply laugh at the old man and go about my business, as I always look out for myself and my problems, not worrying about helping others (I know what you're thinking—that is not the way a monk to be is supposed to act—but I never claimed I wanted to be a monk, did I?). Without understanding why, I agree; after all, I am looking for adventure, a way out of

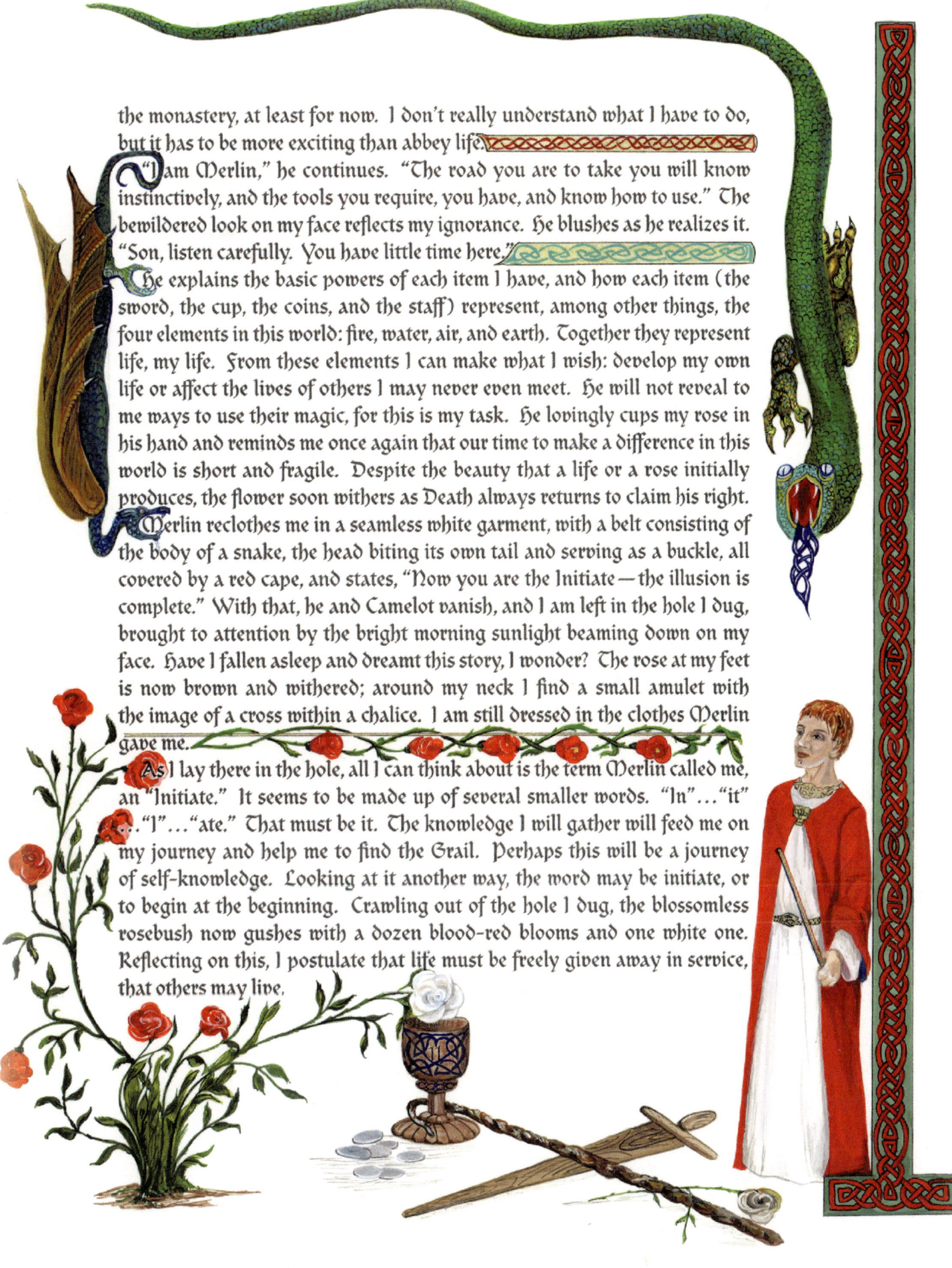

the monastery, at least for now. I don't really understand what I have to do, but it has to be more exciting than abbey life.

"I am Merlin," he continues. "The road you are to take you will know instinctively, and the tools you require, you have, and know how to use." The bewildered look on my face reflects my ignorance. He blushes as he realizes it. "Son, listen carefully. You have little time here."

He explains the basic powers of each item I have, and how each item (the sword, the cup, the coins, and the staff) represent, among other things, the four elements in this world: fire, water, air, and earth. Together they represent life, my life. From these elements I can make what I wish: develop my own life or affect the lives of others I may never even meet. He will not reveal to me ways to use their magic, for this is my task. He lovingly cups my rose in his hand and reminds me once again that our time to make a difference in this world is short and fragile. Despite the beauty that a life or a rose initially produces, the flower soon withers as Death always returns to claim his right.

Merlin reclothes me in a seamless white garment, with a belt consisting of the body of a snake, the head biting its own tail and serving as a buckle, all covered by a red cape, and states, "Now you are the Initiate—the illusion is complete." With that, he and Camelot vanish, and I am left in the hole I dug, brought to attention by the bright morning sunlight beaming down on my face. Have I fallen asleep and dreamt this story, I wonder? The rose at my feet is now brown and withered; around my neck I find a small amulet with the image of a cross within a chalice. I am still dressed in the clothes Merlin gave me.

As I lay there in the hole, all I can think about is the term Merlin called me, an "Initiate." It seems to be made up of several smaller words. "In"…"it" …"I"…"ate." That must be it. The knowledge I will gather will feed me on my journey and help me to find the Grail. Perhaps this will be a journey of self-knowledge. Looking at it another way, the word may be initiate, or to begin at the beginning. Crawling out of the hole I dug, the blossomless rosebush now gushes with a dozen blood-red blooms and one white one. Reflecting on this, I postulate that life must be freely given away in service, that others may live.

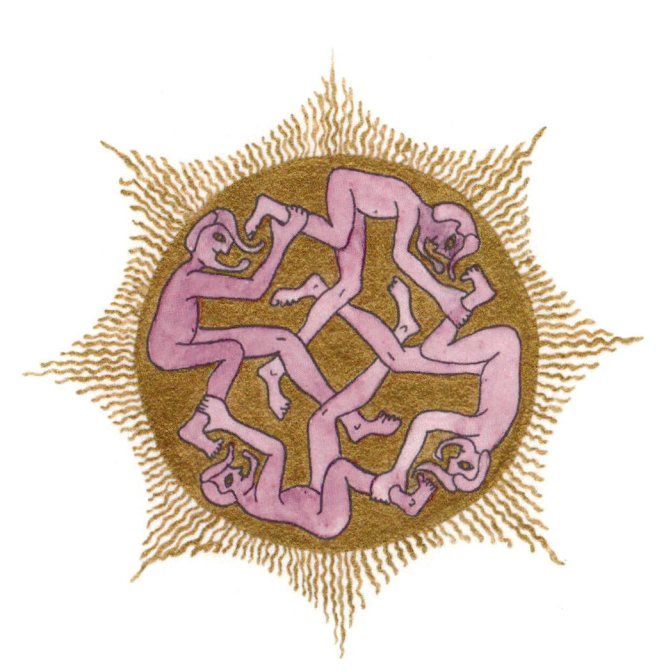

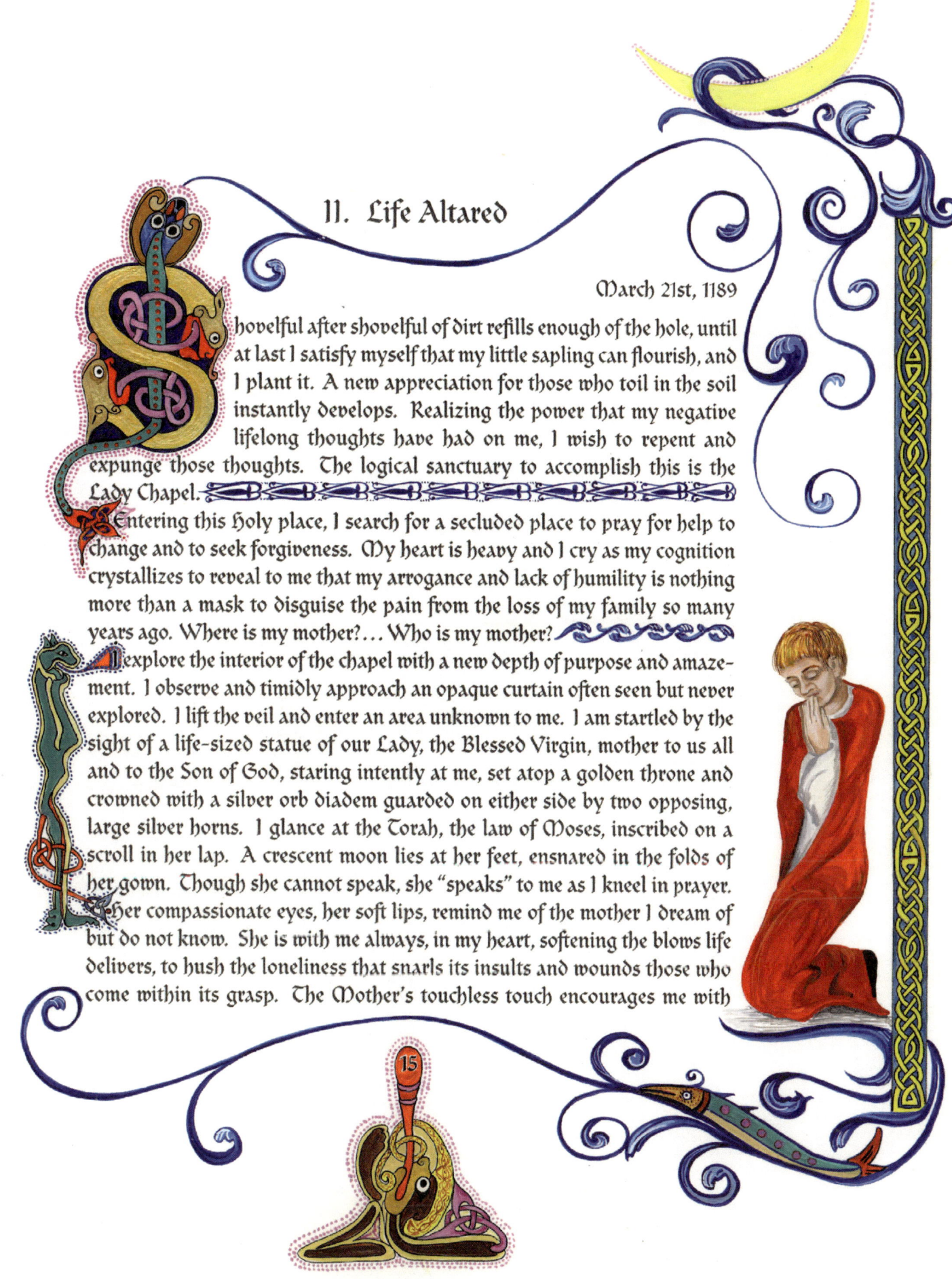

11. Life Altared

March 21st, 1189

Shovelful after shovelful of dirt refills enough of the hole, until at last I satisfy myself that my little sapling can flourish, and I plant it. A new appreciation for those who toil in the soil instantly develops. Realizing the power that my negative lifelong thoughts have had on me, I wish to repent and expunge those thoughts. The logical sanctuary to accomplish this is the Lady Chapel.

Entering this holy place, I search for a secluded place to pray for help to change and to seek forgiveness. My heart is heavy and I cry as my cognition crystallizes to reveal to me that my arrogance and lack of humility is nothing more than a mask to disguise the pain from the loss of my family so many years ago. Where is my mother?... Who is my mother?

I explore the interior of the chapel with a new depth of purpose and amazement. I observe and timidly approach an opaque curtain often seen but never explored. I lift the veil and enter an area unknown to me. I am startled by the sight of a life-sized statue of our Lady, the Blessed Virgin, mother to us all and to the Son of God, staring intently at me, set atop a golden throne and crowned with a silver orb diadem guarded on either side by two opposing, large silver horns. I glance at the Torah, the law of Moses, inscribed on a scroll in her lap. A crescent moon lies at her feet, ensnared in the folds of her gown. Though she cannot speak, she "speaks" to me as I kneel in prayer. Her compassionate eyes, her soft lips, remind me of the mother I dream of but do not know. She is with me always, in my heart, softening the blows life delivers, to hush the loneliness that snarls its insults and wounds those who come within its grasp. The Mother's touchless touch encourages me with

15

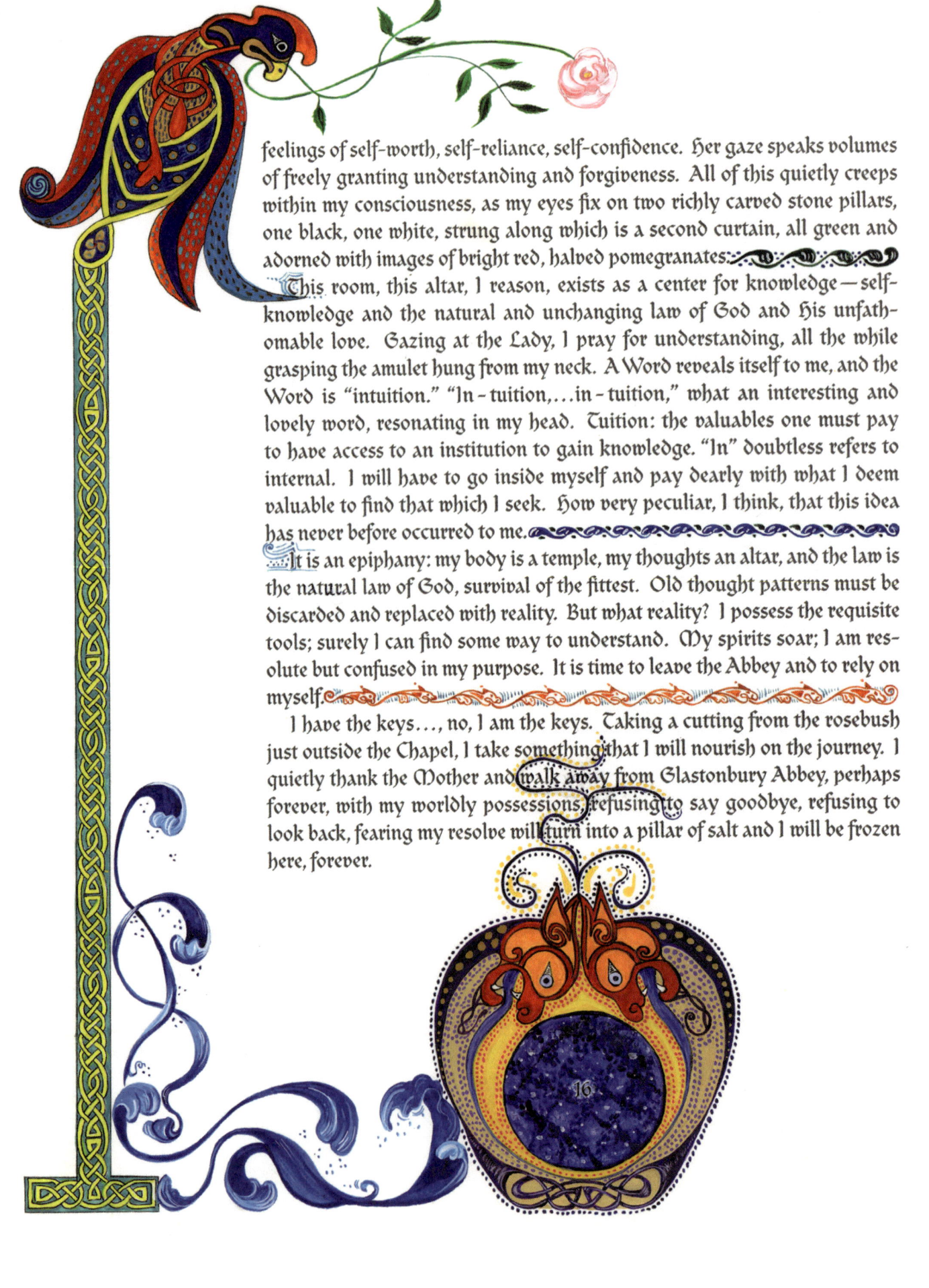

feelings of self-worth, self-reliance, self-confidence. Her gaze speaks volumes of freely granting understanding and forgiveness. All of this quietly creeps within my consciousness, as my eyes fix on two richly carved stone pillars, one black, one white, strung along which is a second curtain, all green and adorned with images of bright red, halved pomegranates.

This room, this altar, I reason, exists as a center for knowledge—self-knowledge and the natural and unchanging law of God and His unfathomable love. Gazing at the Lady, I pray for understanding, all the while grasping the amulet hung from my neck. A Word reveals itself to me, and the Word is "intuition." "In-tuition,…in-tuition," what an interesting and lovely word, resonating in my head. Tuition: the valuables one must pay to have access to an institution to gain knowledge. "In" doubtless refers to internal. I will have to go inside myself and pay dearly with what I deem valuable to find that which I seek. How very peculiar, I think, that this idea has never before occurred to me.

It is an epiphany: my body is a temple, my thoughts an altar, and the law is the natural law of God, survival of the fittest. Old thought patterns must be discarded and replaced with reality. But what reality? I possess the requisite tools; surely I can find some way to understand. My spirits soar; I am resolute but confused in my purpose. It is time to leave the Abbey and to rely on myself.

I have the keys…, no, I am the keys. Taking a cutting from the rosebush just outside the Chapel, I take something that I will nourish on the journey. I quietly thank the Mother and walk away from Glastonbury Abbey, perhaps forever, with my worldly possessions, refusing to say goodbye, refusing to look back, fearing my resolve will turn into a pillar of salt and I will be frozen here, forever.

16

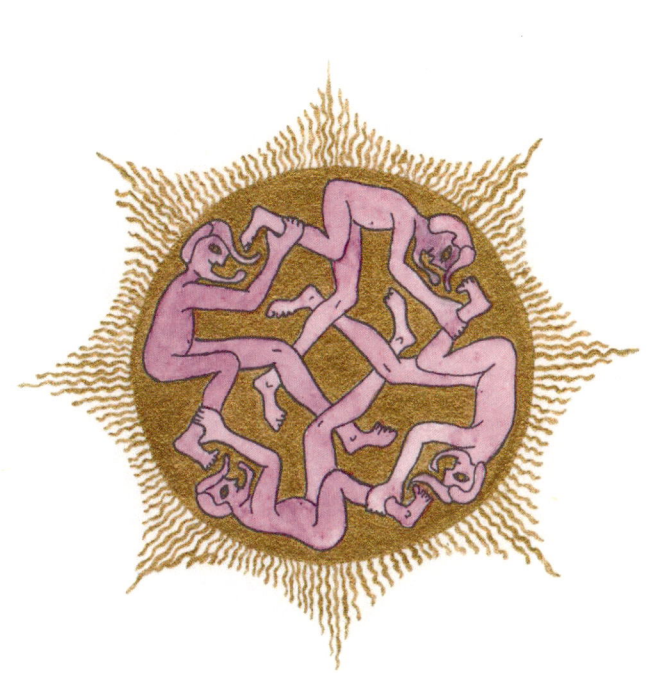

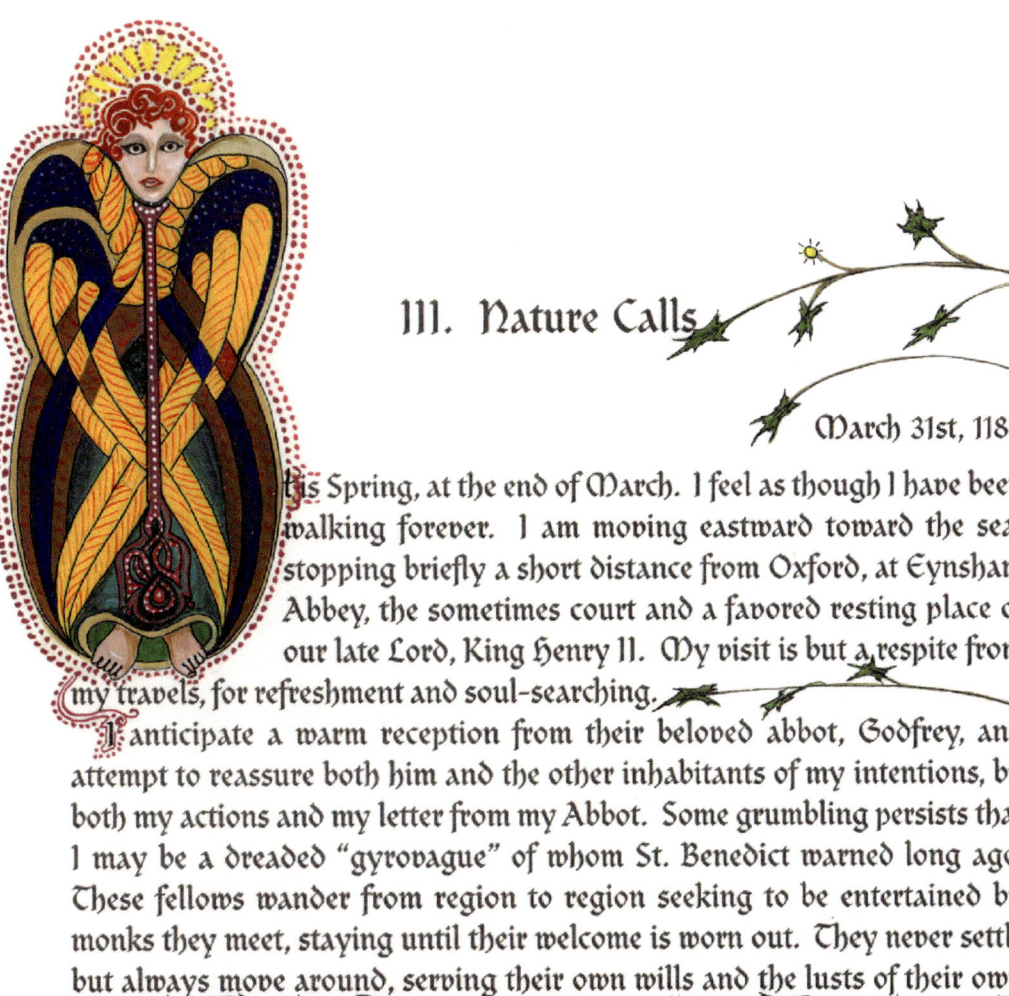

III. Nature Calls

March 31st, 1189

Tis Spring, at the end of March. I feel as though I have been walking forever. I am moving eastward toward the sea, stopping briefly a short distance from Oxford, at Eynsham Abbey, the sometimes court and a favored resting place of our late Lord, King Henry II. My visit is but a respite from my travels, for refreshment and soul-searching.

I anticipate a warm reception from their beloved abbot, Godfrey, and attempt to reassure both him and the other inhabitants of my intentions, by both my actions and my letter from my Abbot. Some grumbling persists that I may be a dreaded "gyrovague" of whom St. Benedict warned long ago. These fellows wander from region to region seeking to be entertained by monks they meet, staying until their welcome is worn out. They never settle but always move around, serving their own wills and the lusts of their own bellies.

My explanation that I am on my way somewhere unknown, to find something I know nothing about, and have absolutely no way to identify, does not enhance my stature here. They are busy enlarging structures dedicated to the glory of God, and I am at the least, a distraction. I bid them peace and set out again, to find my way to God only knows where.

April 1st, 1189

The forests and fields reverberate with rich colors. Surrounded by radiant flora of every conceivable variety, each with an intoxicating fragrance that overwhelms my nose as I plod toward Canterbury. Content to enjoy the warmth of the Sun and the beauty God provided, my thoughts are basically an empty set. An army of flowers and trees covers this Cotswold forest and seem to march in lock step on either side of me. Life is so beautiful and good. The feast that consumes my senses is interrupted when my eyes are assaulted by the most radiantly beautiful damsel I have ever seen. Clothed in robes heavily embroidered with vivid images of the forest flowers and a diadem topped with stars from the heavens, this angel sits regally ensconced on a bench crafted from the branches of a gnarled and ancient oak. She smiles impishly as I move toward her. I am beguiled by her countenance and I know instantly that I am in love. This must be the forbidden love I've never known. I can think of nothing else. I am sick. An ethereal, eternal mystery, she permits me to kneel near her. She is my Empress, she is my goddess, she is my heart's sole desire.

We smile, communing only with our eyes. In my mind, I call her "Terra," for she is the woman with whom I want to spend my life. She is perfection. Hours and days pass and it seems as though we have always known one another. Is she my mother? Is she my sister? Is she a hidden part of me? This radiant being of mercy so completes me; her smiles pierce my heart. I sit with her on her bench, perhaps forever.

Questions of life and death that have always seemed so simple, so black and white, now take on a new and more profound meaning and I see a reason for life beyond mere existence. I will serve her beauty and kindness forever, for she is the soul of every living thing around me. But even as she reveals herself to me, she begins to change. The grass surrounding us changes as well, suffering patches of brown from the heat. She is feverish and somehow older now, much older than me. But this does not disturb me, for I have never known any woman on any level.

I am content, but as I become comfortable, she begins to change once again. She is aging rapidly and her temperature begins to fall. She appears weaker and somewhat sadder as she stares intently into my eyes. Many of the flowers that seemed so vibrant now fade and the leaves of the trees turn red and gold. The image of a split pomegranate returns to me, and in my innocence I run around the fields seeking what I believe will cure her, only to return to a very old woman, shivering in the cold. Like her, the flowers and grasses

shrivel and die as trees are denuded, their golden leaves turning brown and falling, returning to Mother Earth to be buried in the forest floor.

Though not a word passes between us, she promises to return to me someday before long, as a young and innocent flower. She begs me not to be sad or bitter, for she is Nature and she reminds me that the great Wheel of Life turns and the Winter of life is always followed by the Spring. She is the naturally occurring cycle of seasons, part of the Universal Law. Tears fall from my face to the ground like drops of rain. She withers, her body turns to dead and decaying leaves and then to dust, slowly fading from my sight. Ashes to ashes, dust to dust.

Profound sadness overwhelms me. I am insecure, alone again. Hmmm… "insecure"—internally secure—in myself? "Is this a lesson too?" I wonder aloud. If so, it is an excruciatingly bitter one. Grief and shock keep me from wondering too long. I cannot speak again until I reach the Cathedral at Canterbury, a pilgrimage for many, a place of refuge for those who ache inside. The Brothers of this temple empathize, counsel me, and leave me alone to contemplate and learn what I must from this experience.

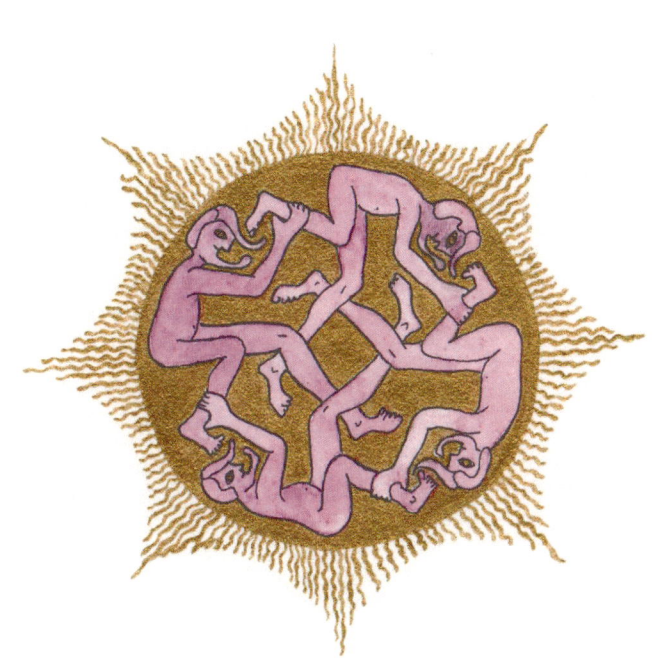

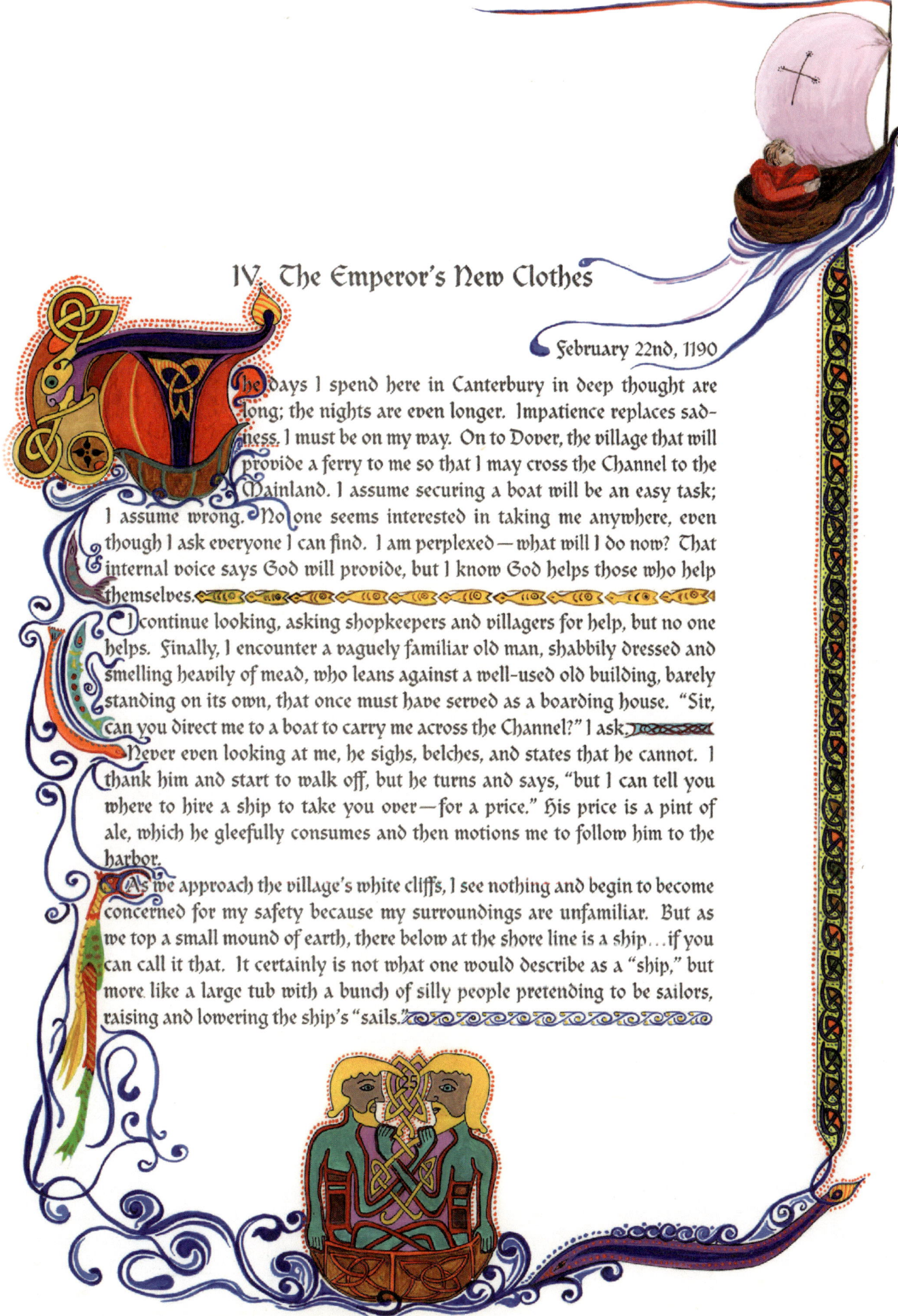

IV. The Emperor's New Clothes

February 22nd, 1190

The days I spend here in Canterbury in deep thought are long; the nights are even longer. Impatience replaces sadness. I must be on my way. On to Dover, the village that will provide a ferry to me so that I may cross the Channel to the Mainland. I assume securing a boat will be an easy task; I assume wrong. No one seems interested in taking me anywhere, even though I ask everyone I can find. I am perplexed—what will I do now? That internal voice says God will provide, but I know God helps those who help themselves.

I continue looking, asking shopkeepers and villagers for help, but no one helps. Finally, I encounter a vaguely familiar old man, shabbily dressed and smelling heavily of mead, who leans against a well-used old building, barely standing on its own, that once must have served as a boarding house. "Sir, can you direct me to a boat to carry me across the Channel?" I ask.

Never even looking at me, he sighs, belches, and states that he cannot. I thank him and start to walk off, but he turns and says, "but I can tell you where to hire a ship to take you over—for a price." His price is a pint of ale, which he gleefully consumes and then motions me to follow him to the harbor.

As we approach the village's white cliffs, I see nothing and begin to become concerned for my safety because my surroundings are unfamiliar. But as we top a small mound of earth, there below at the shore line is a ship…if you can call it that. It certainly is not what one would describe as a "ship," but more like a large tub with a bunch of silly people pretending to be sailors, raising and lowering the ship's "sails."

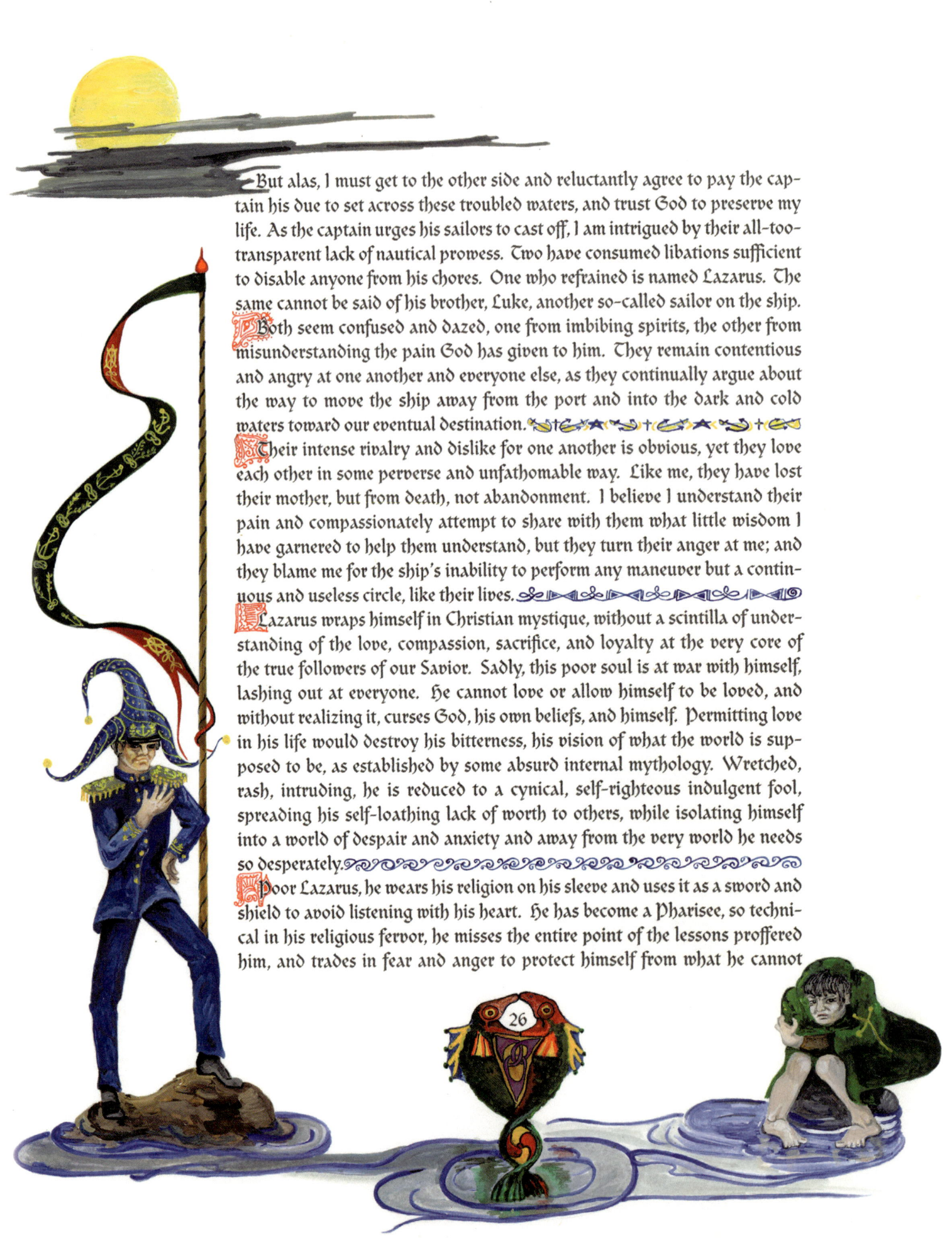

But alas, I must get to the other side and reluctantly agree to pay the captain his due to set across these troubled waters, and trust God to preserve my life. As the captain urges his sailors to cast off, I am intrigued by their all-too-transparent lack of nautical prowess. Two have consumed libations sufficient to disable anyone from his chores. One who refrained is named Lazarus. The same cannot be said of his brother, Luke, another so-called sailor on the ship. Both seem confused and dazed, one from imbibing spirits, the other from misunderstanding the pain God has given to him. They remain contentious and angry at one another and everyone else, as they continually argue about the way to move the ship away from the port and into the dark and cold waters toward our eventual destination.

Their intense rivalry and dislike for one another is obvious, yet they love each other in some perverse and unfathomable way. Like me, they have lost their mother, but from death, not abandonment. I believe I understand their pain and compassionately attempt to share with them what little wisdom I have garnered to help them understand, but they turn their anger at me; and they blame me for the ship's inability to perform any maneuver but a continuous and useless circle, like their lives.

Lazarus wraps himself in Christian mystique, without a scintilla of understanding of the love, compassion, sacrifice, and loyalty at the very core of the true followers of our Savior. Sadly, this poor soul is at war with himself, lashing out at everyone. He cannot love or allow himself to be loved, and without realizing it, curses God, his own beliefs, and himself. Permitting love in his life would destroy his bitterness, his vision of what the world is supposed to be, as established by some absurd internal mythology. Wretched, rash, intruding, he is reduced to a cynical, self-righteous indulgent fool, spreading his self-loathing lack of worth to others, while isolating himself into a world of despair and anxiety and away from the very world he needs so desperately.

Poor Lazarus, he wears his religion on his sleeve and uses it as a sword and shield to avoid listening with his heart. He has become a Pharisee, so technical in his religious fervor, he misses the entire point of the lessons proffered him, and trades in fear and anger to protect himself from what he cannot

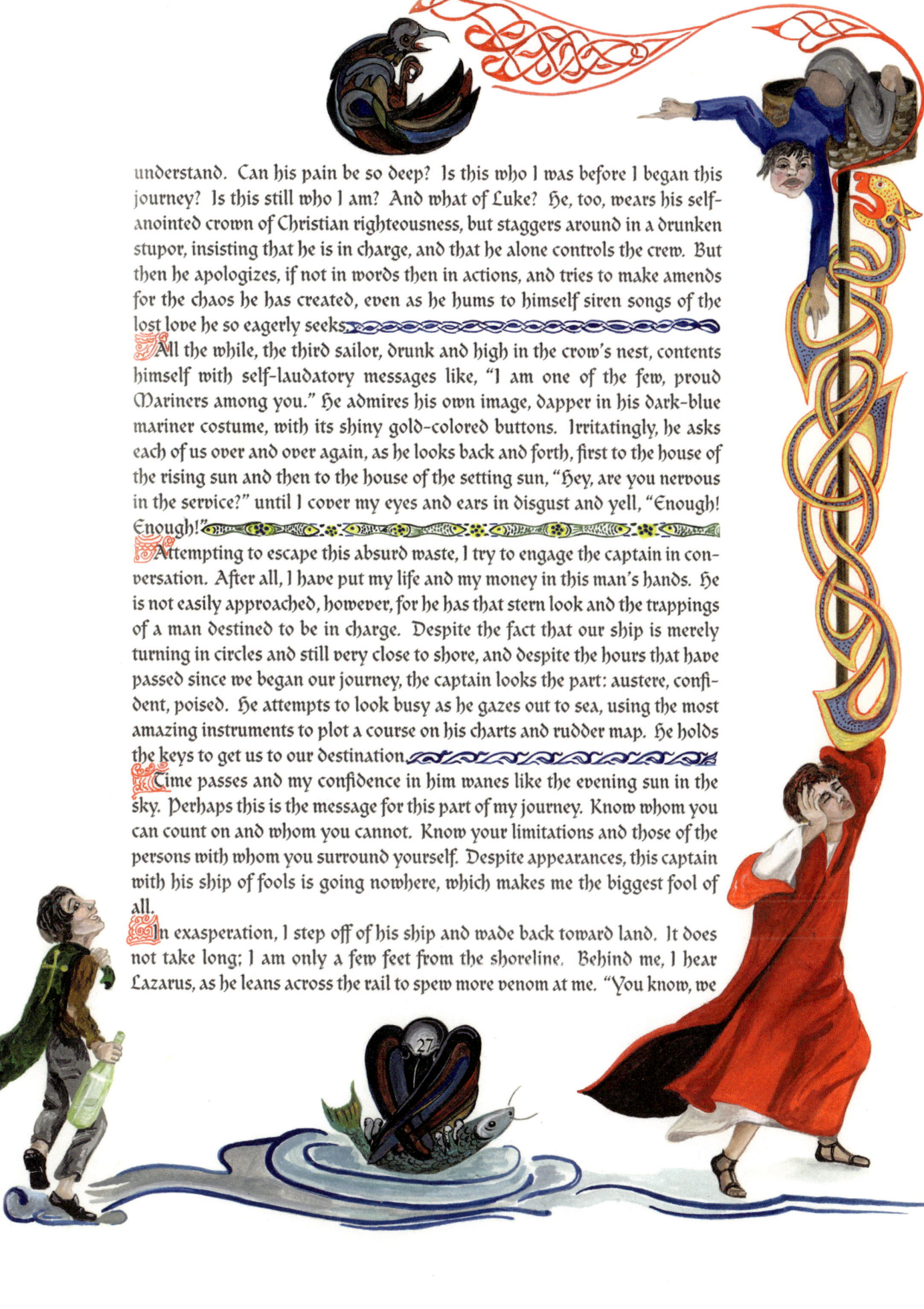

understand. Can his pain be so deep? Is this who I was before I began this journey? Is this still who I am? And what of Luke? He, too, wears his self-anointed crown of Christian righteousness, but staggers around in a drunken stupor, insisting that he is in charge, and that he alone controls the crew. But then he apologizes, if not in words then in actions, and tries to make amends for the chaos he has created, even as he hums to himself siren songs of the lost love he so eagerly seeks.

All the while, the third sailor, drunk and high in the crow's nest, contents himself with self-laudatory messages like, "I am one of the few, proud Mariners among you." He admires his own image, dapper in his dark-blue mariner costume, with its shiny gold-colored buttons. Irritatingly, he asks each of us over and over again, as he looks back and forth, first to the house of the rising sun and then to the house of the setting sun, "Hey, are you nervous in the service?" until I cover my eyes and ears in disgust and yell, "Enough! Enough!"

Attempting to escape this absurd waste, I try to engage the captain in conversation. After all, I have put my life and my money in this man's hands. He is not easily approached, however, for he has that stern look and the trappings of a man destined to be in charge. Despite the fact that our ship is merely turning in circles and still very close to shore, and despite the hours that have passed since we began our journey, the captain looks the part: austere, confident, poised. He attempts to look busy as he gazes out to sea, using the most amazing instruments to plot a course on his charts and rudder map. He holds the keys to get us to our destination.

Time passes and my confidence in him wanes like the evening sun in the sky. Perhaps this is the message for this part of my journey. Know whom you can count on and whom you cannot. Know your limitations and those of the persons with whom you surround yourself. Despite appearances, this captain with his ship of fools is going nowhere, which makes me the biggest fool of all.

In exasperation, I step off of his ship and wade back toward land. It does not take long; I am only a few feet from the shoreline. Behind me, I hear Lazarus, as he leans across the rail to spew more venom at me. "You know, we

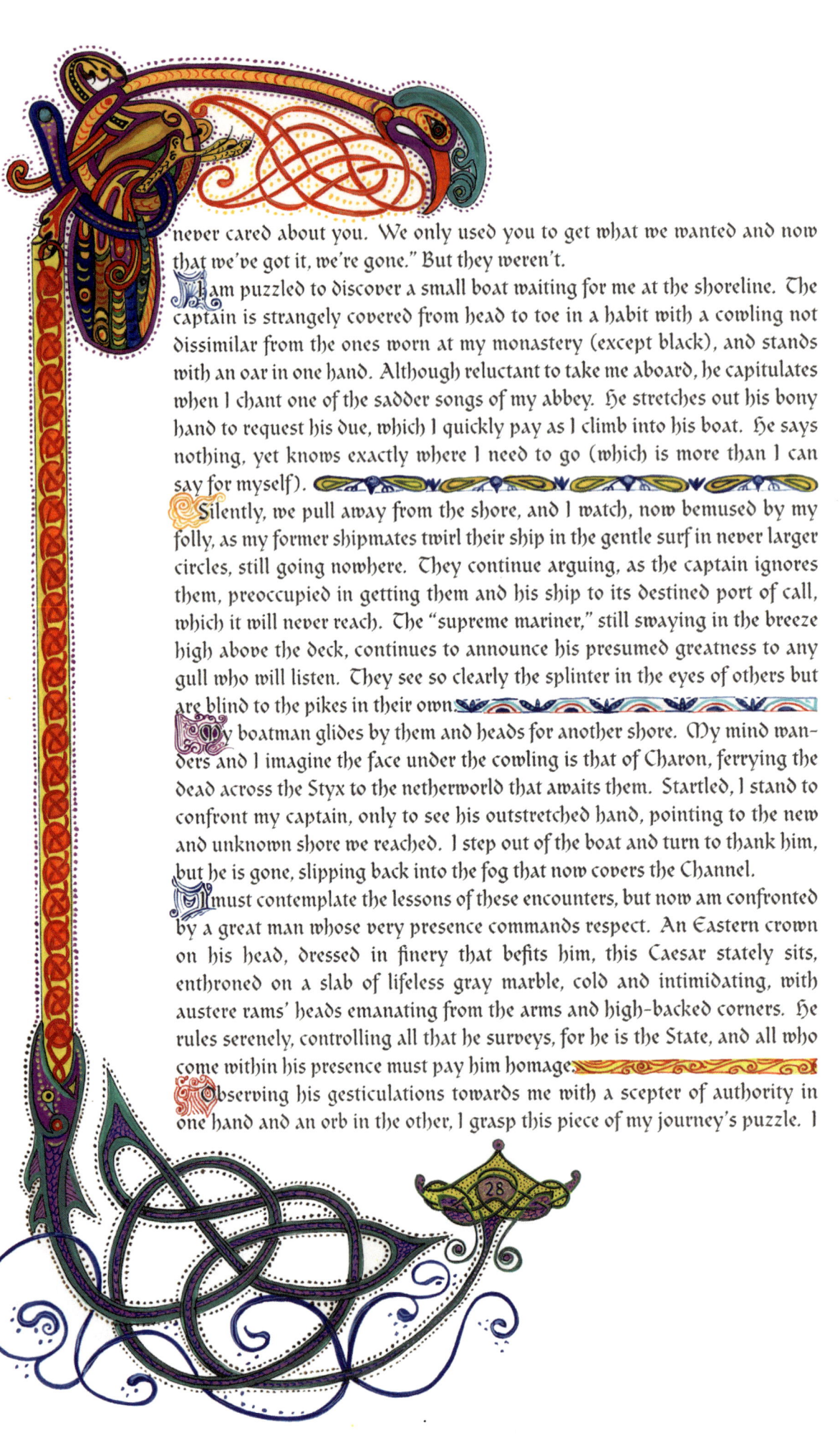

never cared about you. We only used you to get what we wanted and now that we've got it, we're gone." But they weren't.

I am puzzled to discover a small boat waiting for me at the shoreline. The captain is strangely covered from head to toe in a habit with a cowling not dissimilar from the ones worn at my monastery (except black), and stands with an oar in one hand. Although reluctant to take me aboard, he capitulates when I chant one of the sadder songs of my abbey. He stretches out his bony hand to request his due, which I quickly pay as I climb into his boat. He says nothing, yet knows exactly where I need to go (which is more than I can say for myself).

Silently, we pull away from the shore, and I watch, now bemused by my folly, as my former shipmates twirl their ship in the gentle surf in never larger circles, still going nowhere. They continue arguing, as the captain ignores them, preoccupied in getting them and his ship to its destined port of call, which it will never reach. The "supreme mariner," still swaying in the breeze high above the deck, continues to announce his presumed greatness to any gull who will listen. They see so clearly the splinter in the eyes of others but are blind to the pikes in their own.

My boatman glides by them and heads for another shore. My mind wanders and I imagine the face under the cowling is that of Charon, ferrying the dead across the Styx to the netherworld that awaits them. Startled, I stand to confront my captain, only to see his outstretched hand, pointing to the new and unknown shore we reached. I step out of the boat and turn to thank him, but he is gone, slipping back into the fog that now covers the Channel.

I must contemplate the lessons of these encounters, but now am confronted by a great man whose very presence commands respect. An Eastern crown on his head, dressed in finery that befits him, this Caesar stately sits, enthroned on a slab of lifeless gray marble, cold and intimidating, with austere rams' heads emanating from the arms and high-backed corners. He rules serenely, controlling all that he surveys, for he is the State, and all who come within his presence must pay him homage.

Observing his gesticulations towards me with a scepter of authority in one hand and an orb in the other, I grasp this piece of my journey's puzzle. I acknowledge his gesture, lifting my staff toward the heavens with my right hand and holding forth a coin in the other. He appears to notice, but then simply turns towards others as he continues to hold his worldly court.

He is an alternate way to see myself: a window that I may look inside. I will use this vision as a compass to travel the light. Through introspection, investigation, analysis, calculation, energy, leadership, and courage I may escape the fate of the mariners, who no doubt, continue to spin around and around in their tub of self-induced misery, urging others to join their pointless journey to nowhere; they are without vision, as lifeless phantasms, except in their own minds and those they continue to seduce.

I will pray for them, that like a fine wine, they will mature with age and reach their destinies. Only God can help them to see the folly they have created and now live: unhappy, but unwilling to change a thing. This king turns once more towards me and nods, as if to acknowledge my thoughts. It is time to travel on east to the Ile de Paris. Nothing is said; nothing is left to say. I glance once more at his face and realize this is the self-same beggar that directed me to the ship I first took. Only now... now he has clothes that befit his position, and he is the Emperor.

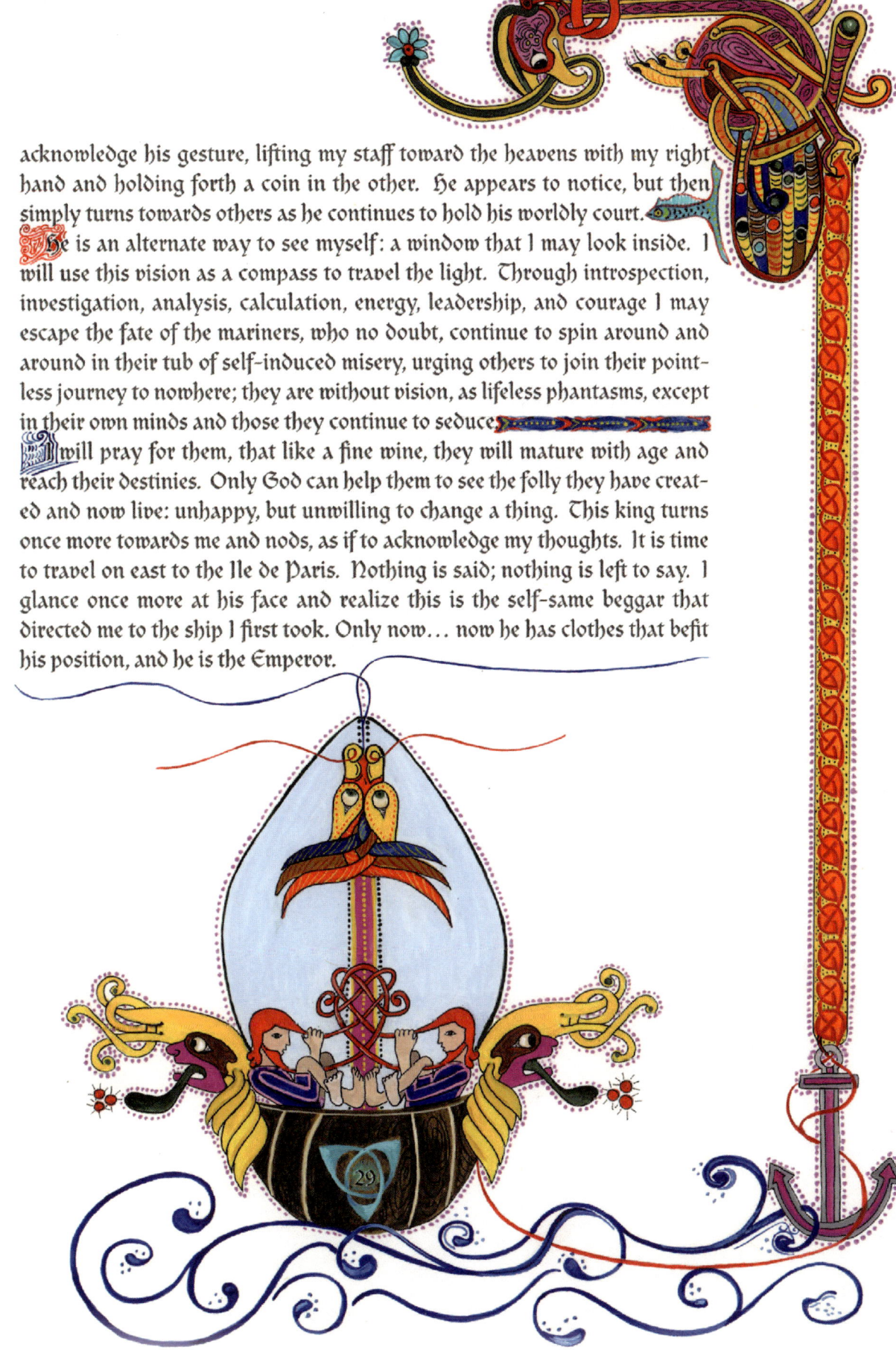

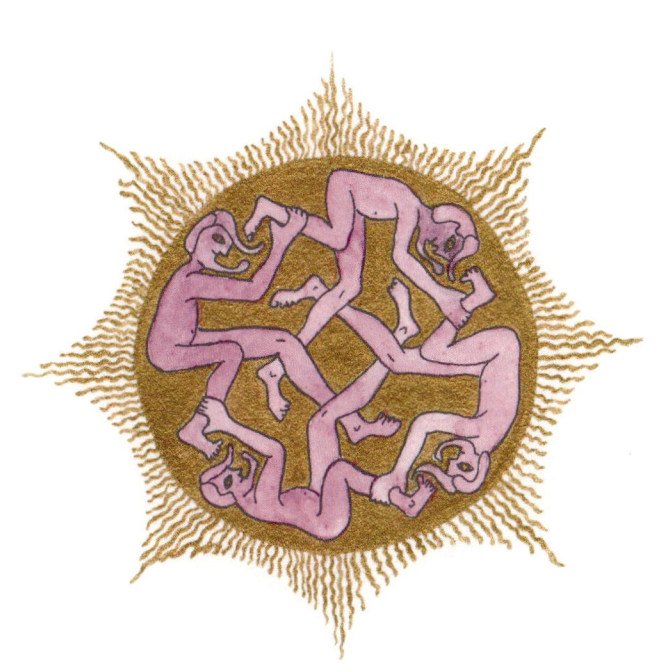

V. Fires Burn, Cauldrons Bubble

March 3rd, 1190

Recognizing the great distance I must traverse to reach the Holy city of Jerusalem where I believe I will discover the treasure I seek, I purchase a donkey and small cart just on the outskirts of town, shortly after leaving the Emperor's presence. Not only will I be able to reach Jerusalem more quickly, the wear and tear I save on my sandals and my feet will be inestimable. Rouen looms in the distance, the only town of any size before Paris. My little donkey is amiable enough, plodding along on an even pace, step by step. Although I certainly could never walk in His shoes, I cannot help but think of the Lord's triumphant entry into Jerusalem on the back of an ass and compare it with my journey of discovery with this little donkey.

Maybe I'll be welcomed with palm branches lining my way and people cheering as they did Him. Not likely, but it would be a nice touch. Daydreaming away, I take time to nibble on a snack, some cheese and a small loaf of bread, just enough to sustain me for now, and wash it down with a little spring water.

Just ahead of me, a cloud of dust obscures the road. Someone is coming towards me, someone in quite a hurry. Before I can think much about it, a huge golden chariot, its front decorated with the image of a spinning top within a white shield, wheels to an abrupt halt in front of me. The chariot is pulled by two gargantuan and very muscular sphinxes: one a black and silver female, and the other a lapis and gold-colored male.

The sphinxes answer to a proud and stately young man, covered in golden armor, topped by a golden diadem fashioned like the crown of olive branches awarded to ancient Olympian champions. A cape of purest golden silk covers

33

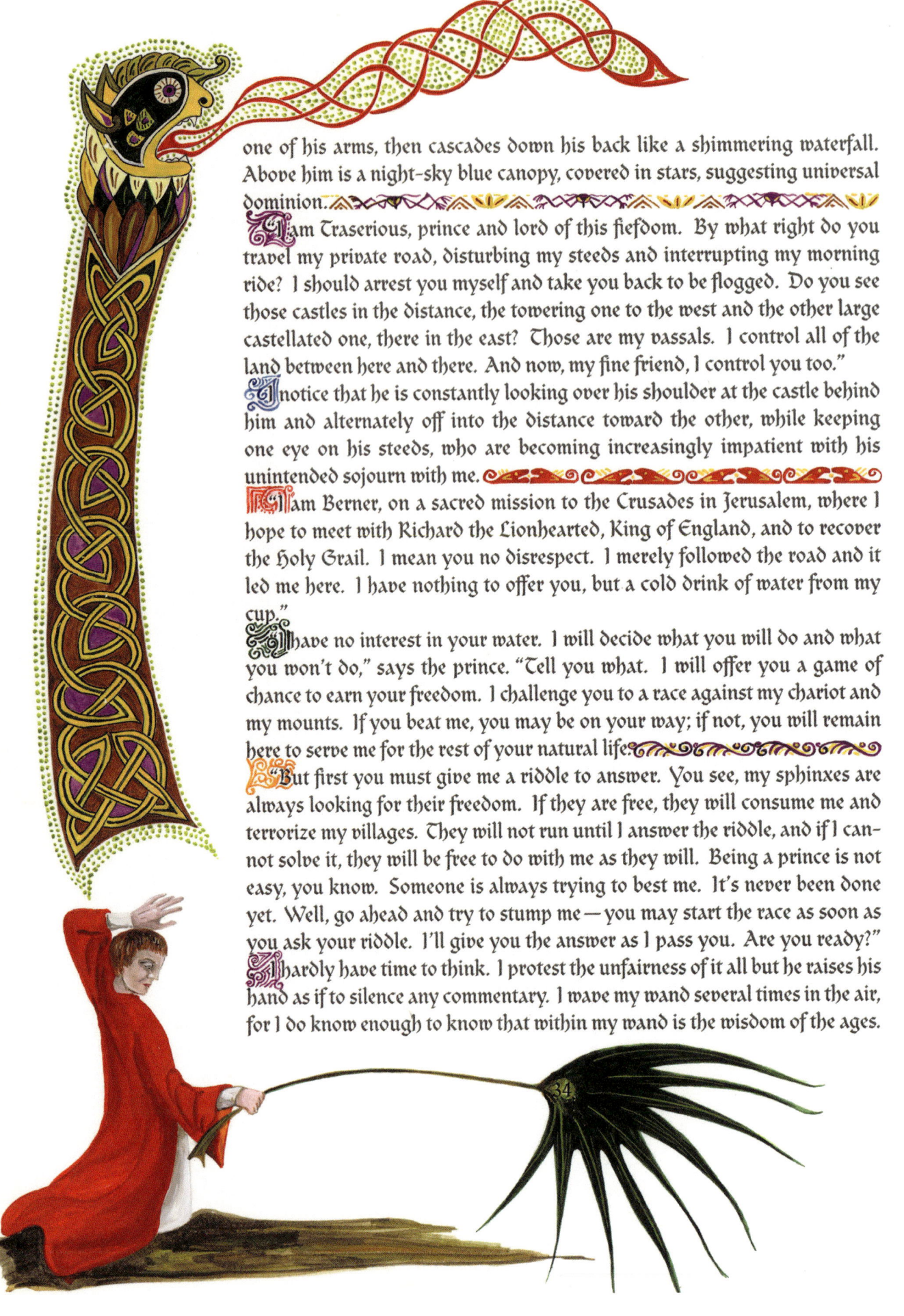

one of his arms, then cascades down his back like a shimmering waterfall. Above him is a night-sky blue canopy, covered in stars, suggesting universal dominion.

"I am Traserious, prince and lord of this fiefdom. By what right do you travel my private road, disturbing my steeds and interrupting my morning ride? I should arrest you myself and take you back to be flogged. Do you see those castles in the distance, the towering one to the west and the other large castellated one, there in the east? Those are my vassals. I control all of the land between here and there. And now, my fine friend, I control you too."

I notice that he is constantly looking over his shoulder at the castle behind him and alternately off into the distance toward the other, while keeping one eye on his steeds, who are becoming increasingly impatient with his unintended sojourn with me.

"I am Berner, on a sacred mission to the Crusades in Jerusalem, where I hope to meet with Richard the Lionhearted, King of England, and to recover the Holy Grail. I mean you no disrespect. I merely followed the road and it led me here. I have nothing to offer you, but a cold drink of water from my cup."

"I have no interest in your water. I will decide what you will do and what you won't do," says the prince. "Tell you what. I will offer you a game of chance to earn your freedom. I challenge you to a race against my chariot and my mounts. If you beat me, you may be on your way; if not, you will remain here to serve me for the rest of your natural life.

"But first you must give me a riddle to answer. You see, my sphinxes are always looking for their freedom. If they are free, they will consume me and terrorize my villages. They will not run until I answer the riddle, and if I cannot solve it, they will be free to do with me as they will. Being a prince is not easy, you know. Someone is always trying to best me. It's never been done yet. Well, go ahead and try to stump me—you may start the race as soon as you ask your riddle. I'll give you the answer as I pass you. Are you ready?"

I hardly have time to think. I protest the unfairness of it all but he raises his hand as if to silence any commentary. I wave my wand several times in the air, for I do know enough to know that within my wand is the wisdom of the ages.

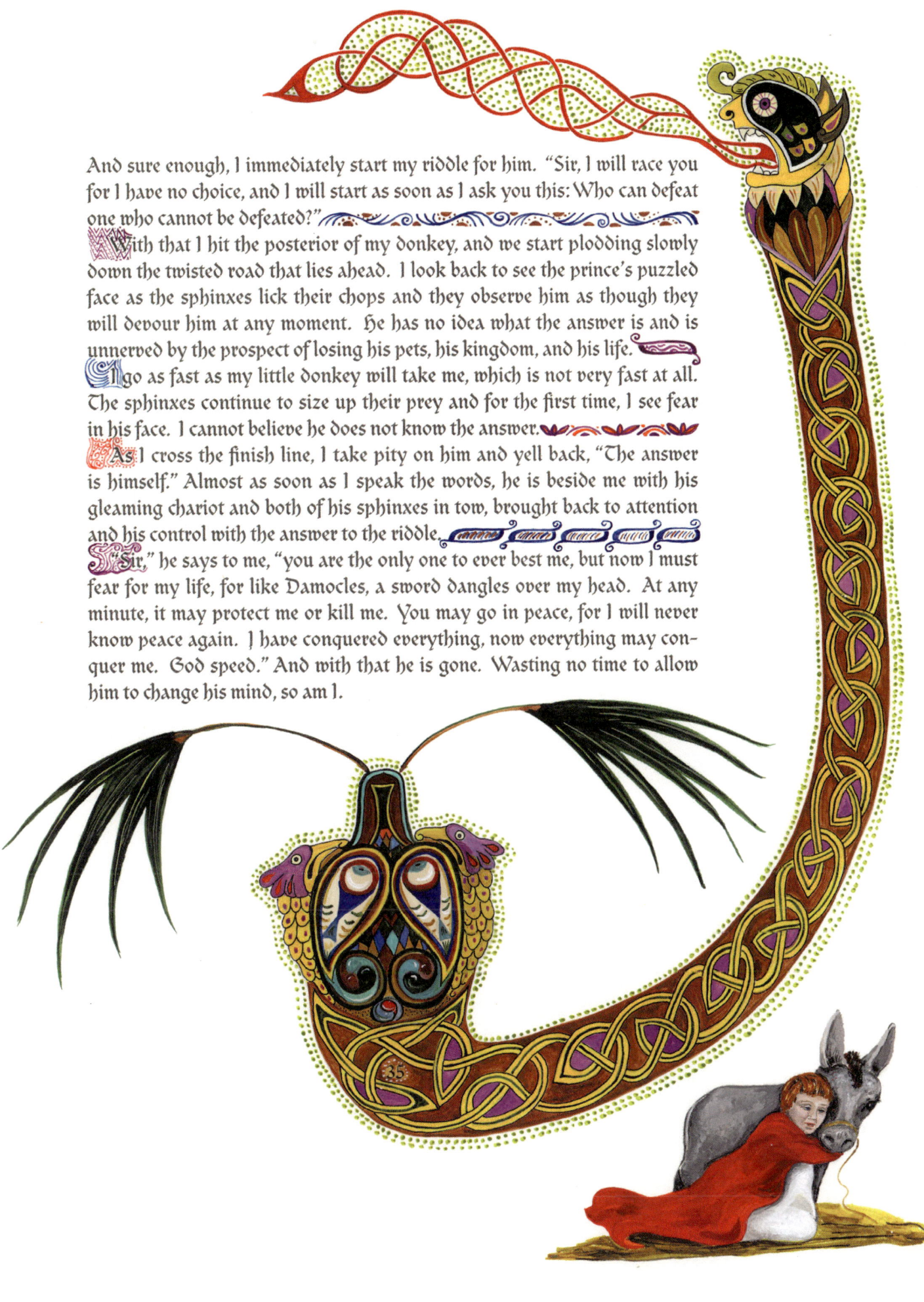

And sure enough, I immediately start my riddle for him. "Sir, I will race you for I have no choice, and I will start as soon as I ask you this: Who can defeat one who cannot be defeated?"

With that I hit the posterior of my donkey, and we start plodding slowly down the twisted road that lies ahead. I look back to see the prince's puzzled face as the sphinxes lick their chops and they observe him as though they will devour him at any moment. He has no idea what the answer is and is unnerved by the prospect of losing his pets, his kingdom, and his life.

I go as fast as my little donkey will take me, which is not very fast at all. The sphinxes continue to size up their prey and for the first time, I see fear in his face. I cannot believe he does not know the answer.

As I cross the finish line, I take pity on him and yell back, "The answer is himself." Almost as soon as I speak the words, he is beside me with his gleaming chariot and both of his sphinxes in tow, brought back to attention and his control with the answer to the riddle.

"Sir," he says to me, "you are the only one to ever best me, but now I must fear for my life, for like Damocles, a sword dangles over my head. At any minute, it may protect me or kill me. You may go in peace, for I will never know peace again. I have conquered everything, now everything may conquer me. God speed." And with that he is gone. Wasting no time to allow him to change his mind, so am I.

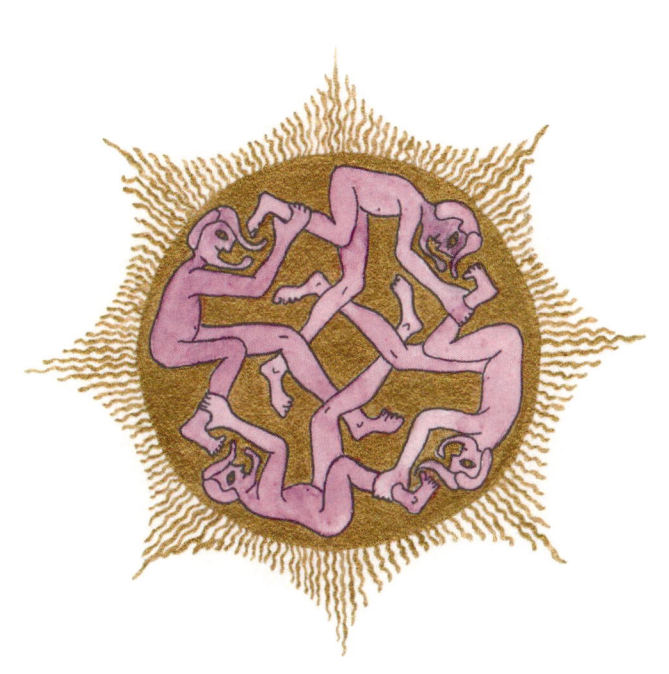

VI. Wild Things

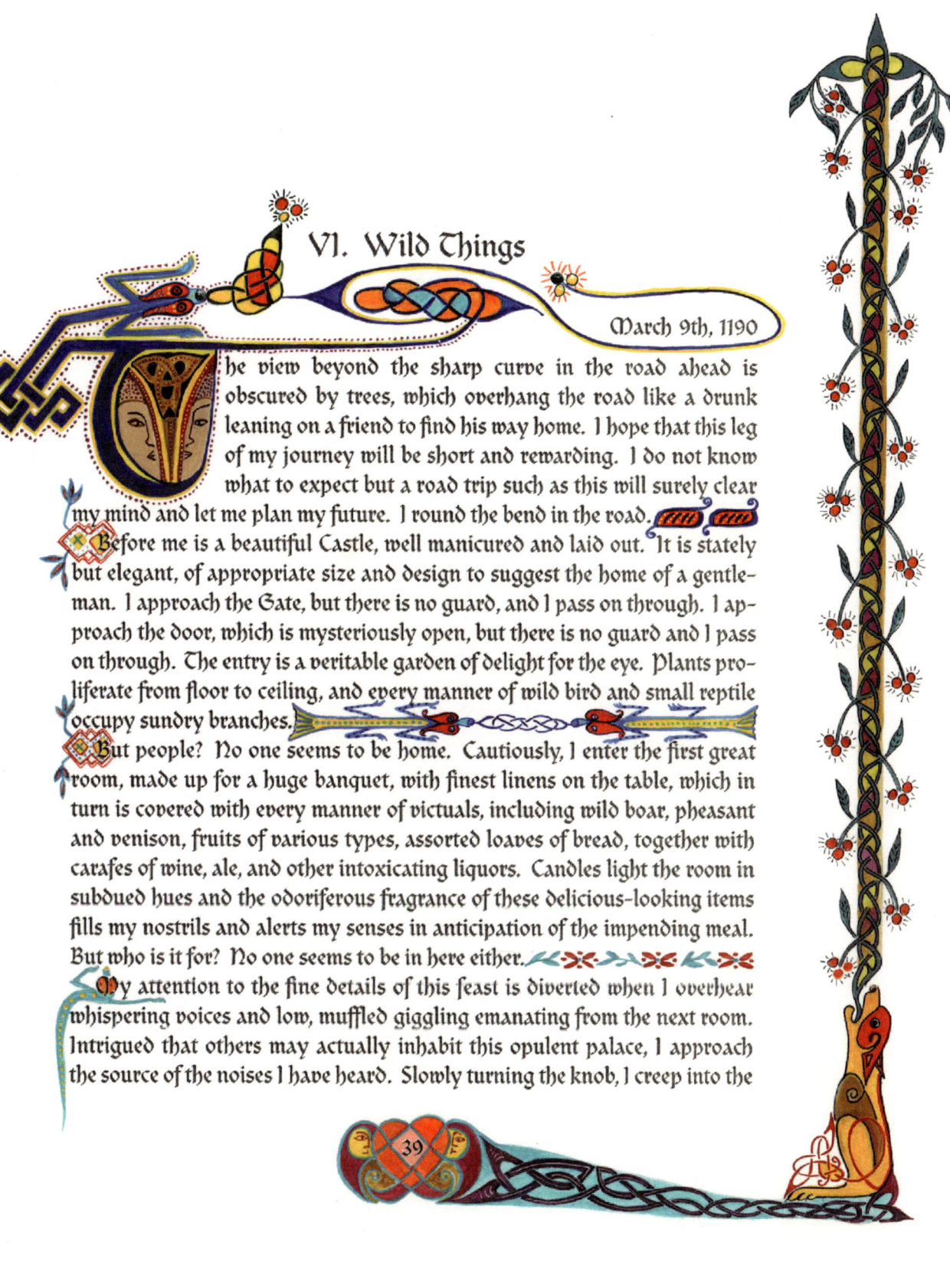

March 9th, 1190

he view beyond the sharp curve in the road ahead is obscured by trees, which overhang the road like a drunk leaning on a friend to find his way home. I hope that this leg of my journey will be short and rewarding. I do not know what to expect but a road trip such as this will surely clear my mind and let me plan my future. I round the bend in the road. Before me is a beautiful Castle, well manicured and laid out. It is stately but elegant, of appropriate size and design to suggest the home of a gentleman. I approach the Gate, but there is no guard, and I pass on through. I approach the door, which is mysteriously open, but there is no guard and I pass on through. The entry is a veritable garden of delight for the eye. Plants proliferate from floor to ceiling, and every manner of wild bird and small reptile occupy sundry branches. But people? No one seems to be home. Cautiously, I enter the first great room, made up for a huge banquet, with finest linens on the table, which in turn is covered with every manner of victuals, including wild boar, pheasant and venison, fruits of various types, assorted loaves of bread, together with carafes of wine, ale, and other intoxicating liquors. Candles light the room in subdued hues and the odoriferous fragrance of these delicious-looking items fills my nostrils and alerts my senses in anticipation of the impending meal. But who is it for? No one seems to be in here either. My attention to the fine details of this feast is diverted when I overhear whispering voices and low, muffled giggling emanating from the next room. Intrigued that others may actually inhabit this opulent palace, I approach the source of the noises I have heard. Slowly turning the knob, I creep into the

39

room which is painted in pale oranges and yellows, as if to suggest the dawn; and everywhere are paintings of the early morning rising sun.

Two young people, a boy and a girl only slightly older than me, stand at the center of the room facing each other, separated from one another by a thin, silvery veil strung from the ceiling. Clothed only in sunlight, these naturally attired lovers are well-developed, well-nourished, beautiful specimens of God's creative force. He is handsome, long and tall, with keen, blue eyes, high cheekbones and a well built body (except quite skinny); she has shimmering knee-length, jet-black hair to contrast her white-as-snow teeth, that break into a smile sure to win over even the most hard-hearted ogre. Of gentle and pleasing demeanor, her voice charms and disarms, her giggling is most infectious. Her body, so smooth and supple, was no doubt the model for Aphrodite; her lips, pale and soft. She is a vision of loveliness.

The room is lit in soft perfumed candlelight and the talk is of undying love and the beauty they see only in each other. This is indeed curious, because they cannot see each other. Although they can easily lift the veil to see and touch and be with each other, they view only their own reflection of the beauty of the other from behind the veil. They are blind to all else, and see me not, nor seem to sense my presence. They reach out for each other and embrace through the veil. They might as well be blind.

Passing on to the next room, I hear them call out to each other by name and learn that they are Donald and Anne, soon to wed one another. I quietly shut the door behind me so as not to disturb them.

Beyond the door is a magnificent winding staircase, which I follow upward to the second floor. The walls all around are hung with pictures of them both — some together, some separate. Just at the top of the landing is a large picture of Donald, dressed as a knight in chain mail as if ready for war. He holds a red shield, on which are painted three golden Eastern crowns.

A small painting next to it depicts Anne, in tears, proud but defiant, understanding Donald's duty but missing him nonetheless. I contemplate these last two images for quite a while. The sadness in both their faces betrays their loneliness without one another, and leaves me so unhappy for them that I hesitate before daring to enter the adjacent door.

I am shocked. For there is an older Anne on a bed, prostrate, obviously with child. At her side is an older Donald, still dressed in the chain mail of a knight, stroking her hand and telling her how beautiful she is. The curtains are drawn on this pale blue room, and the only light seems to come from the love that radiates from them. Anne is softly crying, for she does not feel beautiful, especially because she realizes her beloved will soon leave her side again. But duty calls, she must cope, and he promises to return. He too, is profoundly saddened by the prospect of being torn away from her once again.

They are older now than before, for several years have passed between them. He speaks his heart to her and she to him, and each promises himself to the other, and to write every day. As they embrace, I know it is time to leave the room and exit quietly but quickly, to give them what little time they have alone together.

The only path I can follow takes me down a narrow dimly lit hall which, like the stairwell before it, is covered in drawings and paintings of the young couple. But now, the two have become four, as I see portrayed first one and then another baby boy in the proud arms of these lovers. Proudly they display these two sons for the world to see as they do.

Each successive picture reflects an older Anne and Donald, and I begin to understand that this castle is a time continuum of their lives, and that I am meant to see their lives unfold. At the end of the hall is a larger than normal door, covered in gold trim and a golden doorknob. A knocker, in the form of a golden, winged griffin looks back at me as if to bar the way of strangers who would dare enter without permission.

As I cautiously open the door, unsure of what to expect, a huge, well-lit room dispels the darkness of the last, for there are no curtains shutting out the daylight. The room is illuminated on three sides by wall-to-wall windows that go from the floor to the high, vaulted ceiling above.

There is an air of contentment as Donald and Anne are observed playing with their two boys who are rapidly growing into young men. Donald has returned from the war, his kingdom safe, his life intact. He is going about his business as a portrait artist to ensure the welfare of his family. Anne, too, works at her job, unusual for a married woman, to ensure the blessings of

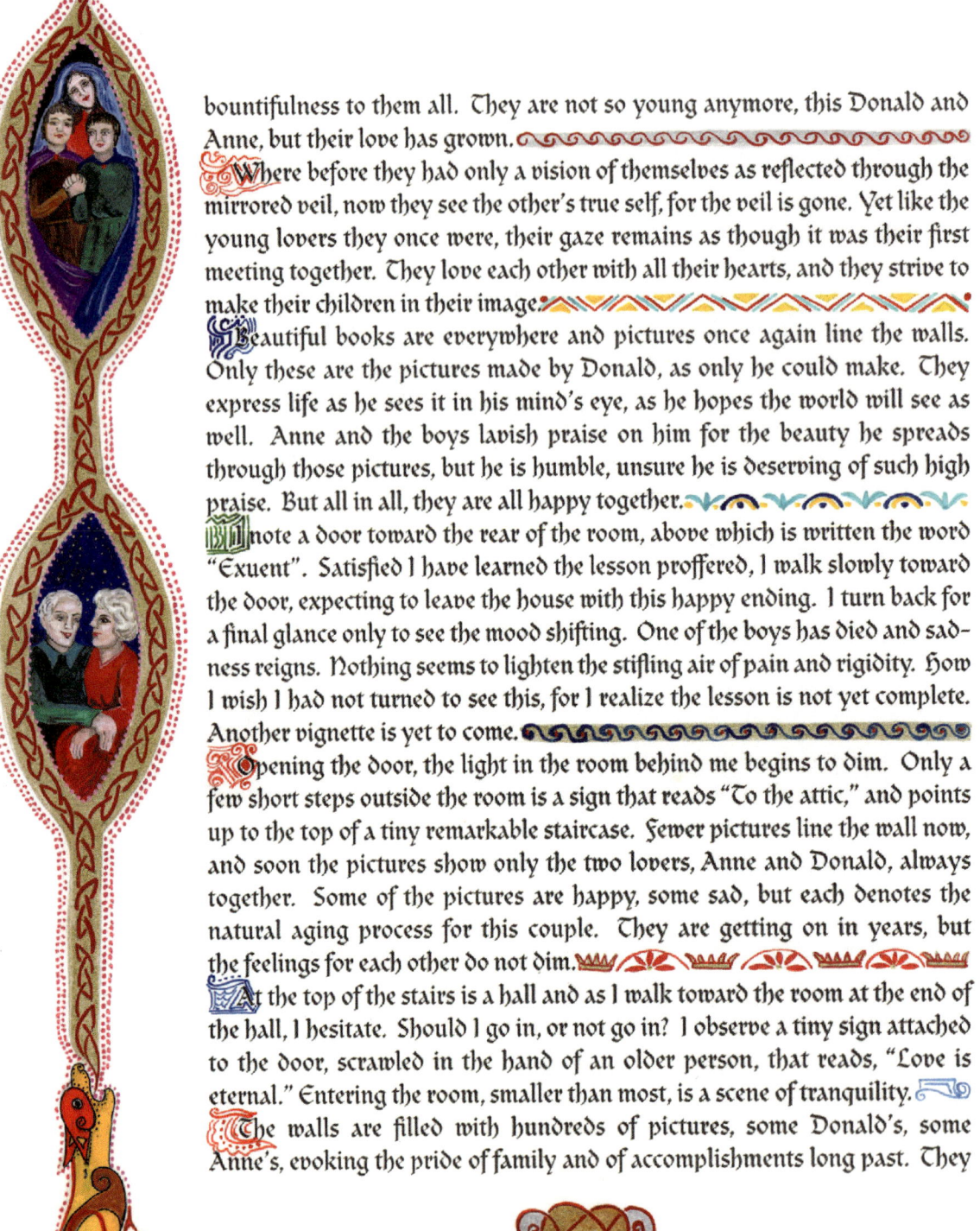

bountifulness to them all. They are not so young anymore, this Donald and Anne, but their love has grown. Where before they had only a vision of themselves as reflected through the mirrored veil, now they see the other's true self, for the veil is gone. Yet like the young lovers they once were, their gaze remains as though it was their first meeting together. They love each other with all their hearts, and they strive to make their children in their image. Beautiful books are everywhere and pictures once again line the walls. Only these are the pictures made by Donald, as only he could make. They express life as he sees it in his mind's eye, as he hopes the world will see as well. Anne and the boys lavish praise on him for the beauty he spreads through those pictures, but he is humble, unsure he is deserving of such high praise. But all in all, they are all happy together. I note a door toward the rear of the room, above which is written the word "Exuent". Satisfied I have learned the lesson proffered, I walk slowly toward the door, expecting to leave the house with this happy ending. I turn back for a final glance only to see the mood shifting. One of the boys has died and sadness reigns. Nothing seems to lighten the stifling air of pain and rigidity. How I wish I had not turned to see this, for I realize the lesson is not yet complete. Another vignette is yet to come. Opening the door, the light in the room behind me begins to dim. Only a few short steps outside the room is a sign that reads "To the attic," and points up to the top of a tiny remarkable staircase. Fewer pictures line the wall now, and soon the pictures show only the two lovers, Anne and Donald, always together. Some of the pictures are happy, some sad, but each denotes the natural aging process for this couple. They are getting on in years, but the feelings for each other do not dim. At the top of the stairs is a hall and as I walk toward the room at the end of the hall, I hesitate. Should I go in, or not go in? I observe a tiny sign attached to the door, scrawled in the hand of an older person, that reads, "Love is eternal." Entering the room, smaller than most, is a scene of tranquility. The walls are filled with hundreds of pictures, some Donald's, some Anne's, evoking the pride of family and of accomplishments long past. They

42

sit quietly in their room, seeing only each other, as angels sing above them, blessing their marriage and their lives together. Though they are somewhat bowed and gnarled, lacking the keen memory each once enjoyed, their eyesight dimmed, their hearing weakened or gone, and unable to do or even remember many of the things they enjoyed in their youth, each sits staring intently at the other. The glint in their eyes tells the rest of the story. They are still very much in love. Love … is … eternal. I take one last look at the scene before me and then walk out the back door and down to the edge of the road. I will contemplate these lives, and enter their experiences in my journal.

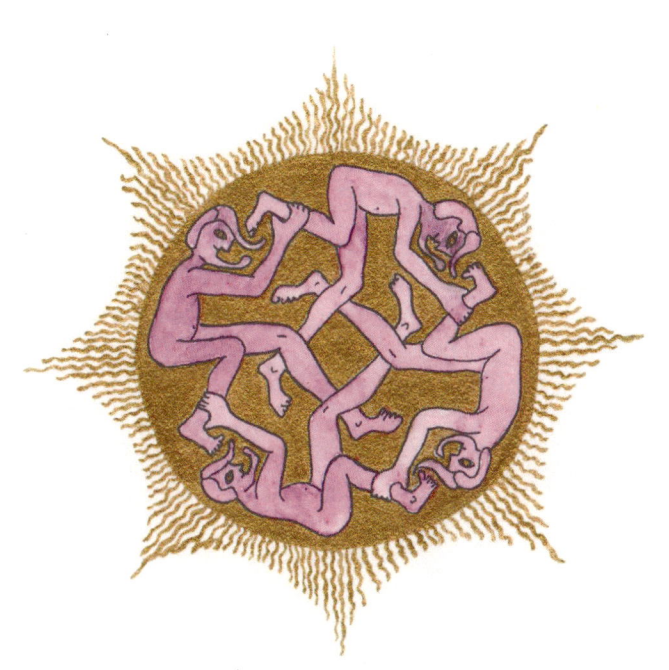

VII. Dream Catcher

May 1st, 1190

he rest of the trip toward Île de la Cité in Paris is, for the most part uneventful, except for the occasional beggar or pilgrim or small groups of Crusaders on their way to the Holy Land to fight for all Christendom in response to Pope Clement III's call to arms. Excitement runs high in the city with rumors of an important visitor. Few are willing to venture even a guess as to the identity of this stranger, and I could not care less. I must be about business and I have no time to gawk at the rich and famous. I am content to seek the hospitality and companionship of the new cathedral, Our Lady of Notre Dame, still under construction by an army of architects and workers, word of which reached Glastonbury years ago. My journey is tiring and I must admit a certain satisfaction at knowing I will sleep in the arms of the Church this night rather than under the stars again. Before I reach it, however, I must run a gauntlet of street vendors, relic and miracle dealers, and indulgence sellers. I have always opposed the concept of the church selling indulgences like farmers selling their chickens and potatoes at market, but then, my opinion doesn't really count in that regard. But someday…someday the Church may recognize the error of this practice. And how people can believe in these miracle sellers and relics of saints confounds me. The discourse with myself comes to a complete standstill when I notice a billboard advertising a piece of the true cross of our Lord, Jesus Christ. I am intrigued and question the seller as to where he got this supposed relic. "Why, in the holy city of Jerusalem," he replies. Incredulous, I ask him for proof. He explains to me that he has been a warrior in the service of Christ on

47

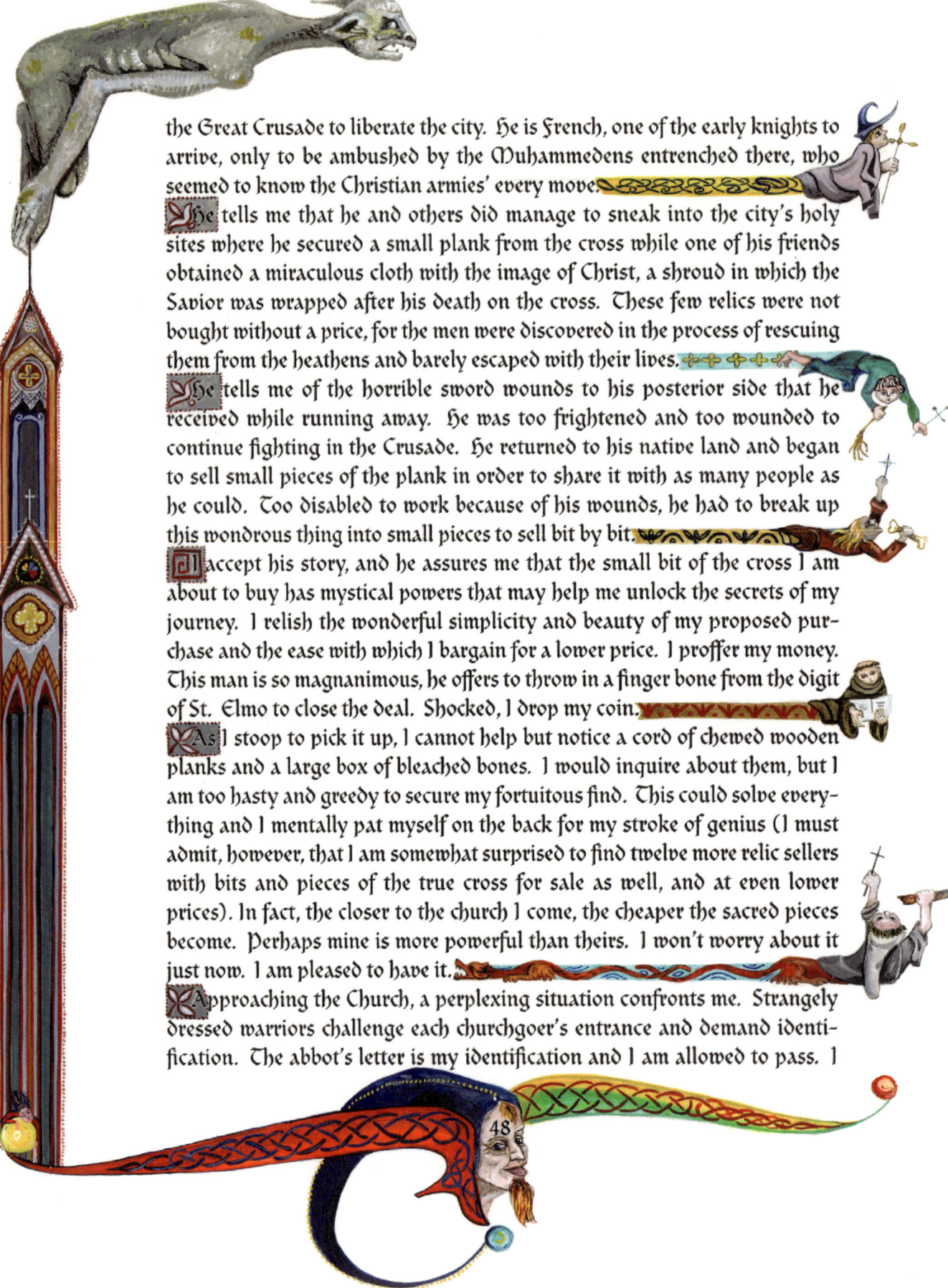

the Great Crusade to liberate the city. He is French, one of the early knights to arrive, only to be ambushed by the Muhammedens entrenched there, who seemed to know the Christian armies' every move.

He tells me that he and others did manage to sneak into the city's holy sites where he secured a small plank from the cross while one of his friends obtained a miraculous cloth with the image of Christ, a shroud in which the Savior was wrapped after his death on the cross. These few relics were not bought without a price, for the men were discovered in the process of rescuing them from the heathens and barely escaped with their lives.

He tells me of the horrible sword wounds to his posterior side that he received while running away. He was too frightened and too wounded to continue fighting in the Crusade. He returned to his native land and began to sell small pieces of the plank in order to share it with as many people as he could. Too disabled to work because of his wounds, he had to break up this wondrous thing into small pieces to sell bit by bit.

I accept his story, and he assures me that the small bit of the cross I am about to buy has mystical powers that may help me unlock the secrets of my journey. I relish the wonderful simplicity and beauty of my proposed purchase and the ease with which I bargain for a lower price. I proffer my money. This man is so magnanimous, he offers to throw in a finger bone from the digit of St. Elmo to close the deal. Shocked, I drop my coin.

As I stoop to pick it up, I cannot help but notice a cord of chewed wooden planks and a large box of bleached bones. I would inquire about them, but I am too hasty and greedy to secure my fortuitous find. This could solve everything and I mentally pat myself on the back for my stroke of genius (I must admit, however, that I am somewhat surprised to find twelve more relic sellers with bits and pieces of the true cross for sale as well, and at even lower prices). In fact, the closer to the church I come, the cheaper the sacred pieces become. Perhaps mine is more powerful than theirs. I won't worry about it just now. I am pleased to have it.

Approaching the Church, a perplexing situation confronts me. Strangely dressed warriors challenge each churchgoer's entrance and demand identification. The abbot's letter is my identification and I am allowed to pass. I

48

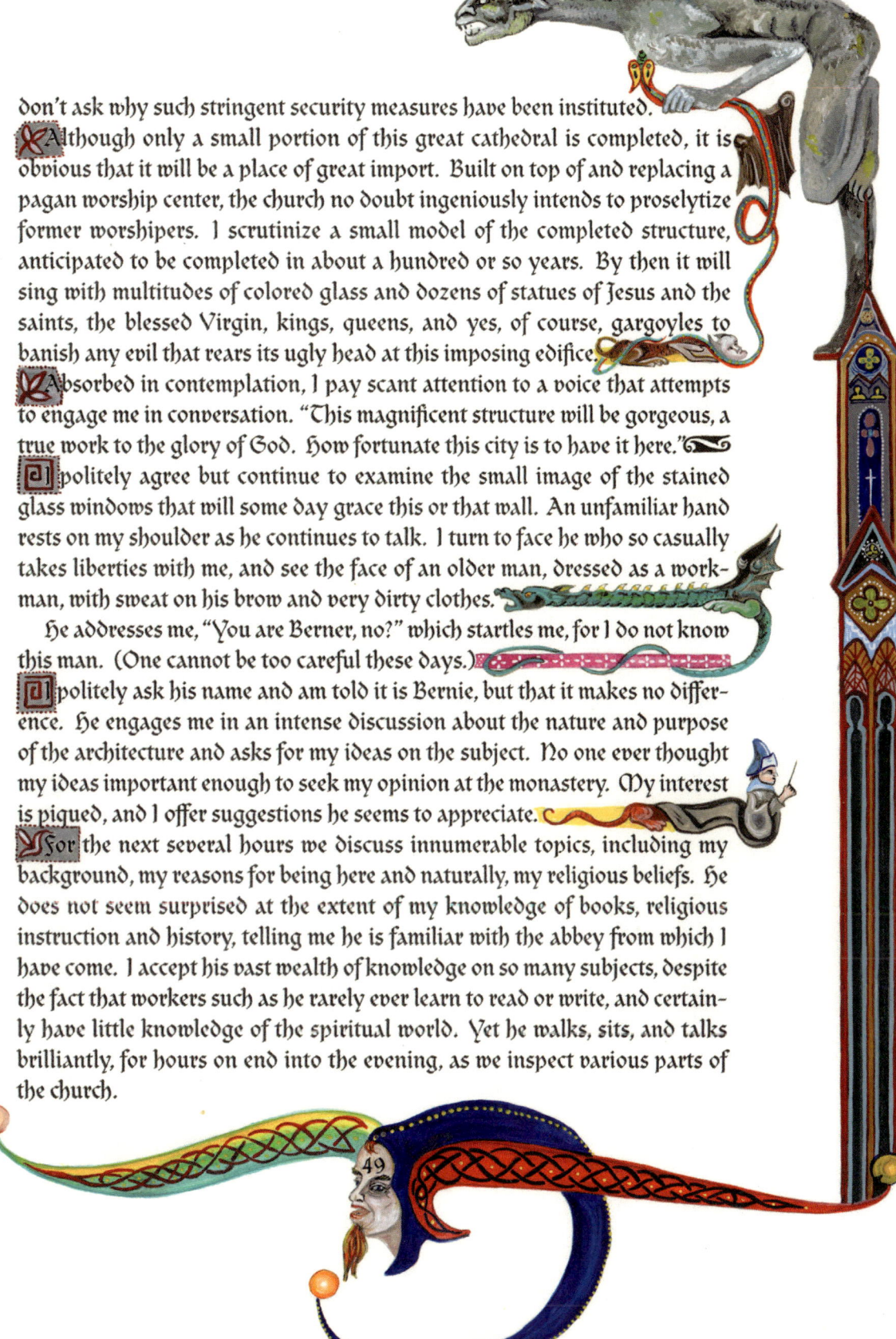

don't ask why such stringent security measures have been instituted. Although only a small portion of this great cathedral is completed, it is obvious that it will be a place of great import. Built on top of and replacing a pagan worship center, the church no doubt ingeniously intends to proselytize former worshipers. I scrutinize a small model of the completed structure, anticipated to be completed in about a hundred or so years. By then it will sing with multitudes of colored glass and dozens of statues of Jesus and the saints, the blessed Virgin, kings, queens, and yes, of course, gargoyles to banish any evil that rears its ugly head at this imposing edifice.

Absorbed in contemplation, I pay scant attention to a voice that attempts to engage me in conversation. "This magnificent structure will be gorgeous, a true work to the glory of God. How fortunate this city is to have it here."

I politely agree but continue to examine the small image of the stained glass windows that will some day grace this or that wall. An unfamiliar hand rests on my shoulder as he continues to talk. I turn to face he who so casually takes liberties with me, and see the face of an older man, dressed as a workman, with sweat on his brow and very dirty clothes.

He addresses me, "You are Berner, no?" which startles me, for I do not know this man. (One cannot be too careful these days.)

I politely ask his name and am told it is Bernie, but that it makes no difference. He engages me in an intense discussion about the nature and purpose of the architecture and asks for my ideas on the subject. No one ever thought my ideas important enough to seek my opinion at the monastery. My interest is piqued, and I offer suggestions he seems to appreciate.

For the next several hours we discuss innumerable topics, including my background, my reasons for being here and naturally, my religious beliefs. He does not seem surprised at the extent of my knowledge of books, religious instruction and history, telling me he is familiar with the abbey from which I have come. I accept his vast wealth of knowledge on so many subjects, despite the fact that workers such as he rarely ever learn to read or write, and certainly have little knowledge of the spiritual world. Yet he walks, sits, and talks brilliantly, for hours on end into the evening, as we inspect various parts of the church.

49

I am amazed at his virility, for all of the workers respectfully genuflect and address him as "Father" as we pass by them. It is only at supper I realize the identity of this man, as he passes me the bread at our communal table filled with workers, parishioners, and priests. The huge gold ring on his finger is unmistakable. Incredulously, I had not noticed it until this moment. I drop to the ground in obeisance.

"You are Peter," I say in almost a whisper.

"No, you are Peter," he replies. I am confused. What does he mean that I am Peter? He is our Father, the Holy See, Pope Clement III. He is Peter. Why has he dressed this way and allowed me to believe he is a simple workman? He seems so at ease as he answers the myriad of questions I have for him, even as I realize I have no right to be asking anything of this Holy man. He chuckles gently as he answers me.

He is so unassuming and disarming and I feel as though I have known him forever. I speak my mind and he is very content to explain patiently everything. His Holiness changes into his vestments, heavily embroidered in gold and silver brocade, and allows me to place his hat upon him like a crown.

Finally, we come to what troubles me from our earlier conversation. I ask him why he called me Peter when he is Peter. His answer will haunt me forever.

"What's in a name?" he asks. "I am known by many. At home in Italy, I was simply Paolo. In Rome, I am Clement. Here, they call me Bernie. It makes no difference what you are called. The only thing that matters is that you recognize the tasks you're called upon to complete. God knows your name, God knows your heart. He asks many sacrifices, like the mission you are on now. What you do about what He calls on you to do, now that really matters. I called you Peter because you will be Peter."

He pulls off his ring and bids me try it on. I tell him I cannot and am shaking, for it is the ring of the first Peter, the favorite male disciple of our Lord. He laughs and places it on my finger. It is so big on my tiny hand. He takes it off and replaces it on his own finger.

"Someday, Berner, it will fit. Until then, keep to your word. These are for you." He hands me two keys, one crossed over the other, like the letter "X". Two cardinals, fully dressed in their vestments, drop to their knees, as if in

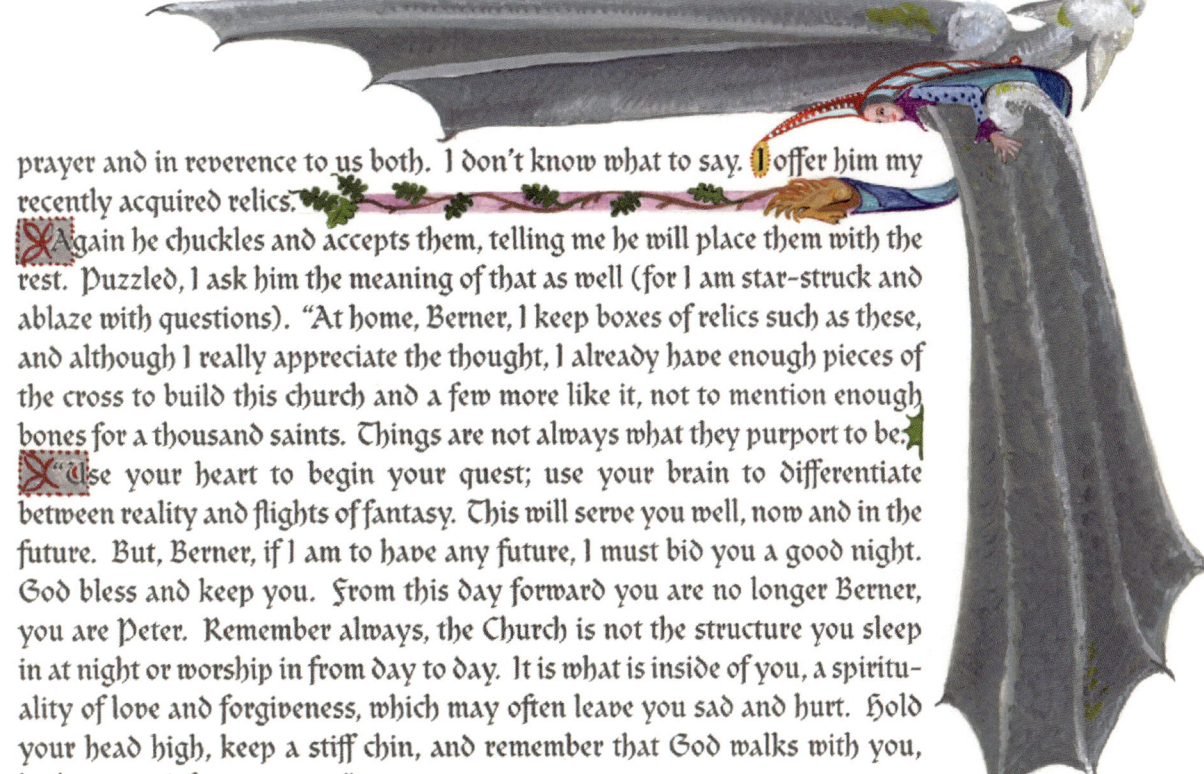

prayer and in reverence to us both. I don't know what to say. I offer him my recently acquired relics.

Again he chuckles and accepts them, telling me he will place them with the rest. Puzzled, I ask him the meaning of that as well (for I am star-struck and ablaze with questions). "At home, Berner, I keep boxes of relics such as these, and although I really appreciate the thought, I already have enough pieces of the cross to build this church and a few more like it, not to mention enough bones for a thousand saints. Things are not always what they purport to be; "Use your heart to begin your quest; use your brain to differentiate between reality and flights of fantasy. This will serve you well, now and in the future. But, Berner, if I am to have any future, I must bid you a good night. God bless and keep you. From this day forward you are no longer Berner, you are Peter. Remember always, the Church is not the structure you sleep in at night or worship in from day to day. It is what is inside of you, a spirituality of love and forgiveness, which may often leave you sad and hurt. Hold your head high, keep a stiff chin, and remember that God walks with you, both now and forever more."

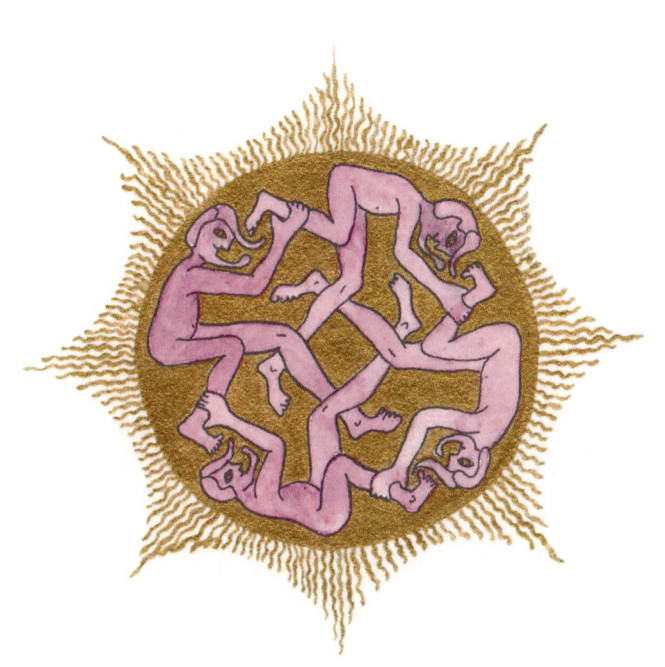

VIII. But for a Feather

May 12th, 1190

I awaken to the sounds of birds chattering their morning songs as they go about their daily business. I feel really good about myself, especially after the inspirational words of encouragement I received the night before from Clement. I know, however, that I must not tarry, for I have much to do and a long way to go.

After morning devotional prayers, a small bag is passed to me containing sufficient victuals for the next few days. I am grateful for this bounty and bless the inhabitants of this place. I pray for Clement's health, for his heart is weak and his future unclear. I cleanse myself with the refreshing waters brought to my cell and ready myself to leave, meditating silently.

As I exit, I am struck at the renaissance of emotions others exhibit towards me this morning. Quiet but reverent respect from the workers and monks inside, and by the soldiers and the general populace outside, who genuflect as I pass, surprise me. I try to remain humble. They act as though I have a shining halo on my head and a glowing body they dare not approach.

This dissipates the farther I get from the church and head eastward out of the city. People begin to make fun of me as I go through their towns and villages — of my clothes, my looks, my quest. They call me a fool and their children begin to spit at me and throw rotten food at me. I try to ignore them and turn the other cheek. But as the din of the crowds increases and they carelessly spew their vitriolic rhetoric at me, I begin to lose the very confidence bestowed on me by Clement last night.

I resent this uncalled-for treatment. I am lost in my own feelings of anger and shame. To regain control, I decide to rest in a shaded area just up the

55

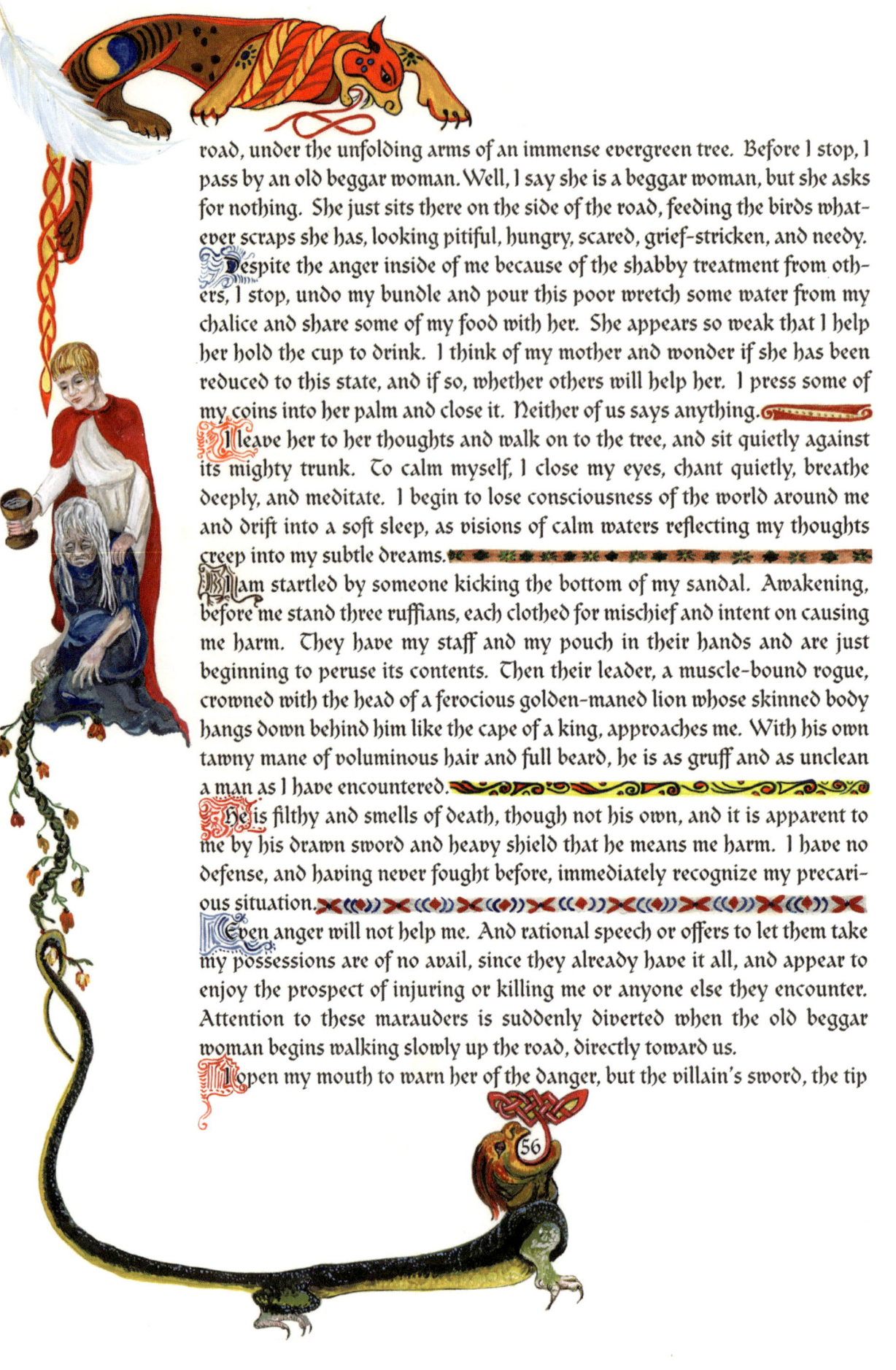

road, under the unfolding arms of an immense evergreen tree. Before I stop, I pass by an old beggar woman. Well, I say she is a beggar woman, but she asks for nothing. She just sits there on the side of the road, feeding the birds whatever scraps she has, looking pitiful, hungry, scared, grief-stricken, and needy. Despite the anger inside of me because of the shabby treatment from others, I stop, undo my bundle and pour this poor wretch some water from my chalice and share some of my food with her. She appears so weak that I help her hold the cup to drink. I think of my mother and wonder if she has been reduced to this state, and if so, whether others will help her. I press some of my coins into her palm and close it. Neither of us says anything.

I leave her to her thoughts and walk on to the tree, and sit quietly against its mighty trunk. To calm myself, I close my eyes, chant quietly, breathe deeply, and meditate. I begin to lose consciousness of the world around me and drift into a soft sleep, as visions of calm waters reflecting my thoughts creep into my subtle dreams.

I am startled by someone kicking the bottom of my sandal. Awakening, before me stand three ruffians, each clothed for mischief and intent on causing me harm. They have my staff and my pouch in their hands and are just beginning to peruse its contents. Then their leader, a muscle-bound rogue, crowned with the head of a ferocious golden-maned lion whose skinned body hangs down behind him like the cape of a king, approaches me. With his own tawny mane of voluminous hair and full beard, he is as gruff and as unclean a man as I have encountered.

He is filthy and smells of death, though not his own, and it is apparent to me by his drawn sword and heavy shield that he means me harm. I have no defense, and having never fought before, immediately recognize my precarious situation.

Even anger will not help me. And rational speech or offers to let them take my possessions are of no avail, since they already have it all, and appear to enjoy the prospect of injuring or killing me or anyone else they encounter. Attention to these marauders is suddenly diverted when the old beggar woman begins walking slowly up the road, directly toward us.

I open my mouth to warn her of the danger, but the villain's sword, the tip

of which is rested on my tongue, is prepared to rip it out just as would have the predator whose skin he now wears as a trophy. The situation appears hopeless for us as the woman approaches, walking the slow and deliberate walk of an infirm old woman of her age.

The wind blows and a feather floats down from the sky, drifting this way and that. The rogues notice it too. The feather travels where the wind carries it. The old woman does not notice. And then, the strangest thing happens. The feather comes to rest directly on the top of the old woman's shoulder.

My captors turn their gaze back to me, but I stare at the face of the old woman. A halo, shaped like the sign of infinity appears above her head as she transforms somehow. Signs of age in her disappear, as she becomes young, beautiful, and infinitely powerful. Her head is covered with a crown of flowers; around her waist, a triple wreath of roses, all brilliantly shimmering in prismatic colors in the bright sun. On each of her arms hang elongated garlands of roses, all made up of blooms without thorns, like magical chains of love.

Rising off of the ground, she glides through the air towards us, casting a garland over each of these hapless fellows. She saves the last and longest one for their leader, casting this vegetal chain across his head and down his side. Peace and calm exude from her even as she casts her web over them. The action is not vengeful, but rather displays unity of purpose, desire, and aspiration, which creates such power that these wild men and their undisciplined force are instantly subdued.

They fall to the ground, and as she hovers and lands amongst them, they lay at her feet like obedient pets awaiting their master's touch. I am humbled as I realize the message, that love alone, not hate, conquers hate.

My mouth is agape, and all I can think to say is, "Who are you?"

"The Abbess Hildegard von Bingen," she replies.

"But," I respond, "she passed this life more than ten years ago."

"Yes, this is true, but be assured, I am here in spirit form, dropped from the heavens as a feather on the breath of God to protect you, even as you protected the weak, the poor, the helpless. God watches. You battle the Nemean lion from within, and sometimes the struggle with yourself becomes too great. You must not be afraid to ask for help. My trophy is this skin." With that, she grabs the lion skin by its head and removes it from the not-so-tough-looking figure at her feet, and places it over her arm.

"Yours is to realize that you have the power over urges that sometimes lead you away from the light. Your acts of kindness towards me, a complete stranger, have showered me with viriditas, greening power. Greening love hastens to the aid of all. With the passion of heavenly yearning, people who breathe this dew produce rich fruit. … To make the spiritual journey requires passion. My gift to you is knowledge to help imbue you with this passion."

Then she sits patiently beside me as I try to absorb all she is saying. Although I know of her many works in music, medicine, prose, and plays, she reminds me that her life was not too different from mine. Her parents, like mine, dedicated their daughter to a lifetime of service to God and gave her to the Benedictines (when she was eight). But it was not until she attained the age of 42 years when she says the heavens opened up and shone a light upon her that filled her with understanding and a sense of her talents and her obligations to God.

Each of us has his own duties, but must conquer the unconscious fears and anger within before he can meet them. Some never do. I hope I am not one of them. To her, God gave visions and revelations. Whenever she disobeyed her mandate, she fell ill. With great reluctance she caused her thoughts to be put down in writing as God told her to do. Now she is here to protect me.

She explains the power of plants, animals, and mineral life lovingly put here by Nature to heal man and to keep him strong. The explanation is described in terms of the elements, as being hot, cold, wet, or dry. She warns me to be wary of the dry and lifeless tree that oppresses the mind of the sufferer, prevents contrition, and leaves him "blind and deaf to the recognition of God and empty of good works."

She chides me to godly actions by reminding me of the blackbird of the north that afflicted our late sovereign, Henry, as she had warned him before his words initiated the tragic murder of Becket. I thank her for her kindness, tell her I will contemplate her wisdom all of my days, and set out on my way. She touches the end of my rosebush cutting and it immediately begins to bloom brilliant red roses, and she is gone.

58

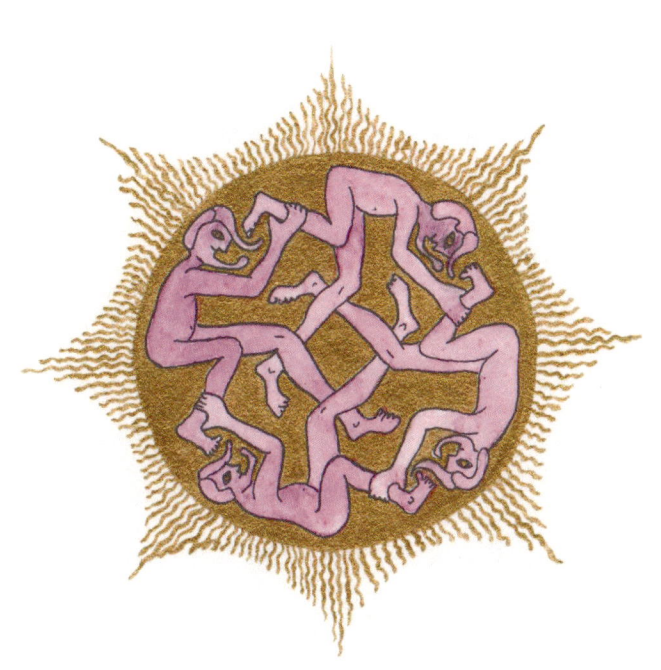

IX. All Alone Again

My encounter with Hildegard represents the closest direct connection I have yet experienced with God. I feel peaceful and happy inside. I lie back under the tree once more and fall fast asleep, a deep, abiding sleep. It is late afternoon, and as I drift off in slumber, I remember that I have not eaten and think about the fine meal I will prepare in a little while for my dinner.

Hours pass as I dream dreams of never-before-conceived magnitude. In one, I seem to be at the foot of the Throne of God Almighty Himself, watching approvingly as life goes on below here on earth, all according to His Plan. From this vantage point, earth seems so small and its inhabitants minuscule, but each so important to Him.

As I wander through the Kingdom of God, I am allowed to approach a council attended by Our Lord, Jesus of Nazareth, and Muhammed, Buddha, Zoroaster, Krishna, and so many others. They discuss calmly and lovingly the scenes I have just seen. All are saddened by the strife on earth and conceive plans to get a message of peace and harmony to those below. Everyone here lives in harmony and good will. There is no war, no autocratic and didactic theology, no anger. Peace truly reigns.

Like a baby in the womb, I am secure and warm inside, knowing that I am protected and safe here. But this is short-lived, as I begin to feel myself drifting back toward earth, falling like Hildegard's feather from His heavenly sanctuary. A smell…a smell of food is bringing me back, and although it is a wonderful smell, I resent its intrusion into this comfort zone I've never experienced before.

The smell is interrupted by sounds, like the crackling of food on an open

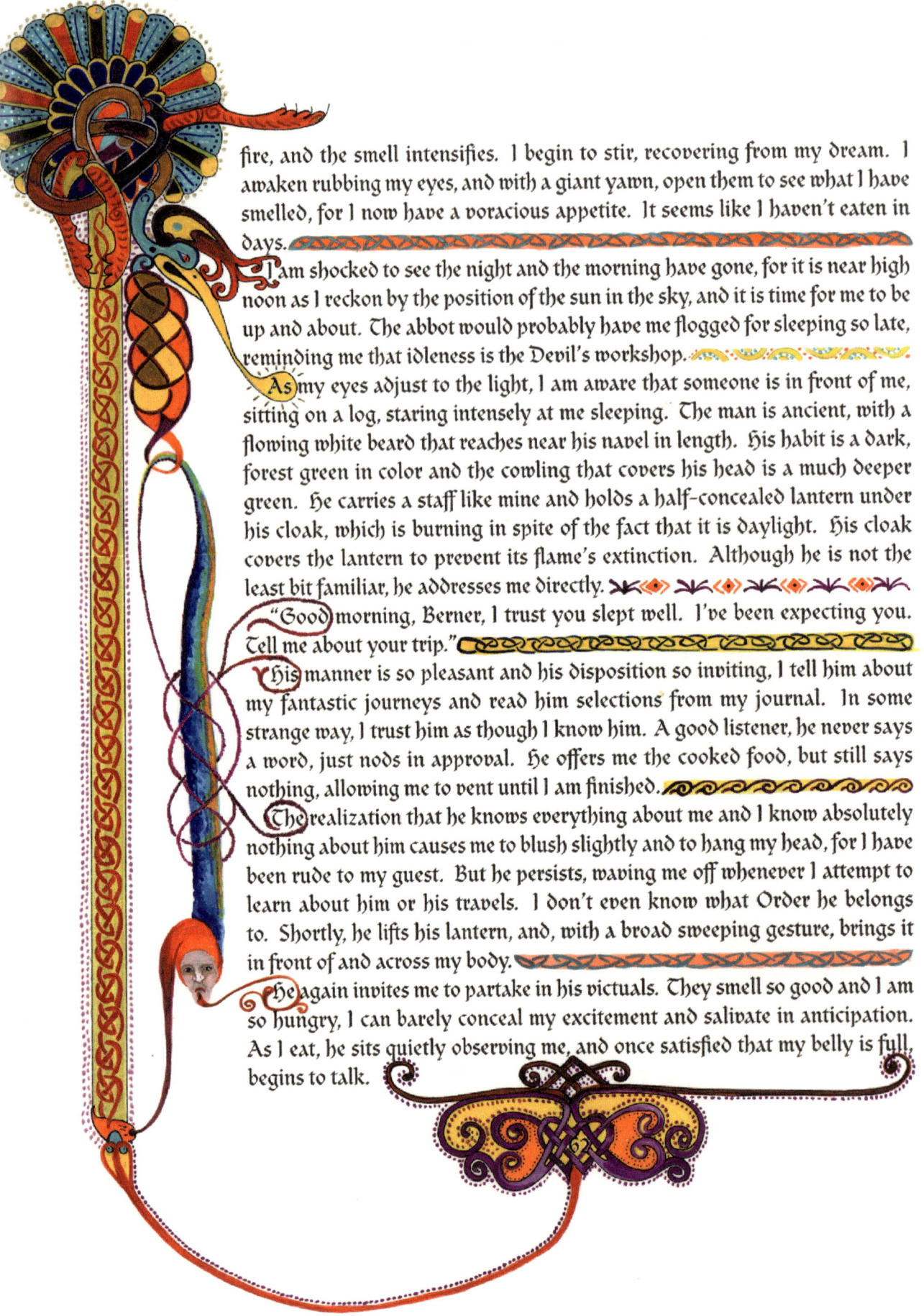

fire, and the smell intensifies. I begin to stir, recovering from my dream. I awaken rubbing my eyes, and with a giant yawn, open them to see what I have smelled, for I now have a voracious appetite. It seems like I haven't eaten in days.

I am shocked to see the night and the morning have gone, for it is near high noon as I reckon by the position of the sun in the sky, and it is time for me to be up and about. The abbot would probably have me flogged for sleeping so late, reminding me that idleness is the Devil's workshop.

As my eyes adjust to the light, I am aware that someone is in front of me, sitting on a log, staring intensely at me sleeping. The man is ancient, with a flowing white beard that reaches near his navel in length. His habit is a dark, forest green in color and the cowling that covers his head is a much deeper green. He carries a staff like mine and holds a half-concealed lantern under his cloak, which is burning in spite of the fact that it is daylight. His cloak covers the lantern to prevent its flame's extinction. Although he is not the least bit familiar, he addresses me directly.

"Good morning, Berner, I trust you slept well. I've been expecting you. Tell me about your trip."

His manner is so pleasant and his disposition so inviting, I tell him about my fantastic journeys and read him selections from my journal. In some strange way, I trust him as though I know him. A good listener, he never says a word, just nods in approval. He offers me the cooked food, but still says nothing, allowing me to vent until I am finished.

The realization that he knows everything about me and I know absolutely nothing about him causes me to blush slightly and to hang my head, for I have been rude to my guest. But he persists, waving me off whenever I attempt to learn about him or his travels. I don't even know what Order he belongs to. Shortly, he lifts his lantern, and, with a broad sweeping gesture, brings it in front of and across my body.

He again invites me to partake in his victuals. They smell so good and I am so hungry, I can barely conceal my excitement and salivate in anticipation. As I eat, he sits quietly observing me, and once satisfied that my belly is full, begins to talk.

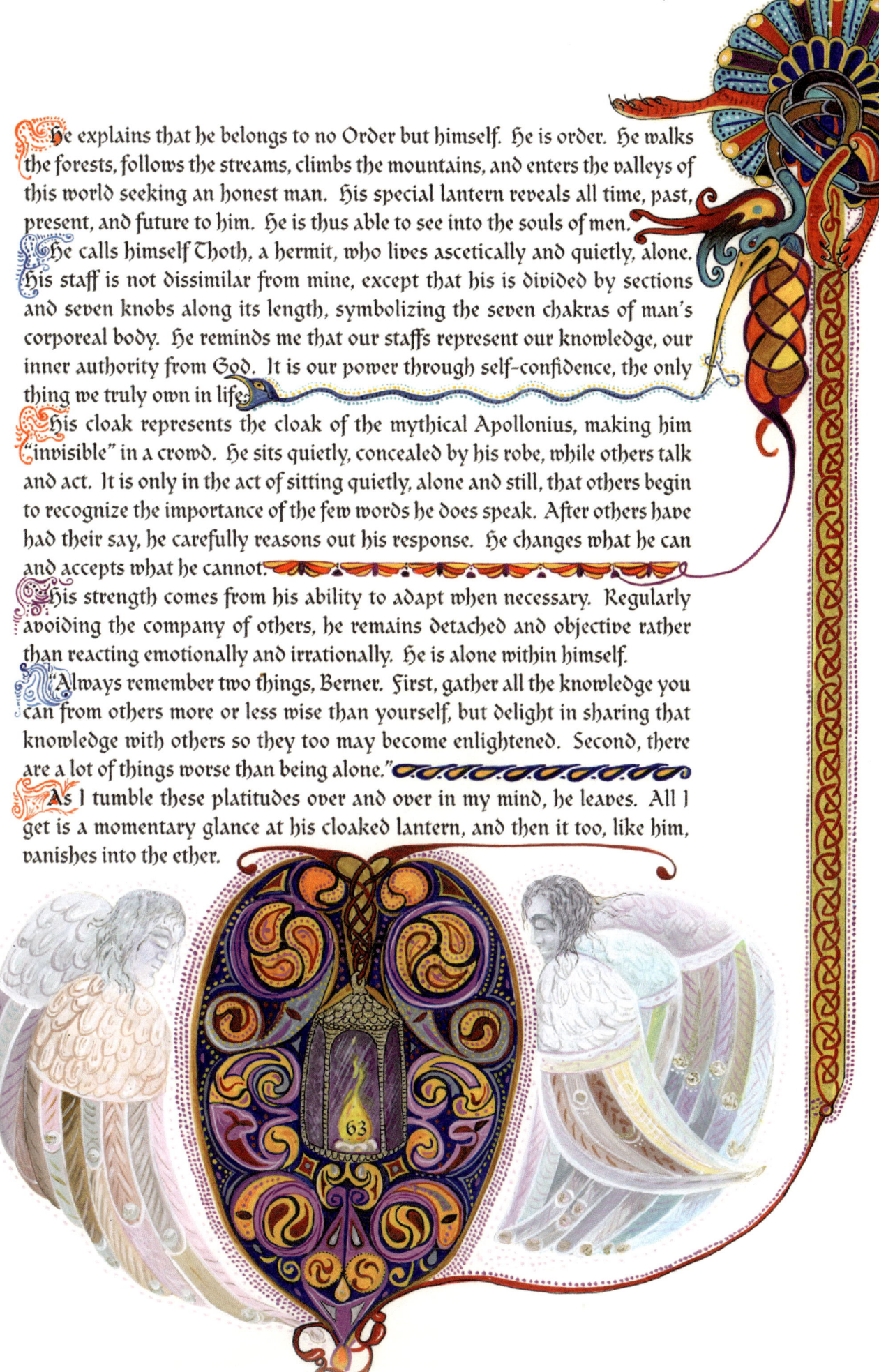

He explains that he belongs to no Order but himself. He is order. He walks the forests, follows the streams, climbs the mountains, and enters the valleys of this world seeking an honest man. His special lantern reveals all time, past, present, and future to him. He is thus able to see into the souls of men.

He calls himself Thoth, a hermit, who lives ascetically and quietly, alone. His staff is not dissimilar from mine, except that his is divided by sections and seven knobs along its length, symbolizing the seven chakras of man's corporeal body. He reminds me that our staffs represent our knowledge, our inner authority from God. It is our power through self-confidence, the only thing we truly own in life.

His cloak represents the cloak of the mythical Apollonius, making him "invisible" in a crowd. He sits quietly, concealed by his robe, while others talk and act. It is only in the act of sitting quietly, alone and still, that others begin to recognize the importance of the few words he does speak. After others have had their say, he carefully reasons out his response. He changes what he can and accepts what he cannot.

His strength comes from his ability to adapt when necessary. Regularly avoiding the company of others, he remains detached and objective rather than reacting emotionally and irrationally. He is alone within himself.

"Always remember two things, Berner. First, gather all the knowledge you can from others more or less wise than yourself, but delight in sharing that knowledge with others so they too may become enlightened. Second, there are a lot of things worse than being alone."

As I tumble these platitudes over and over in my mind, he leaves. All I get is a momentary glance at his cloaked lantern, and then it too, like him, vanishes into the ether.

63

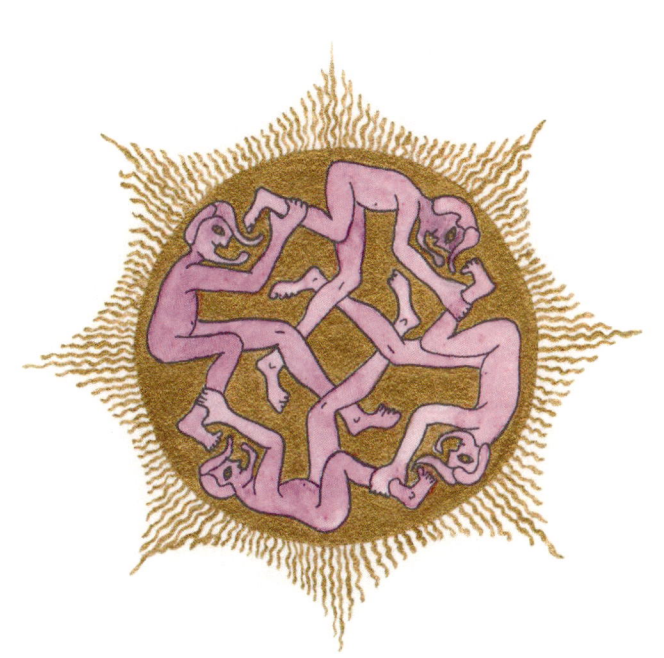

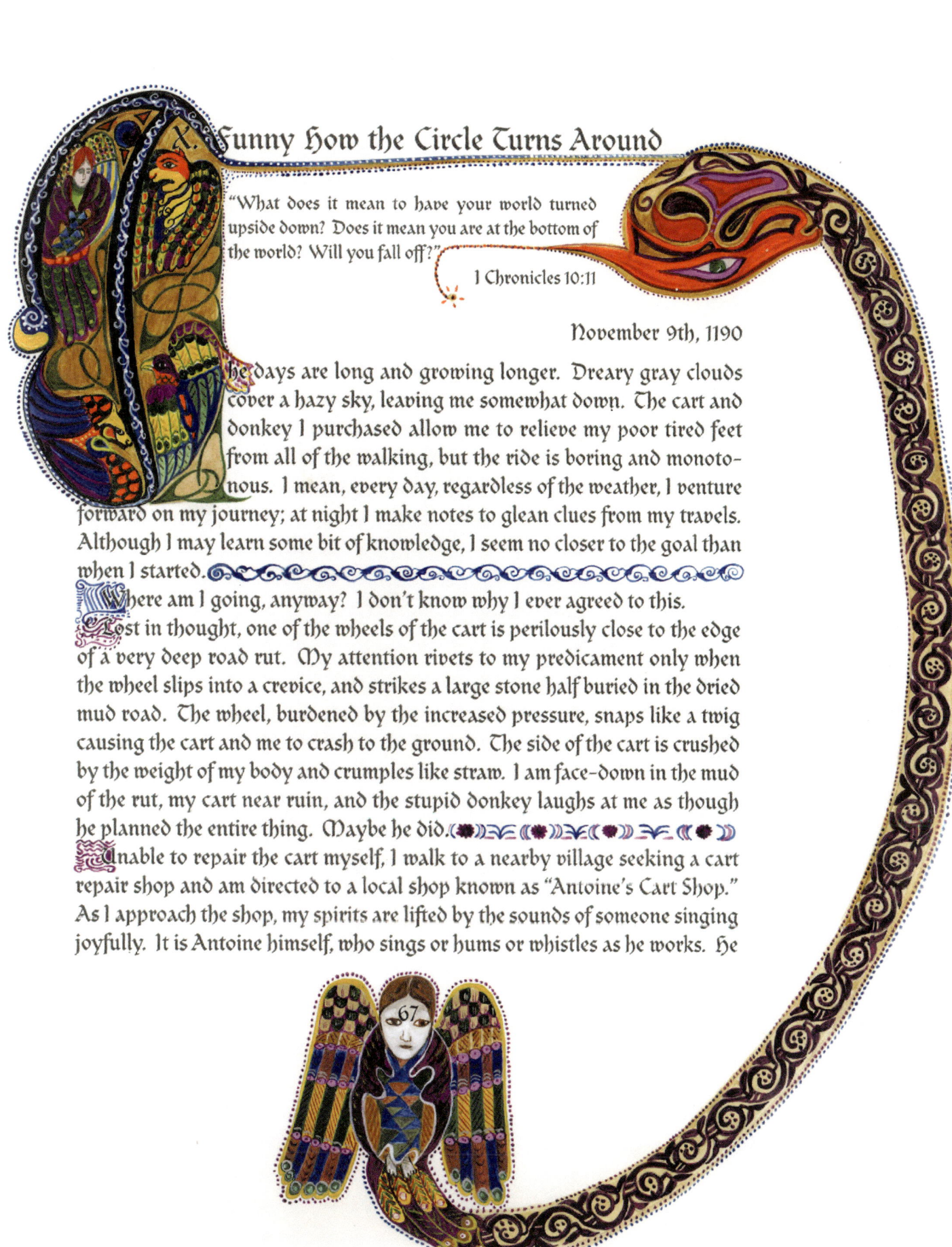

Funny How the Circle Turns Around

"What does it mean to have your world turned upside down? Does it mean you are at the bottom of the world? Will you fall off?"

1 Chronicles 10:11

November 9th, 1190

The days are long and growing longer. Dreary gray clouds cover a hazy sky, leaving me somewhat down. The cart and donkey I purchased allow me to relieve my poor tired feet from all of the walking, but the ride is boring and monotonous. I mean, every day, regardless of the weather, I venture forward on my journey; at night I make notes to glean clues from my travels. Although I may learn some bit of knowledge, I seem no closer to the goal than when I started.

Where am I going, anyway? I don't know why I ever agreed to this. Lost in thought, one of the wheels of the cart is perilously close to the edge of a very deep road rut. My attention rivets to my predicament only when the wheel slips into a crevice, and strikes a large stone half buried in the dried mud road. The wheel, burdened by the increased pressure, snaps like a twig causing the cart and me to crash to the ground. The side of the cart is crushed by the weight of my body and crumples like straw. I am face-down in the mud of the rut, my cart near ruin, and the stupid donkey laughs at me as though he planned the entire thing. Maybe he did.

Unable to repair the cart myself, I walk to a nearby village seeking a cart repair shop and am directed to a local shop known as "Antoine's Cart Shop." As I approach the shop, my spirits are lifted by the sounds of someone singing joyfully. It is Antoine himself, who sings or hums or whistles as he works. He is a happy man of medium height, mustachioed, with graying hair and maybe just a few pounds over average weight. A humble man, Antoine takes considerable pride in his work, as is very evident in the finished product. All about his shop are cart parts of varying sizes, placed in neatly arranged stacks. He directs me to leave everything to him, and sends one of his workers to retrieve my donkey and what's left of my cart. "Don't worry, we fix you up in no time and have you on your way." His soothing voice, his foreign accent and the ease with which he carries himself reassure me that everything is going to be all right.

"Come with me, we are going to eat a nice meal and I will show you something I'll bet you've never seen before." We pass by stall after stall of his workmen, each working feverishly to repair a damaged cart or carriage. "You see that one there?" he asks as he points to the same fine, two-wheeled chariot gilded in gold whose owner insisted on racing me some days ago.

"That one belongs to a bull-headed prince. Although he is nearly 30, he is still trying to prove himself. He rides around in that thing every day, all day, trying to find someone he can bully into a race, anyone he thinks might be a challenge. And, so fine a vehicle to be reduced to this state. It deserves better treatment.

"It's the fifth one he's destroyed. Someday, maybe he will grow up and realize that a fast cart, physical strength, an athletic body, and a smart mouth do not necessarily make you all that powerful. His father must hope for that, at least… but for now, he indulges him. What a pity."

He leads me out to the back of his shop, where the din of clanging hammers striking the iron frames of cart wheels is suddenly silenced. The world out back is totally different. It is calm, peaceful. Beautiful flowers buttress the walls of his shop and flora like that of the Cotswolds is abundant all around. But my eyes focus on a giant wheel firmly secured upright on an axle, sticking out of a large pole that is anchored in the ground. The wheel is decorated with the most amazing and colorful devices on it.

At each of the four quarters are angels, one with the head of a man, another with the head of an eagle, yet another with the head of a lion, and the last with the head of a bull, all of which I recognize as symbolic of the Apostles of the

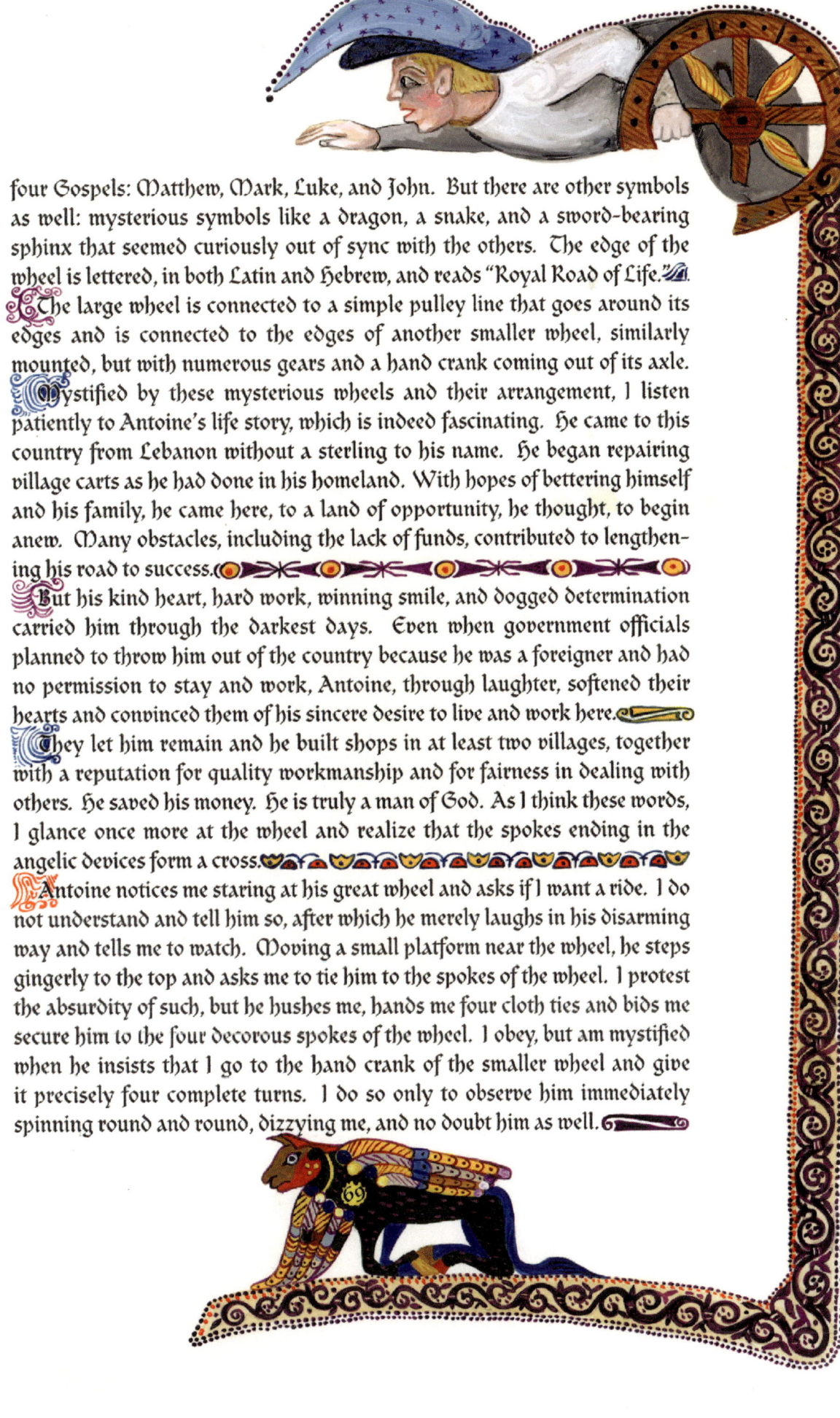

four Gospels: Matthew, Mark, Luke, and John. But there are other symbols as well: mysterious symbols like a dragon, a snake, and a sword-bearing sphinx that seemed curiously out of sync with the others. The edge of the wheel is lettered, in both Latin and Hebrew, and reads "Royal Road of Life."

The large wheel is connected to a simple pulley line that goes around its edges and is connected to the edges of another smaller wheel, similarly mounted, but with numerous gears and a hand crank coming out of its axle.

Mystified by these mysterious wheels and their arrangement, I listen patiently to Antoine's life story, which is indeed fascinating. He came to this country from Lebanon without a sterling to his name. He began repairing village carts as he had done in his homeland. With hopes of bettering himself and his family, he came here, to a land of opportunity, he thought, to begin anew. Many obstacles, including the lack of funds, contributed to lengthening his road to success.

But his kind heart, hard work, winning smile, and dogged determination carried him through the darkest days. Even when government officials planned to throw him out of the country because he was a foreigner and had no permission to stay and work, Antoine, through laughter, softened their hearts and convinced them of his sincere desire to live and work here.

They let him remain and he built shops in at least two villages, together with a reputation for quality workmanship and for fairness in dealing with others. He saved his money. He is truly a man of God. As I think these words, I glance once more at the wheel and realize that the spokes ending in the angelic devices form a cross.

Antoine notices me staring at his great wheel and asks if I want a ride. I do not understand and tell him so, after which he merely laughs in his disarming way and tells me to watch. Moving a small platform near the wheel, he steps gingerly to the top and asks me to tie him to the spokes of the wheel. I protest the absurdity of such, but he hushes me, hands me four cloth ties and bids me secure him to the four decorous spokes of the wheel. I obey, but am mystified when he insists that I go to the hand crank of the smaller wheel and give it precisely four complete turns. I do so only to observe him immediately spinning round and round, dizzying me, and no doubt him as well.

Curiously he laughs and laughs throughout the experience until the wheel stops and he asks me to release him, which I immediately do. He insists that I be next. I do not understand, but he seemed to have so much fun, that I think, "Why not?"

Suddenly, it is I who am questioning the natural laws of the universe, spinning like a planet in the cosmos above…no…below…no…above me. I marvel as I see images flickering about of the world all around me, including places and events I've been and places I'm likely to go. Although little more than a blur, I catch glimpses of Glastonbury Abbey and all of my friends there, of the beautiful lady in the forest I earlier encountered and lost, and of things that have been, and are yet to be. Liberated from space and time, I do not want the ride to end and beg like a child, bargaining with Antoine for just one more turn of the wheel. He chuckles to himself, but the wheel comes to a grinding halt, leaving me headfirst toward the ground. He rights me by slowly advancing the wheel a half turn and unties my bonds.

"You see, my boy, life is not always what you expect. You have already experienced the past and you will experience the future. You have no control over those times. The only time you control is now. The round wheel is a great spinning calendar of life. Round and round and round you go, where you gonna stop, nobody knows.

"But the ride, the ride…that's the thing. It can be as glorious or as sad (or a little of both) as you make it. It is your life, what are you going to do with it? If you constantly live in the past or project your future, you may lose the experience of the present.

Fools do nothing more than complain and throw life away like spoiled children that discard useless toys they are tired of. Others work hard but find no pleasure or pride in their toils. They say that if you plant your seeds, the harvest will come. Me, I'm very happy. God has granted me a beautiful wife and three lovely daughters. I work hard every day to provide them the best life possible, always telling them how much I love them and always remembering God and my wheel of life. Good times today can turn to dust tomorrow. Even that dust is what I choose to make of it. The masses do not understand the completeness of the wheel, the great circle, with no beginning or

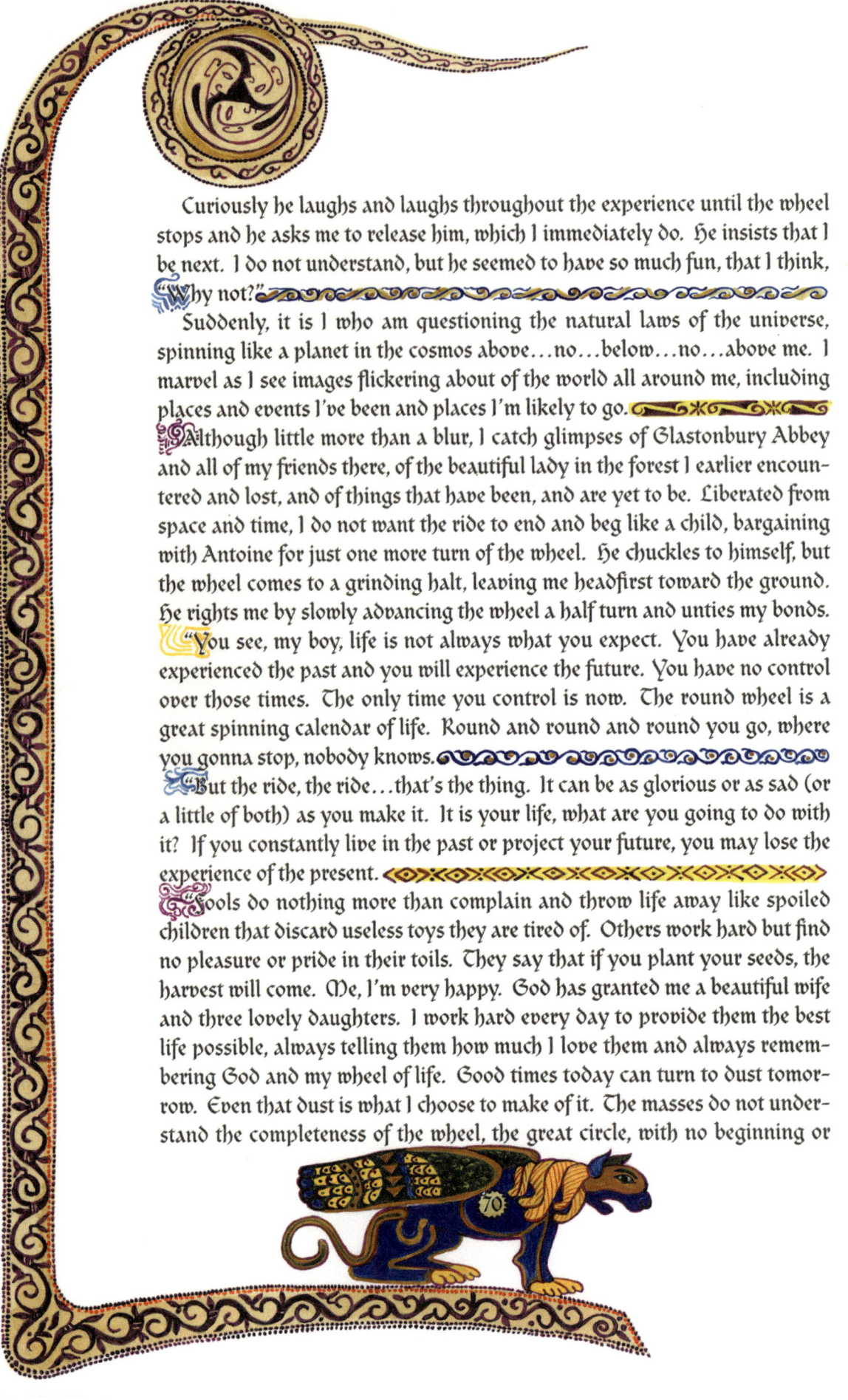

end, yet their number, the number zero, describes it perfectly for them. A pity they cannot see this aspect of the great Mystery. They close their eyes and pretend happiness."

"But how do you know they aren't happy, Antoine?"

"Because they all end up here at my shop, their carts broken, needing mending. (Isn't that why you're really here?) Their carts represent their lives; I merely repair them the best I can and offer them a vision of what life can be. Some see it, others cannot. Those that do are offered a ride on the Wheel, but few accept, for they are afraid of altering their pre-conceived notions of how life is supposed to be. Thoughtful change is not for the faint of heart. It requires a true inner faith, an internal moral compass, and a willingness to examine carefully what one encounters, without prejudice.

The keystone is individuality, the keys are the children. They alone accept people and situations on faith and trust, until the grownups damage them forever by filling them with fear for life and its multitudinous variations. Each person can grow if he decides what is right and what is wrong for him, and not merely be victimized by currently imposed social mores and misconstrued dogmatic religious pronouncements of how things are supposed to be. Come on Berner, let's eat."

With that, he fed me a sumptuous meal that included apricots, acorns, grapes, figs, olives, anise, and cinnamon, for which I praised God in his mercy, and I set off in my newly repaired cart, happier in spirit and soul for this lucky encounter.

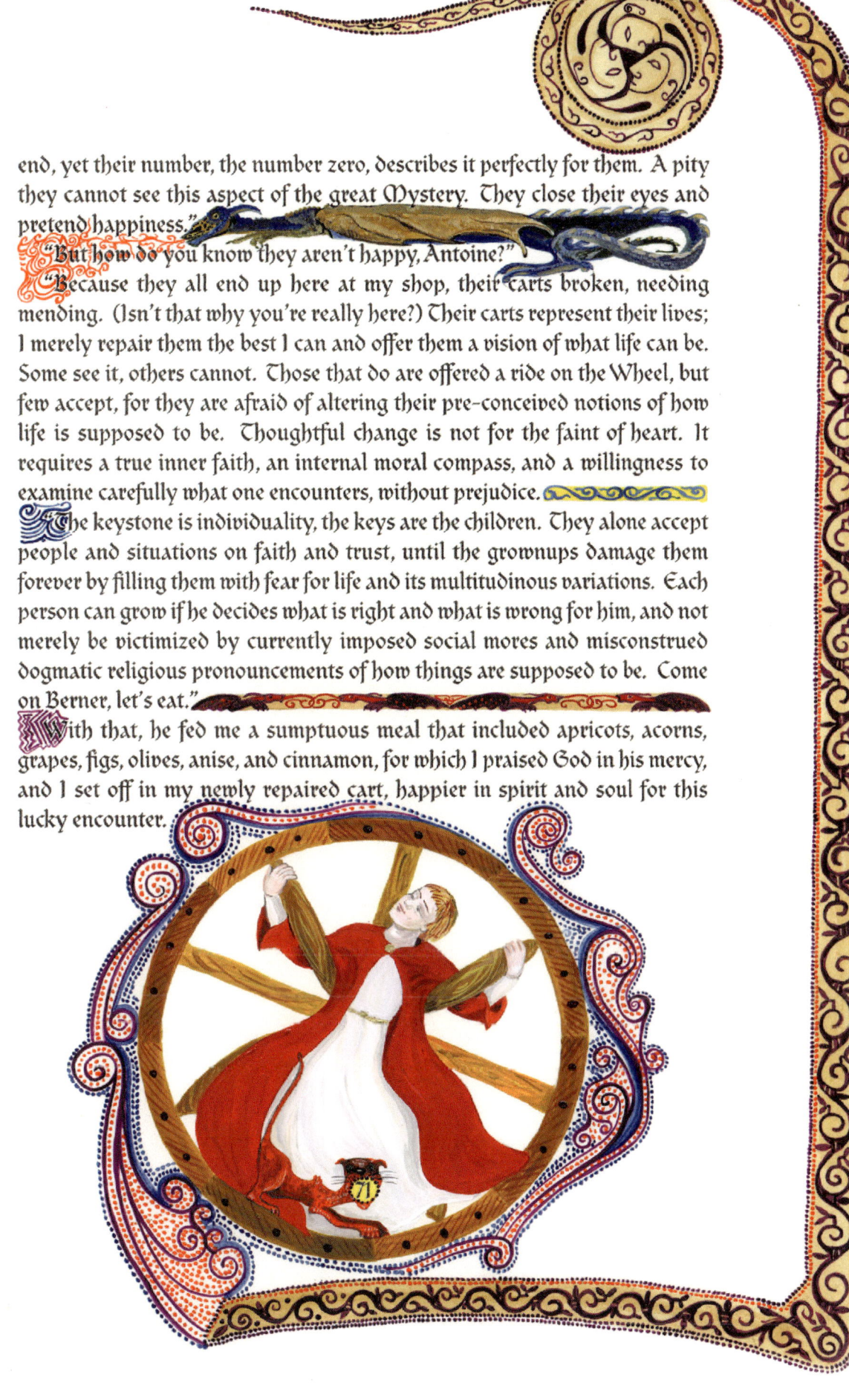

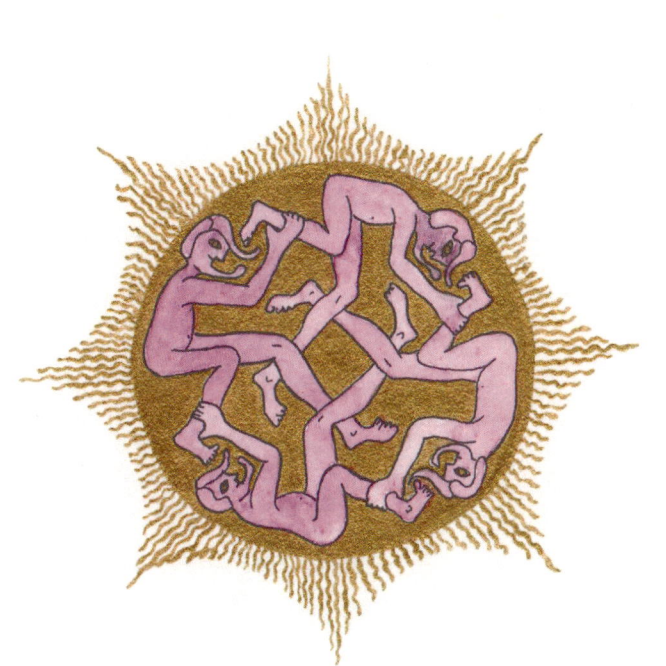

XI. Overruled

pproaching a large city inhabited by thousands of souls, intimidation overtakes me. Unaccustomed to such a large center of habitation, I determine my best strategy for a speedy trip through it to the other side. Fearful, I try to appear confident and sure. I pass by its denizens, but none appear to be the type to help a stranger in these parts; that is, until I accidentally meet Palmer. He is seated high in his ivory tower, close enough to the clouds to be above most of the town, looking out his window and watching the vagaries of the world.

Palmer is an older gentleman, with an empty pate save small vestiges of thin white hair on the sides and a distinctive handlebar mustache. Married more than 50 years, his lovely wife, Eleanor of Aquitaine, deports herself as a lady fit for a prince — charming, supportive, and kind, attending his every need. Aristocratic in his dapper suit of clothes, and possessing an ease with words uncommon to most, Palmer can read as well.

His charming wit captivates me and his kindness in inviting a total stranger to his perch so far above the fray comforts me as I sit and listen to his melodious voice. I am amazed to see his flexibility as he sits relaxed on a bench, in all of his finery, cross-legged, just to talk with me.

"So, what brings you to these parts, young man?"

"I seek the Holy Grail, sir," I replied with as much dignity as I could muster.

"The Holy Grail, eh? That's quite an undertaking for a young man. Many wise and brave persons pass this way with a similar quest, but never return. Most don't understand the nature of that which they seek, eventually abandon all hope and slink back home dejected and empty-handed. By the

way, have you been through your trial?" he asks with a gleam in his eye that lets me know he knows I have not.

"No sir, I don't even know what that is."

Patiently, he explains the intricacies of complicated judicial proceedings. Palmer, a barrister practicing in the chancellor's equity court for more than a half century, defends those poor souls heavily indebted to others and unable to meet their obligation to repay them. Most of these people are jailed and live out their miserable existence in deplorable conditions. Using various strategies, he salvages his clients' lives and freedom often enough that his colleagues fondly address him as "Dean" out of respect.

The older barristers regale me with stories of his renowned triumphs in the courtroom, and chortle about the high esteem in which the Court holds him. I beg him to teach me what he can, which he attempts to do, as a kindness to me. Hours turn into days until he turns and tells me, "You are ready." Although I protest and insist on the need for more training, he escorts me out of his tower, and with a gentle push out of doors, bids me well and points me toward the local chancery.

His directions instantly lead me to the Hall of Justice. An admirer of fine architecture, I stand outside looking leisurely about, marveling at this demonstration of strength and character. It is, I believe, the home of Truth, Justice, and the Way. Statues and other representations dedicated to those beings abound here.

Entering inside, a throng of people line the halls and fill the Courtroom. They seem to expect me, for I am called by name and seized straight away. I thought they were welcoming me, but quickly realize that this is a lynch mob, unruly and intent on doing me bodily harm. Vitriolic diatribes against me pour from their mouths like venom from a serpent. The allegations are so outrageous they sound more like cheap mythology than actual transgressions. I do not understand.

Everyone is taking this seriously. No amount of preparation could have led me to anticipate what was occurring. I am dazed and confused as they lead me before the chancellor, who asks me how I wish to plead to the trumped up charges against me.

76

"Plead?" I ask. "Prithee sir, plead to what?"

"To the unspecified high crimes you're accused of committing. Are you guilty of owing money or services to others? Did you kill someone? Answer wisely, for you may spend the rest of your life in prison, or worse."

"Kill him! Burn him! Beat him! Off with his head!" the crowd shouts. "Put him away forever, show no mercy. Justice! Justice!"

Recalling Palmer's teachings, I merely smile, deny the accusations, plead my innocence and advise the chancellor I plan to challenge these absurd charges by filing certain timely motions. I show no fear, though I recognize my helplessness in that I am a stranger in a strange land. I don't comprehend their customs or their reaction to my presence here. Nonetheless, I remain calm and keep my wits about me.

Suddenly, the doors swing open wide and in strides Palmer, dressed in his finest ermine robes. The auspicious appearance of this great man hushes the courtroom and overwhelms me. The Chancellor insists on an immediate trial on the merits and commences to swear witnesses.

One after another, townspeople bear false witness. They accuse me of breaking all of God's great commandments and a few I've never heard of. Lies, all lies.

Palmer, even without time for preparation, presents a brilliant defense.

"Objection sustained." "Objection overruled." "Order in the Court! Order in the Court!" were heard so often, the words reverberated throughout the corridors. Prosecutors volleyed and thundered each trying to best Palmer. But he was unflappable, unmovable, and unbeatable. Methodically, one by one, he demolishes their theories, their charges and their witnesses, suggesting that they, rather than I, should be punished.

The Chancellor has heard enough.

"Justice delayed is Justice denied!" he finally remarks. The tide is turned.

The clear champion this day is Palmer, who forces the Chancellor to withdraw the charges and allow me to walk out of the Courthouse a free man. Amid the jeers of many who are clearly pained that I have escaped their Justice, I leave the chancery, my head held high.

I am grateful and know I owe Palmer my life. I go to his loft to thank him for establishing the truth.

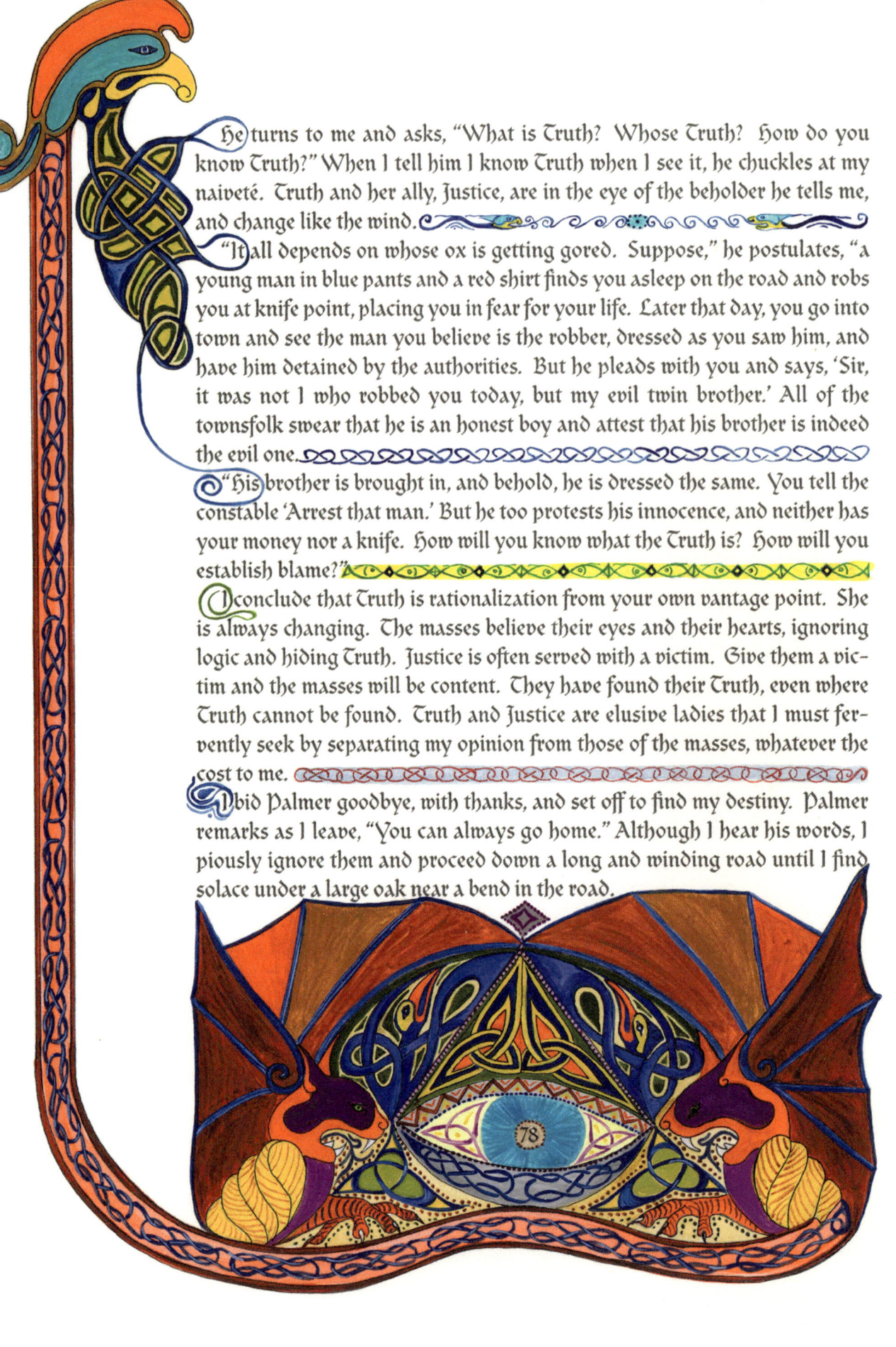

He turns to me and asks, "What is Truth? Whose Truth? How do you know Truth?" When I tell him I know Truth when I see it, he chuckles at my naiveté. Truth and her ally, Justice, are in the eye of the beholder he tells me, and change like the wind.

"It all depends on whose ox is getting gored. Suppose," he postulates, "a young man in blue pants and a red shirt finds you asleep on the road and robs you at knife point, placing you in fear for your life. Later that day, you go into town and see the man you believe is the robber, dressed as you saw him, and have him detained by the authorities. But he pleads with you and says, 'Sir, it was not I who robbed you today, but my evil twin brother.' All of the townsfolk swear that he is an honest boy and attest that his brother is indeed the evil one.

"His brother is brought in, and behold, he is dressed the same. You tell the constable 'Arrest that man.' But he too protests his innocence, and neither has your money nor a knife. How will you know what the Truth is? How will you establish blame?"

I conclude that Truth is rationalization from your own vantage point. She is always changing. The masses believe their eyes and their hearts, ignoring logic and hiding Truth. Justice is often served with a victim. Give them a victim and the masses will be content. They have found their Truth, even where Truth cannot be found. Truth and Justice are elusive ladies that I must fervently seek by separating my opinion from those of the masses, whatever the cost to me.

I bid Palmer goodbye, with thanks, and set off to find my destiny. Palmer remarks as I leave, "You can always go home." Although I hear his words, I piously ignore them and proceed down a long and winding road until I find solace under a large oak near a bend in the road.

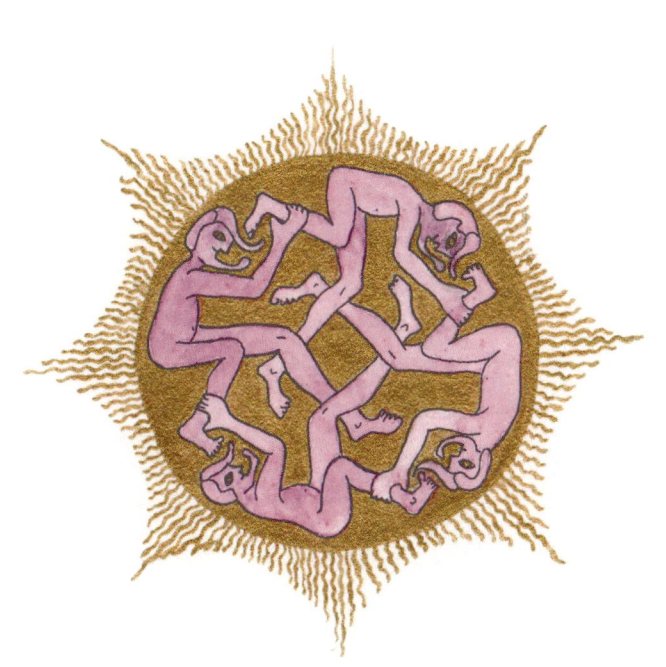

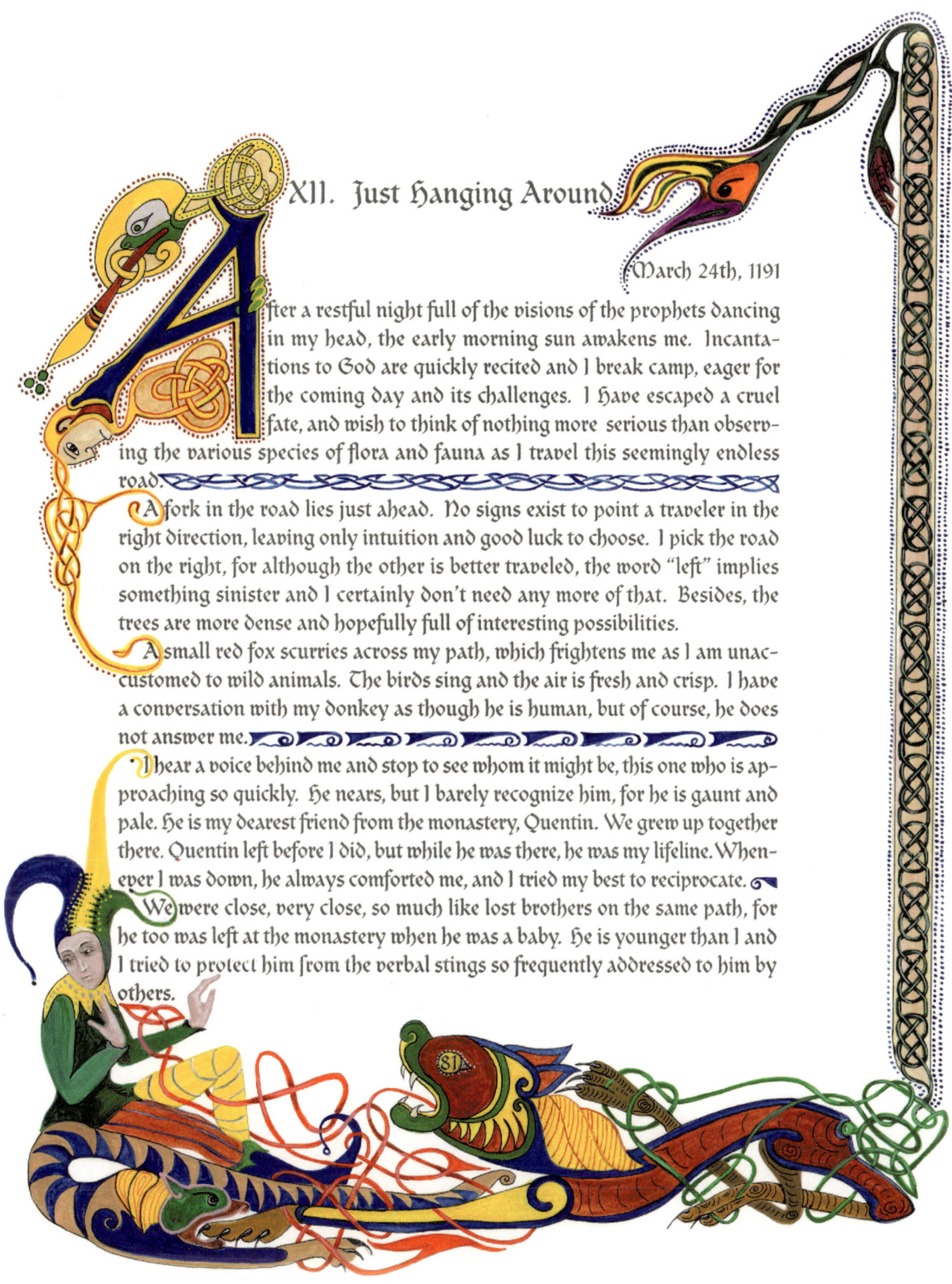

XII. Just Hanging Around

March 24th, 1191

After a restful night full of the visions of the prophets dancing in my head, the early morning sun awakens me. Incantations to God are quickly recited and I break camp, eager for the coming day and its challenges. I have escaped a cruel fate, and wish to think of nothing more serious than observing the various species of flora and fauna as I travel this seemingly endless road.

A fork in the road lies just ahead. No signs exist to point a traveler in the right direction, leaving only intuition and good luck to choose. I pick the road on the right, for although the other is better traveled, the word "left" implies something sinister and I certainly don't need any more of that. Besides, the trees are more dense and hopefully full of interesting possibilities.

A small red fox scurries across my path, which frightens me as I am unaccustomed to wild animals. The birds sing and the air is fresh and crisp. I have a conversation with my donkey as though he is human, but of course, he does not answer me.

I hear a voice behind me and stop to see whom it might be, this one who is approaching so quickly. He nears, but I barely recognize him, for he is gaunt and pale. He is my dearest friend from the monastery, Quentin. We grew up together there. Quentin left before I did, but while he was there, he was my lifeline. Whenever I was down, he always comforted me, and I tried my best to reciprocate.

We were close, very close, so much like lost brothers on the same path, for he too was left at the monastery when he was a baby. He is younger than I and I tried to protect him from the verbal stings so frequently addressed to him by others.

We were both very sensitive, easily hurt by the actions of the others. People were so cruel. But we, we got lost in our own world, a world we shared with no one. We shared everything together — there were no secrets, no jealousies, no tragedies, or comedies too great to be shared together. We could talk about anything, anytime, and in so doing, escape if only for a little while from the vagaries of the world we knew. We were united together in mind and spirit in a bond that transcended the human experience.

In the early days, before we knew each other, he rarely spoke to me or to anyone else. Once he got to know someone he wouldn't stop talking. His speech was very rapid, and one had to listen quickly to the words or at least the concepts. It was as though his mind ran faster than his words and he was always racing to put them together again.

Deep-set, dark black eyes revealed an aura of sadness about him. He was very lazy, but an avid reader and inventor, who quickly and easily grasped any concept thrown at him by the monks or anyone else. He irritated them constantly because he was much brighter than any of us or them, even without studying. His logical analysis made problem-solving a joke to him. In short, he was a tragic genius.

Just after he turned 15, Quentin seemed unable to take life at the monastery any more. By this time he spoke his mind, especially to me, and lost his civility with those who attempted to control or instruct him.

Though we disagreed on many things, he was always respectful, but not so with those in authority. They considered his thinking dangerous and heretical and regularly told him so, threatening frequently to punish him or banish him or even worse, to try him as a heretic and have him put to death. The more he spoke out on his own beliefs, the more upset they became. To him, they were demons, stifling his creativity and his existence. When he could take their control and their threats no longer, he left. No good-byes, no regrets, he merely left.

We heard he was drinking a lot of ale and wine and hanging out with the wrong sort. But I didn't care; he was my friend. So when Quentin reaches me, I stop the donkey and run to him, my arms extended to embrace him warmly, since it is the very first time I have seen him in nearly two years. His eyes are hollow and sunken and depression beyond anything I have ever seen in him prevails. He holds up his hand as I approach, as if to rebuff my advance. His first words pain me, for we had always been as close as any brothers and he is my heart and soul.

"I love you dearly, brother Berner, but please do not touch me for I seek acceptance from no one. If you believe what they have taught you, then I have sinned, for I have fathered a child, a son, out of wedlock. He is called Jason. Others will raise him, but I pray that you will always consider him your son, too."

I readily agree and invite Quentin to come sup with me and to sit and talk with me as we always have and he reluctantly agrees. Our talk goes long into the night and it is like old times once again. Sweet memories of childhood together, shared once more. The embers of our fire begin to dim and then turn cold. Night casts its heavy, shadowy web upon us, causing us to fall asleep, even though we would prefer to talk forever.

The crisp, cold morning sends jolting chills down my spine. I sit straight up, awake and ready to converse with Quentin some more. He is not here. All I find to greet me is a note, staked on a low-lying branch of a nearby tree like a rapier piercing the heart and flesh of a man. As I read the words, tears begin to flow down my cheeks and sadness overcomes me. The cheeriness of the bright sunlit day gives way to clouds of deep sadness within my soul and the crisp clean air all but chokes me. The words are too much for me.

Berner, my brother, you have been the best friend…no, you are the only real friend I have ever had. I will cherish you forever. But now, I am drowning in the River of Despair. For these last few years, I somehow negotiated my ways through the Forest of Doubt, the Marshes of Anger, and the desert of Lost Children's Souls. But, when I reached the Bridge of Confusion, I could take no more, and so, after taking my leave of you, dear friend, I know I must leave this world.

"The hardest part is the loneliness. I do not like who I am now. I feel like the world's biggest fool, but I'm not pitying myself. What really gets me down is that I traded my youth away. All the years when a person is supposed to grow and mature — the time when you make a start in life, when you get

past your self-indulgence and start to know life for what it is and what it is not. I traded that away for a lot of foolish notions.

"Now I have one last quest, to slay the Dragon that haunts me, so I can rest before I can make the ultimate sacrifice to God. Pray for me Berner, pray for my soul. I am sorry I let you down. Please do not look for me, for the person you knew is gone. God loves you and I love you, Berner. May God countenance you and may His Light shine on you, now and forever more. Farewell."

My heart is wounded and bleeds as though that branch had been stuck into me, rather than into that parchment. I wander around aimlessly trying to find some meaning to this; I am empty, so empty. And as I wander for the next three days, all I can think of are his words to me. What had I done to cause this, how had I let him down so? There are no answers, only more questions.

And then it happens. I come upon a smallish area, cleared of brush and debris, as though it has been set there to relieve the discomfort and to provide solace and rest to those coming along this way. I think to myself that I will rest a while, but it is not to be.

For as I set about to find water to refresh myself, I come upon the most horrible sight of my life. A large inverted cross has been erected near the clearing, and there to my great dismay, hangs my friend, Quentin, crucified upside down, symbolizing that he was not worthy to die as our Lord did so long ago. I rush to his side, but it is too late. He is gone.

The pain is too much and I run as fast and as far as I can. I run till I can run no more. I cry for hours, days, weeks, but nothing changes the fact that he is gone and that I feel responsible in some way. I wander aimlessly. What did I miss? What did I do to cause this? Why didn't he tell me so we could talk about it?

My mind tells me it is not my fault, but my heart says otherwise. It is the only thing I can think about and my distress is crippling. I cannot eat, I cannot sleep, I cannot think, except about him and the path he chose. He is gone. Finally, I can stay awake no more. I fall into a deep trance-like sleep and almost immediately, a vision of him, crying, comes to me.

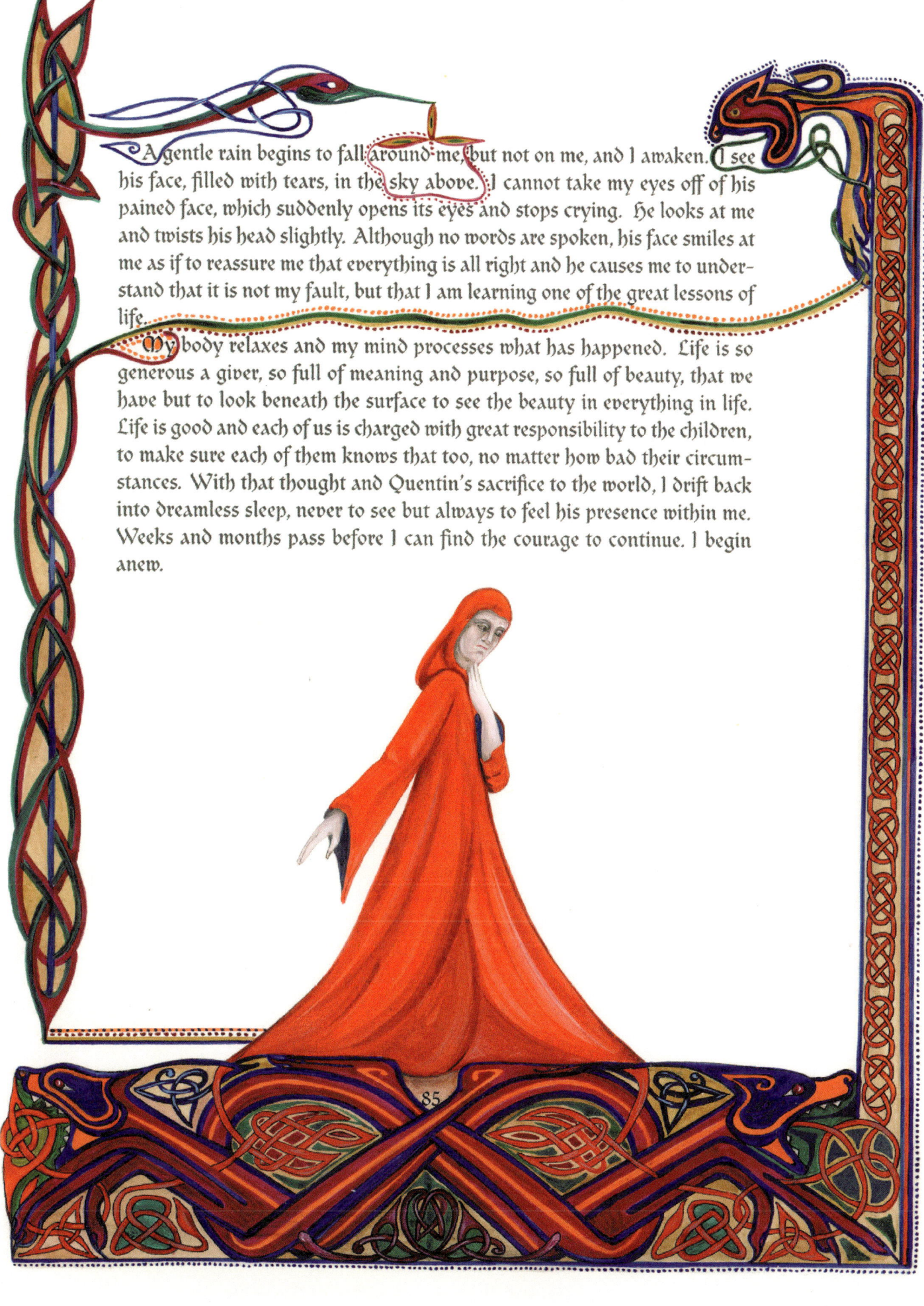

A gentle rain begins to fall around me, but not on me, and I awaken. I see his face, filled with tears, in the sky above. I cannot take my eyes off of his pained face, which suddenly opens its eyes and stops crying. He looks at me and twists his head slightly. Although no words are spoken, his face smiles at me as if to reassure me that everything is all right and he causes me to understand that it is not my fault, but that I am learning one of the great lessons of life.

My body relaxes and my mind processes what has happened. Life is so generous a giver, so full of meaning and purpose, so full of beauty, that we have but to look beneath the surface to see the beauty in everything in life. Life is good and each of us is charged with great responsibility to the children, to make sure each of them knows that too, no matter how bad their circumstances. With that thought and Quentin's sacrifice to the world, I drift back into dreamless sleep, never to see but always to feel his presence within me. Weeks and months pass before I can find the courage to continue. I begin anew.

85

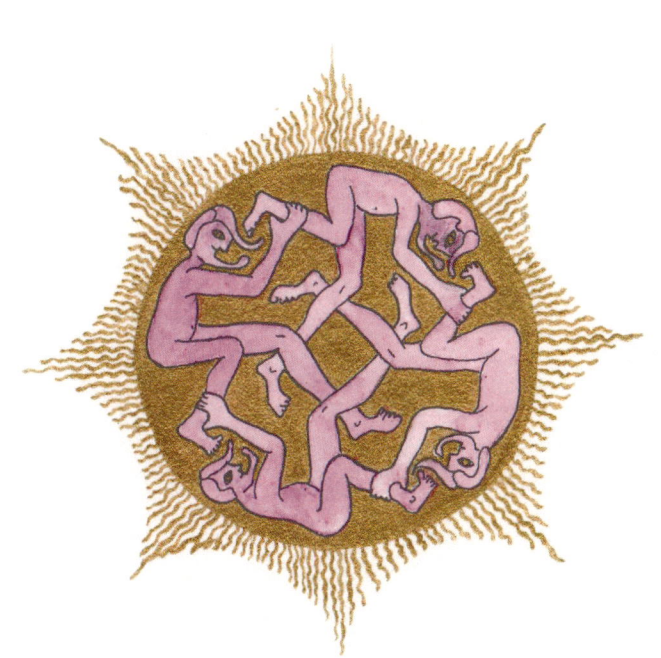

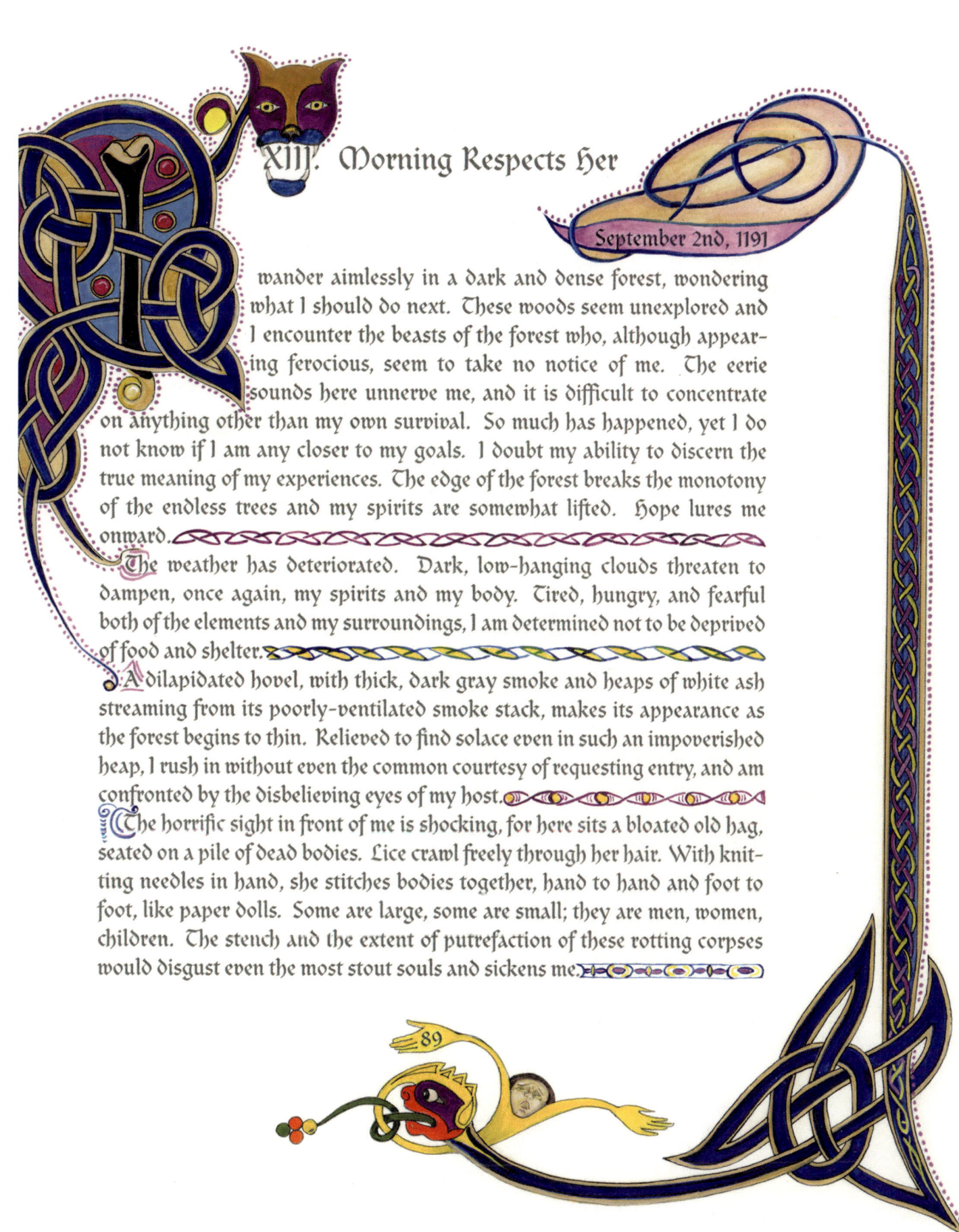

XIII. Morning Respects Her

wander aimlessly in a dark and dense forest, wondering what I should do next. These woods seem unexplored and I encounter the beasts of the forest who, although appearing ferocious, seem to take no notice of me. The eerie sounds here unnerve me, and it is difficult to concentrate on anything other than my own survival. So much has happened, yet I do not know if I am any closer to my goals. I doubt my ability to discern the true meaning of my experiences. The edge of the forest breaks the monotony of the endless trees and my spirits are somewhat lifted. Hope lures me onward.

The weather has deteriorated. Dark, low-hanging clouds threaten to dampen, once again, my spirits and my body. Tired, hungry, and fearful both of the elements and my surroundings, I am determined not to be deprived of food and shelter.

A dilapidated hovel, with thick, dark gray smoke and heaps of white ash streaming from its poorly-ventilated smoke stack, makes its appearance as the forest begins to thin. Relieved to find solace even in such an impoverished heap, I rush in without even the common courtesy of requesting entry, and am confronted by the disbelieving eyes of my host.

The horrific sight in front of me is shocking, for here sits a bloated old hag, seated on a pile of dead bodies. Lice crawl freely through her hair. With knitting needles in hand, she stitches bodies together, hand to hand and foot to foot, like paper dolls. Some are large, some are small; they are men, women, children. The stench and the extent of putrefaction of these rotting corpses would disgust even the most stout souls and sickens me.

Startled by my sudden appearance, the hag jumps slightly and then turns to continue her grisly work. Behind her is a great fireplace stoked by many of the bodies she has sewn together. These bodies are reduced to the ash I saw as I approached this place. Other bodies are carefully set in a large circular basket, presumably for later disposal. Filth and squalor abound. The place is reminiscent of a slaughterhouse, only here our Christian brothers are the slaughtered.

From time to time, without paying the least attention to me, she reaches down to stroke one of her two pet rats, each the size of a boar, that scrounge around her feet to snatch any morsels that might fall from her lap.

She does not seem troubled by my presence but is not given to conversation (but then, I have just barged in). I await her acknowledgment, recognizing that my own initial bad manners and the horror reflected in my eyes are at best, juvenile. She continues to knit for what seems like hours before turning to glance at me as if to ask what it is I want of her.

Before I can find the courage to postulate an answer, she turns and calls for her sons. Like a playful child one enters this place, quickly followed by two others. They are giggling and wrestling like schoolboys at play, dragging in rotting corpses with them, playing with them like children playing stickball. Each is dressed in an individual suit of armor: one jet black, another blood-red, and the third, forest green. They are dangerous looking, and each has his own weapons and shield: a mace, a lance, or a sword. One bears a great black flag and shield decorated with a curiously familiar white rose.

Maggots, flies, and worms crawl on the floor and infest the walls. The exuberant activities of the "boys" comes to a sudden halt when they focus on the presence of a live stranger in their midst. The hag looks at them and swats one hand in their general direction as if to strike one of the multitudes of flies present, and turns and drawls, "Don't stare at 'im, it's impolite." They look thoroughly embarrassed and nervously glance at their feet, shying away from eye contact with me.

She turns back toward me, and with a broad sweep of her hand as if to do me honor, says, "Sir, I am Morgain le Faye, but you may call me Fate. These are my sons, Death, War, and Pestilence. You'll have to forgive their rambunctiousness. They are here to serve me as they bring fuel for my fire. I would not survive without them. I'm always so busy, so much to do."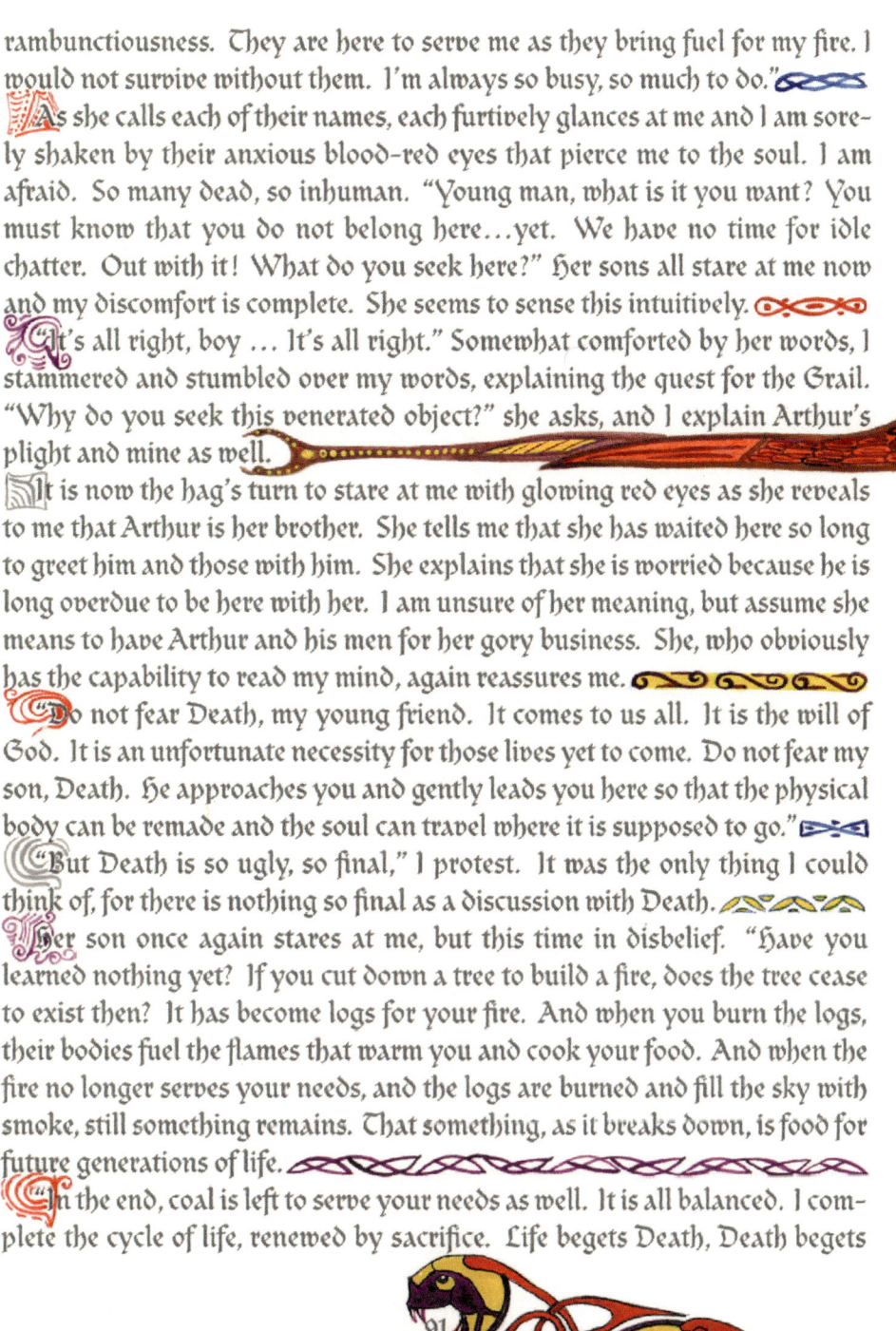

As she calls each of their names, each furtively glances at me and I am sorely shaken by their anxious blood-red eyes that pierce me to the soul. I am afraid. So many dead, so inhuman. "Young man, what is it you want? You must know that you do not belong here…yet. We have no time for idle chatter. Out with it! What do you seek here?" Her sons all stare at me now and my discomfort is complete. She seems to sense this intuitively.

"It's all right, boy … It's all right." Somewhat comforted by her words, I stammered and stumbled over my words, explaining the quest for the Grail. "Why do you seek this venerated object?" she asks, and I explain Arthur's plight and mine as well.

It is now the hag's turn to stare at me with glowing red eyes as she reveals to me that Arthur is her brother. She tells me that she has waited here so long to greet him and those with him. She explains that she is worried because he is long overdue to be here with her. I am unsure of her meaning, but assume she means to have Arthur and his men for her gory business. She, who obviously has the capability to read my mind, again reassures me.

"Do not fear Death, my young friend. It comes to us all. It is the will of God. It is an unfortunate necessity for those lives yet to come. Do not fear my son, Death. He approaches you and gently leads you here so that the physical body can be remade and the soul can travel where it is supposed to go."

"But Death is so ugly, so final," I protest. It was the only thing I could think of, for there is nothing so final as a discussion with Death.

Her son once again stares at me, but this time in disbelief. "Have you learned nothing yet? If you cut down a tree to build a fire, does the tree cease to exist then? It has become logs for your fire. And when you burn the logs, their bodies fuel the flames that warm you and cook your food. And when the fire no longer serves your needs, and the logs are burned and fill the sky with smoke, still something remains. That something, as it breaks down, is food for future generations of life.

"In the end, coal is left to serve your needs as well. It is all balanced. I complete the cycle of life, renewed by sacrifice. Life begets Death, Death begets

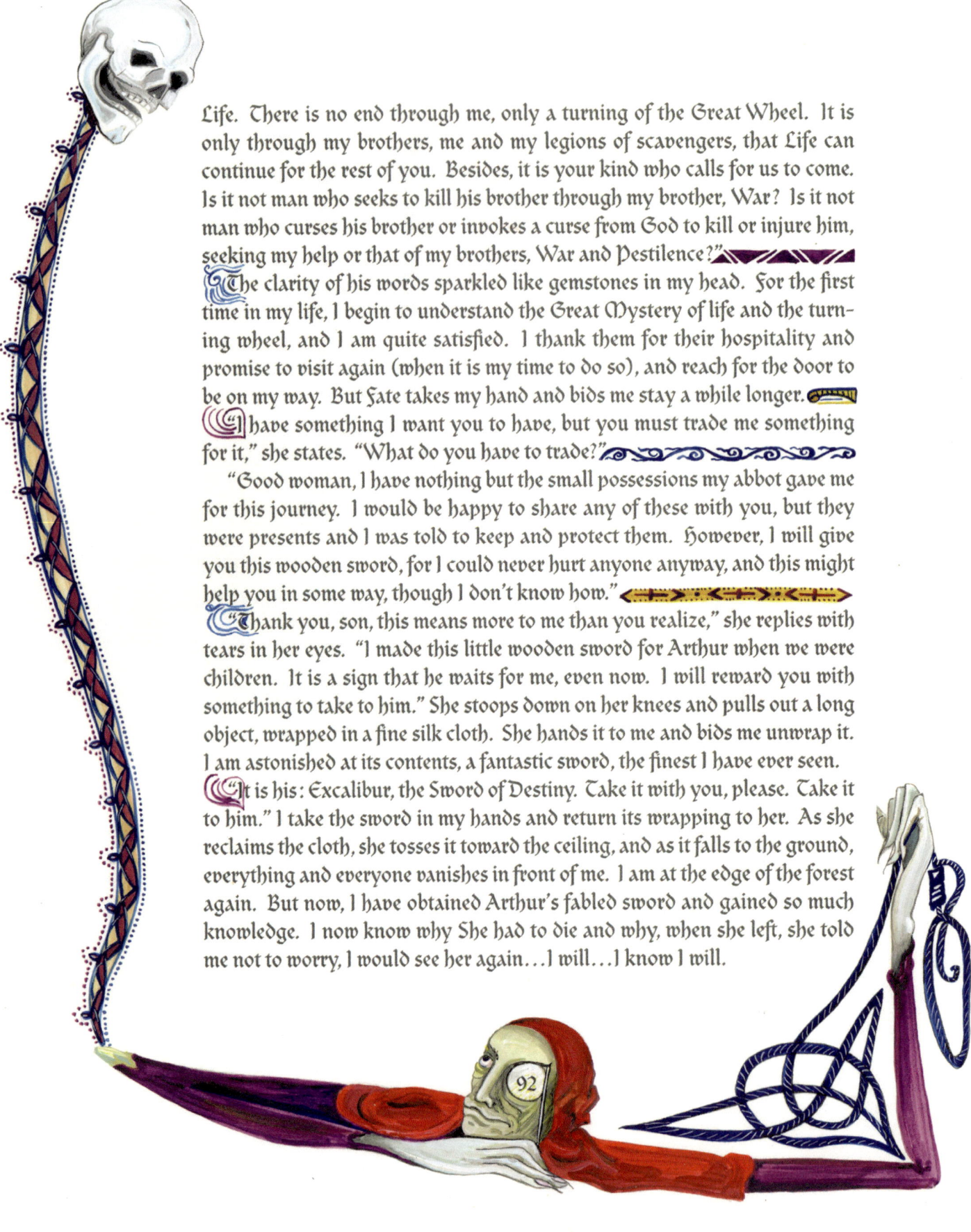

Life. There is no end through me, only a turning of the Great Wheel. It is only through my brothers, me and my legions of scavengers, that Life can continue for the rest of you. Besides, it is your kind who calls for us to come. Is it not man who seeks to kill his brother through my brother, War? Is it not man who curses his brother or invokes a curse from God to kill or injure him, seeking my help or that of my brothers, War and Pestilence?"

The clarity of his words sparkled like gemstones in my head. For the first time in my life, I begin to understand the Great Mystery of life and the turning wheel, and I am quite satisfied. I thank them for their hospitality and promise to visit again (when it is my time to do so), and reach for the door to be on my way. But Fate takes my hand and bids me stay a while longer.

"I have something I want you to have, but you must trade me something for it," she states. "What do you have to trade?"

"Good woman, I have nothing but the small possessions my abbot gave me for this journey. I would be happy to share any of these with you, but they were presents and I was told to keep and protect them. However, I will give you this wooden sword, for I could never hurt anyone anyway, and this might help you in some way, though I don't know how."

"Thank you, son, this means more to me than you realize," she replies with tears in her eyes. "I made this little wooden sword for Arthur when we were children. It is a sign that he waits for me, even now. I will reward you with something to take to him." She stoops down on her knees and pulls out a long object, wrapped in a fine silk cloth. She hands it to me and bids me unwrap it. I am astonished at its contents, a fantastic sword, the finest I have ever seen.

"It is his: Excalibur, the Sword of Destiny. Take it with you, please. Take it to him." I take the sword in my hands and return its wrapping to her. As she reclaims the cloth, she tosses it toward the ceiling, and as it falls to the ground, everything and everyone vanishes in front of me. I am at the edge of the forest again. But now, I have obtained Arthur's fabled sword and gained so much knowledge. I now know why She had to die and why, when she left, she told me not to worry, I would see her again…I will…I know I will.

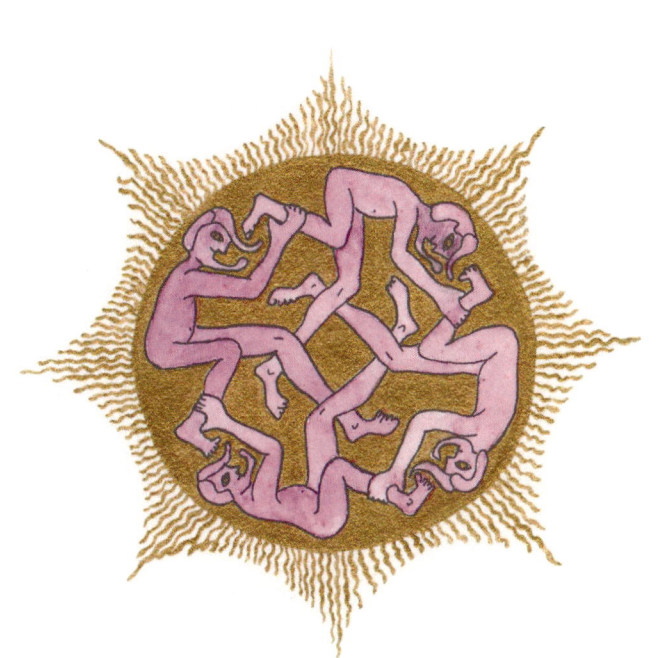

XIV. Dreamscape

Beyond the forest are rolling hills, similar to formations back home. My last experience leaves me shaken, but still in control. I never realized that I had so much to learn and experience in this world. At the outset of this journey I believed that I knew all that I needed to know. Now that appears to have been brash and foolish. Life is much more complicated and difficult than I assumed. Looking back, life at the monastery with all of the hard work and discipline and even being told what to do was easier than attempting to live life out on my own. Nevertheless, these experiences have proved most enlightening to me. Having crossed nearly all of Europe, I am about to enter a point where East meets West, where all of the customs and traditions of the peoples differ greatly from that to which I am accustomed. "Ah, Constantinople, that crown jewel of Christianity, founded by none other than Constantine the Great, the first Roman emperor to accept the inevitable truth of the Divinity of Our Lord and Savior and turn the hearts of the Empire away from their false and bloodthirsty gods of yesterday. (Even if, historically speaking, it looks as though he was merely trying to retain power in an otherwise declining civilization.) It was the capital of the Eastern Roman Empire and has produced some of the most magnificent structures and art of the Christian world. I am most anxious to see it all, but must not tarry long, for I have a job to do. I plan to enter the city by way of the Valley of the Sweet Waters, contiguous to the Golden Horn, to cross over to the other side. Right now, I thirst for a refreshing drink, for the journey is long and the climate hot and sultry. I only hope the waters are true to their name. But first, I must negotiate this little

95

hill. I am fascinated by the many evidences of life in this somewhat arid place. At the top, I look down into a precious valley, filled with lilies, irises, and other plants spilling over into the peaceful waters lying just a little ahead of me. As I contemplate these peaceful waters, a solitary figure glides overhead and gently lands at the water's edge, placing one bare foot ever so softly into the cooling waters. She is a seraphim, beautiful to behold. Bedecked in a luminescent pearl-white robe embroidered over all in tiny indescribable designs of gold and silver thread, she radiates warmth, love, and happiness.

Her long, flowing black hair, intertwined with sprigs of baby's breath and brilliant orange adonis palestinia, drapes over her slender shoulders, perfectly framing the symbols embroidered on her gown, between her breasts. These symbols, different from the rest, are a triangle of gold, a point in its center, and a silver and perfect square circumscribing both. On her forehead, she wears a circle of gold on which is incised a black dot. And her name is Amo, or "Love." Her vibrating wings beat gently sending warm and wonderful, inviting messages to me, offering the sustenance of the water to me. Instinctively, she seems to know that I am a traveler of great distances in need of refreshment. In her hands are two elaborately decorated cups, wrought of gold and silver respectively.

Never even glancing directly at me, she stoops and scoops a cup of this refreshing elixir from the still water, pouring it back and forth into one cup and then the other, a constant glistening stream. The water, rainbow-like, sparkles like liquid silver, reflecting light from her increasingly glowing halo.

In the distance, along the road I must take, glows another object, the silhouette of a golden crown, radiating like the sun above us. She sings quietly to me and bids me to enjoy a respite from the travels that have wearied me so, suggesting that all things come in due course.

Life is not a race; all things should be done in moderation—all in good time. Neither Rome nor the Universe was created in a day. A cool breeze dispels any hesitation I may have had and I truly relax, possibly for the first time in my journey. Time, she tells me, is on my side.

She begins quietly and softly to explain the symbols she wears. She intimates that the serpent belt I wear is an expression similar to that upon her head, that life is a circle, with no beginning or end. Death returns us to birth, which in turns leads us back to Death again. The cups she holds represent the past and the future.

But the flowing water, ah, now that is different. It is the present, which flows in both directions. The liquid present changes constantly, but is influenced both by the things that have been and the things that are yet to be. Man is confused because he thinks of time as a straight line, always moving forward, and it is this fallacy that wreaks havoc with men's souls, especially as they age and come face to face with Death himself.

She points to her chest and enlightens me on the symbols there. The square has four corners, each representing one of the elements of fire, water, air, and earth, like the objects given to me by the abbot that I keep in a bag tied to the end of my staff. The square itself is the world, while the triangle is the Trinity, a representation of God in spirit and physical form. The point within is the soul of man, which God holds and protects from evil, at least when man allows him to do so. All of this and much more than I can comprehend is the extent of God's love.

She takes my cup and pours a little of her water out of each of the two cups and gently moves my hands toward my mouth, implying that I am to drink, which I do. The murmur of the waters soothes my soul. I close my eyes, only for a second, to absorb these revelations. The wind blows in my face, and I open my eyes to see her fluttering away, like a butterfly, into the ether. She turns and blows me a kiss, with love, then sputters away ever so gently till she is gone from my sight, gone with the west winds.

I lie among the wild flowers and fall fast asleep, innocent and oblivious to the troubles of the world, if just for a little while. A rainbow becomes my guardian as I sleep. Tomorrow is another day. Feelings within me ebb and flow like the waters near my feet. Harmony and trust abound within me. I must access and assess these feelings in any decisions I will make, for these feelings are clearly an aspect of me.

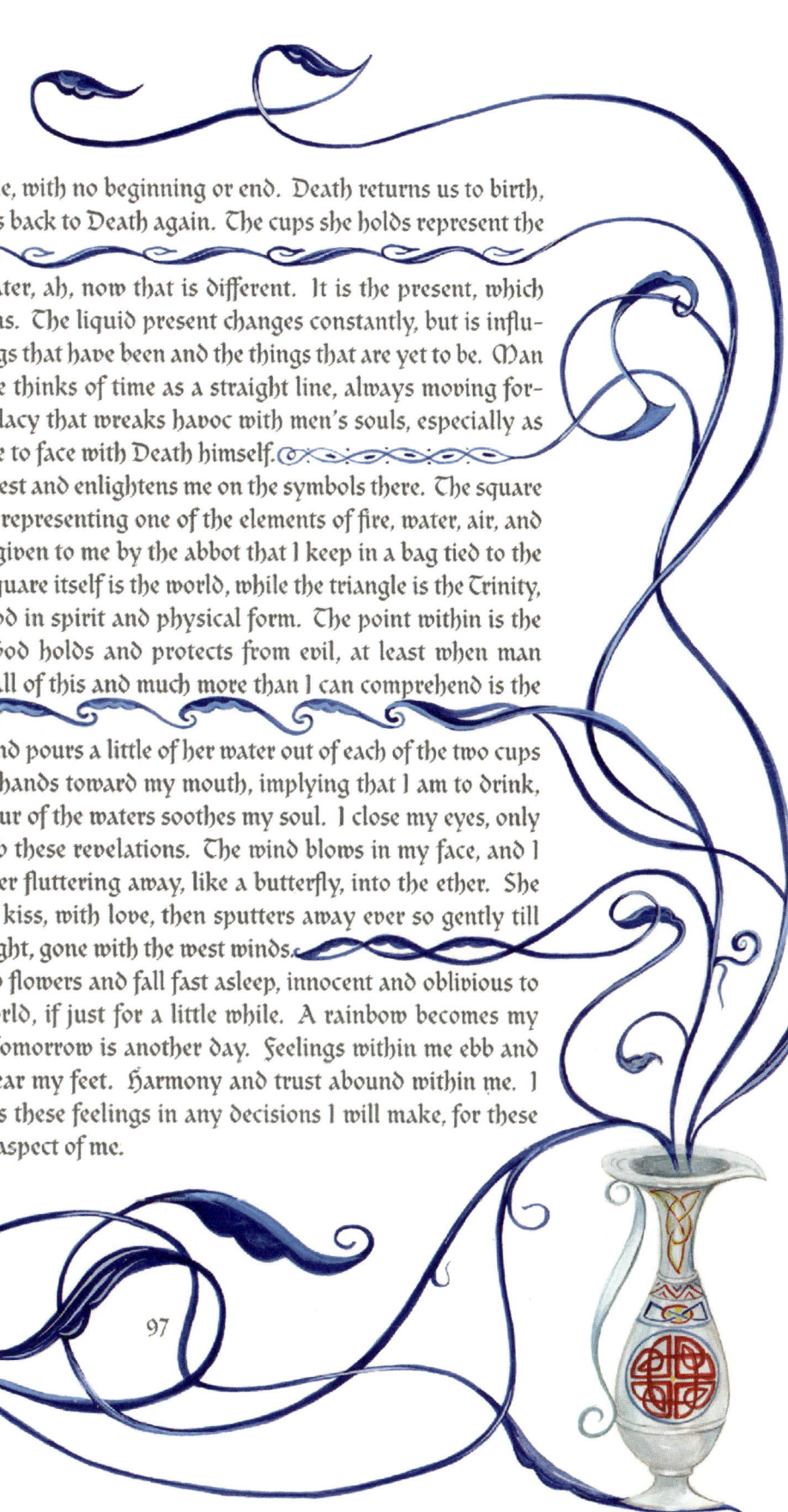

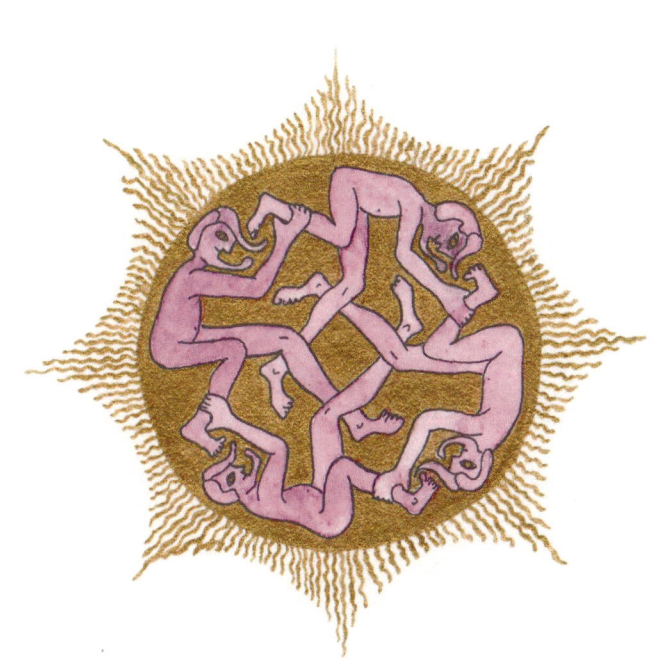

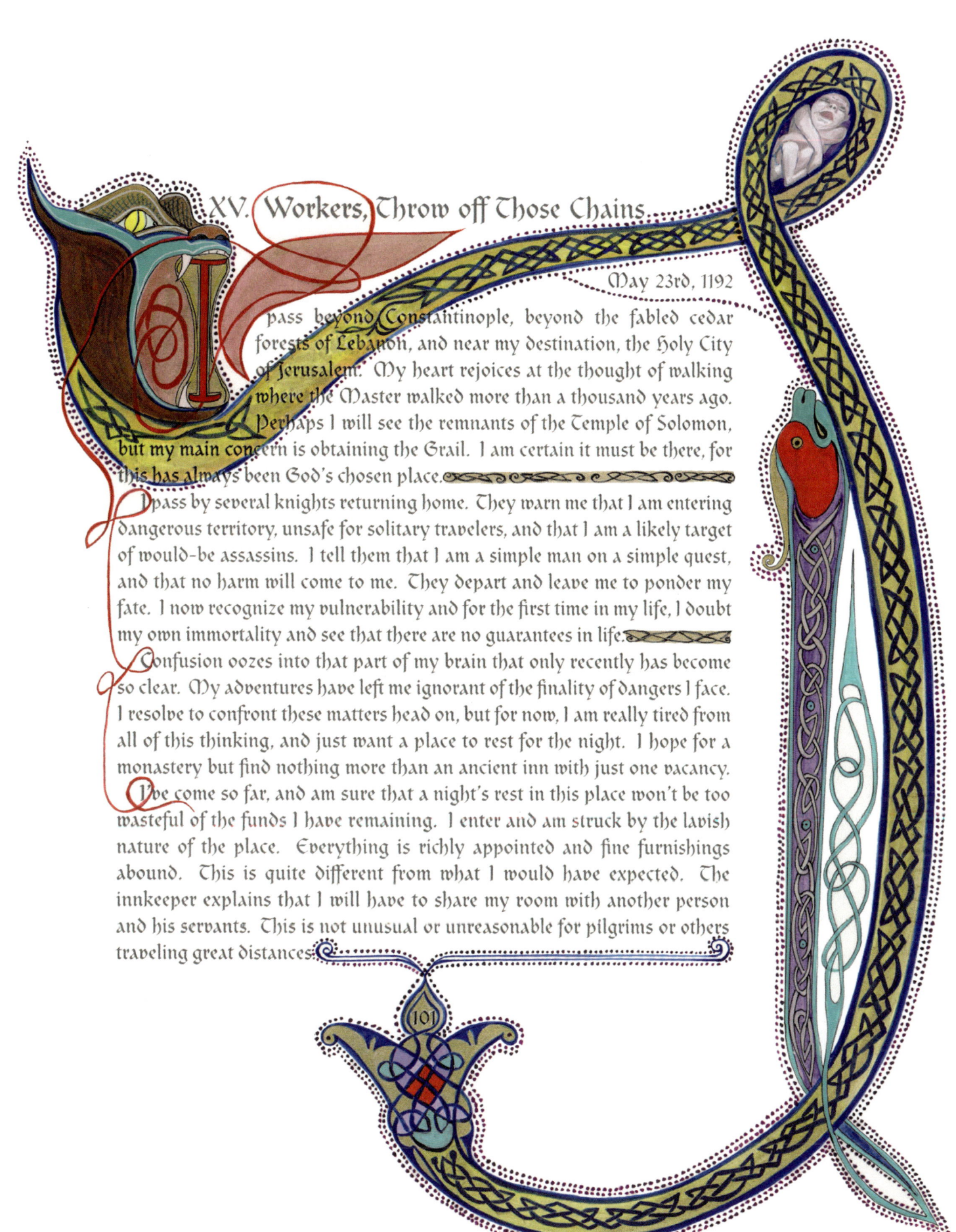

XV. Workers, Throw off Those Chains

May 23rd, 1192

I pass beyond Constantinople, beyond the fabled cedar forests of Lebanon, and near my destination, the Holy City of Jerusalem. My heart rejoices at the thought of walking where the Master walked more than a thousand years ago. Perhaps I will see the remnants of the Temple of Solomon, but my main concern is obtaining the Grail. I am certain it must be there, for this has always been God's chosen place.

I pass by several knights returning home. They warn me that I am entering dangerous territory, unsafe for solitary travelers, and that I am a likely target of would-be assassins. I tell them that I am a simple man on a simple quest, and that no harm will come to me. They depart and leave me to ponder my fate. I now recognize my vulnerability and for the first time in my life, I doubt my own immortality and see that there are no guarantees in life.

Confusion oozes into that part of my brain that only recently has become so clear. My adventures have left me ignorant of the finality of dangers I face. I resolve to confront these matters head on, but for now, I am really tired from all of this thinking, and just want a place to rest for the night. I hope for a monastery but find nothing more than an ancient inn with just one vacancy.

I've come so far, and am sure that a night's rest in this place won't be too wasteful of the funds I have remaining. I enter and am struck by the lavish nature of the place. Everything is richly appointed and fine furnishings abound. This is quite different from what I would have expected. The innkeeper explains that I will have to share my room with another person and his servants. This is not unusual or unreasonable for pilgrims or others traveling great distances.

101

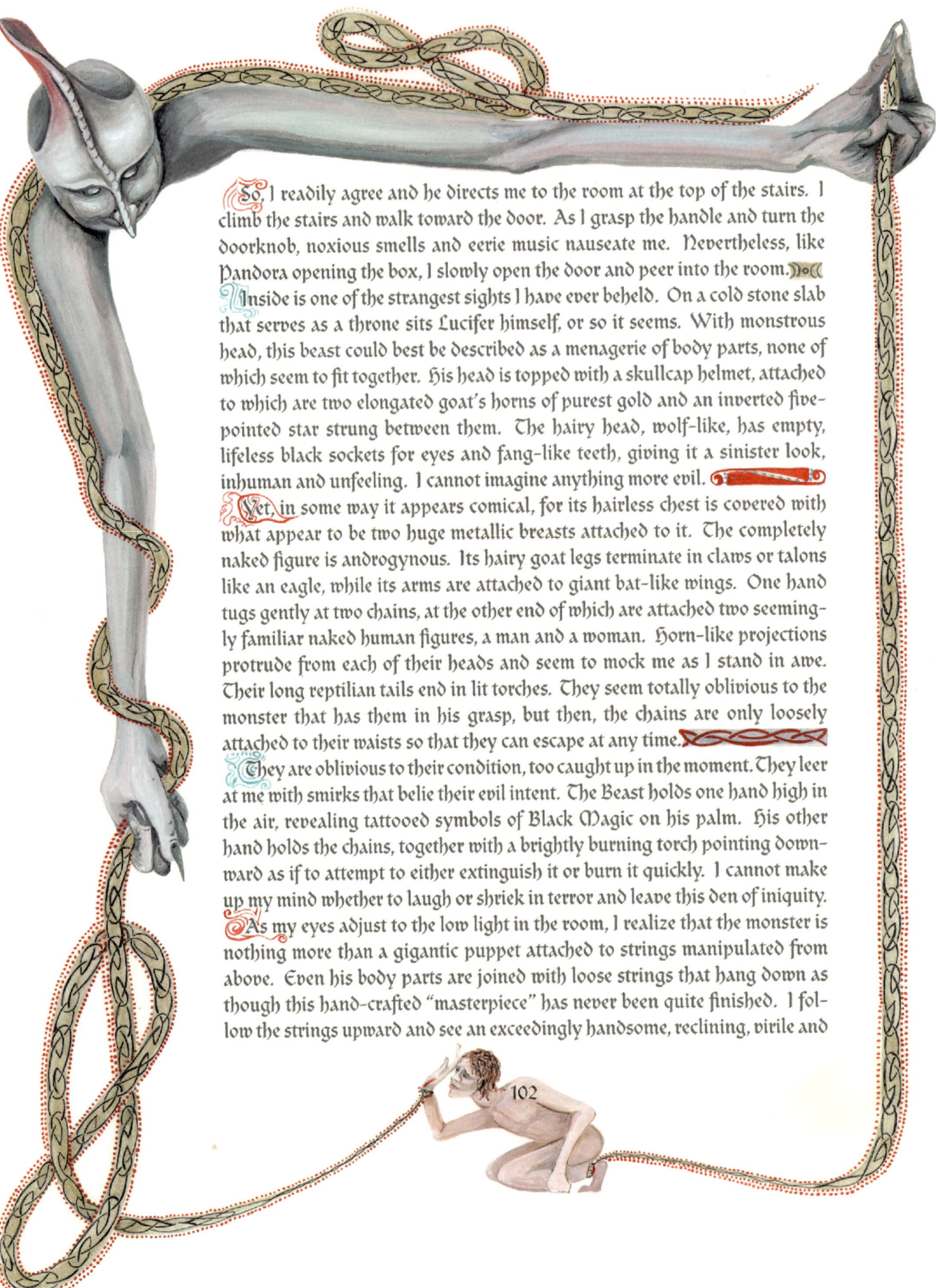

So, I readily agree and he directs me to the room at the top of the stairs. I climb the stairs and walk toward the door. As I grasp the handle and turn the doorknob, noxious smells and eerie music nauseate me. Nevertheless, like Pandora opening the box, I slowly open the door and peer into the room.

Inside is one of the strangest sights I have ever beheld. On a cold stone slab that serves as a throne sits Lucifer himself, or so it seems. With monstrous head, this beast could best be described as a menagerie of body parts, none of which seem to fit together. His head is topped with a skullcap helmet, attached to which are two elongated goat's horns of purest gold and an inverted five-pointed star strung between them. The hairy head, wolf-like, has empty, lifeless black sockets for eyes and fang-like teeth, giving it a sinister look, inhuman and unfeeling. I cannot imagine anything more evil.

Yet, in some way it appears comical, for its hairless chest is covered with what appear to be two huge metallic breasts attached to it. The completely naked figure is androgynous. Its hairy goat legs terminate in claws or talons like an eagle, while its arms are attached to giant bat-like wings. One hand tugs gently at two chains, at the other end of which are attached two seemingly familiar naked human figures, a man and a woman. Horn-like projections protrude from each of their heads and seem to mock me as I stand in awe. Their long reptilian tails end in lit torches. They seem totally oblivious to the monster that has them in his grasp, but then, the chains are only loosely attached to their waists so that they can escape at any time.

They are oblivious to their condition, too caught up in the moment. They leer at me with smirks that belie their evil intent. The Beast holds one hand high in the air, revealing tattooed symbols of Black Magic on his palm. His other hand holds the chains, together with a brightly burning torch pointing downward as if to attempt to either extinguish it or burn it quickly. I cannot make up my mind whether to laugh or shriek in terror and leave this den of iniquity.

As my eyes adjust to the low light in the room, I realize that the monster is nothing more than a gigantic puppet attached to strings manipulated from above. Even his body parts are joined with loose strings that hang down as though this hand-crafted "masterpiece" has never been quite finished. I follow the strings upward and see an exceedingly handsome, reclining, virile and

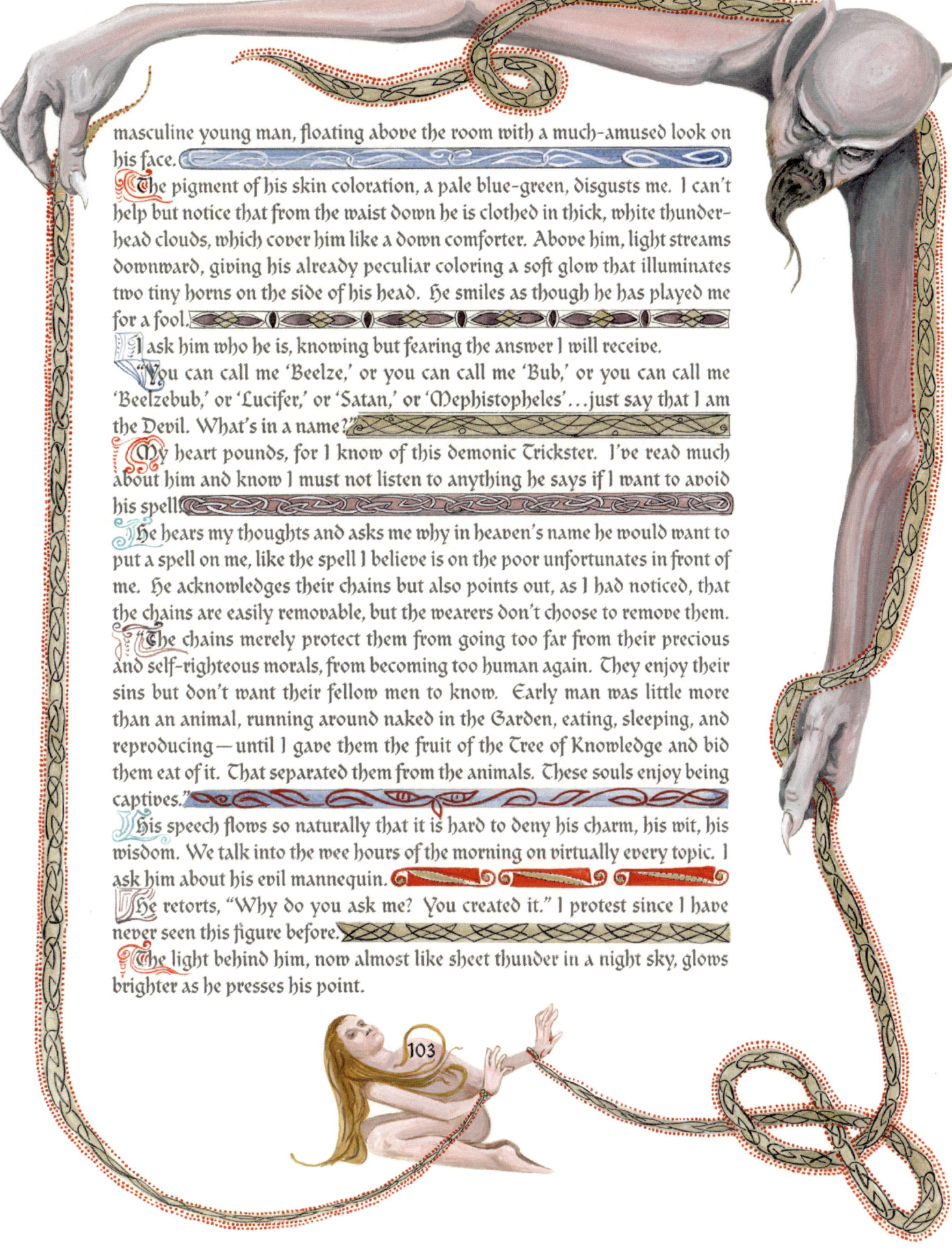

masculine young man, floating above the room with a much-amused look on his face.

The pigment of his skin coloration, a pale blue-green, disgusts me. I can't help but notice that from the waist down he is clothed in thick, white thunderhead clouds, which cover him like a down comforter. Above him, light streams downward, giving his already peculiar coloring a soft glow that illuminates two tiny horns on the side of his head. He smiles as though he has played me for a fool.

I ask him who he is, knowing but fearing the answer I will receive.

"You can call me 'Beelze,' or you can call me 'Bub,' or you can call me 'Beelzebub,' or 'Lucifer,' or 'Satan,' or 'Mephistopheles'...just say that I am the Devil. What's in a name?"

My heart pounds, for I know of this demonic Trickster. I've read much about him and know I must not listen to anything he says if I want to avoid his spell.

He hears my thoughts and asks me why in heaven's name he would want to put a spell on me, like the spell I believe is on the poor unfortunates in front of me. He acknowledges their chains but also points out, as I had noticed, that the chains are easily removable, but the wearers don't choose to remove them.

"The chains merely protect them from going too far from their precious and self-righteous morals, from becoming too human again. They enjoy their sins but don't want their fellow men to know. Early man was little more than an animal, running around naked in the Garden, eating, sleeping, and reproducing—until I gave them the fruit of the Tree of Knowledge and bid them eat of it. That separated them from the animals. These souls enjoy being captives."

His speech flows so naturally that it is hard to deny his charm, his wit, his wisdom. We talk into the wee hours of the morning on virtually every topic. I ask him about his evil mannequin.

He retorts, "Why do you ask me? You created it." I protest since I have never seen this figure before.

The light behind him, now almost like sheet thunder in a night sky, glows brighter as he presses his point.

"Who told you that I am evil?" and I reply that it is well known and written everywhere, even in the Great Holy Book. His easy smile saddens and tears begin to stream down his cheeks.

"I am the most maligned of beings, for it is I, not your great God, Yahweh, who cares for you. I am a humanist, who first brought you fire to warm your bodies and to cook your food. I insisted man and woman eat of the forbidden fruit so they would not remain in the Garden like the ignorant beasts of the forest. It is I who weeps for you when your God sends plagues and swarms of illness-laden flies to strike down young babies and able-bodied souls too young to die, or allows wars to purge whole generations from this planet.

"It is I who care for each of you and help you discover who you really are. My thanks is to be condemned in the pulpit to Hell and eternal damnation. For what? The sin of knowledge, the sin of self-realization, the sins of humanity created by hypocrites and fools? Make no mistake, friend, it is I you should be praying to. The Old Man upstairs doesn't care about you. It is I, Lucifer. I am the Bringer of Light."

"Then why the masquerade of this ugly beast?"

"I told you, you created this in your own mind. Humbly, I merely play a role you ask me to play in your endless, silly morality play. You make me the scapegoat when things go wrong. If you become poor, it is my fault, because I took your money from you. If you are greedy—you say I made you be that way. If you fall ill, you curse me for my wickedness and say I brought the flies or the plague or the other horrible things that doom mankind. And when you do something totally out of character, such that it horrifies even your own sense of right and wrong, you turn and drawl, 'The Devil made me do it.' Can no one take responsibility for his own actions?

"Who is the Creator? By definition, I cannot create those evil things that cause you harm. You worship the Being that created everything (even me), who destroys you, hurts you, leaves you begging for mercy. Yet you hate me, insult me, blame me. Oh, I am a most misunderstood being. I don't even know why I continue to try.

"To each of you, I am only a boogeyman, and I have to create one to show to you to satisfy your preposterous ideas of who or what I am, else I will never

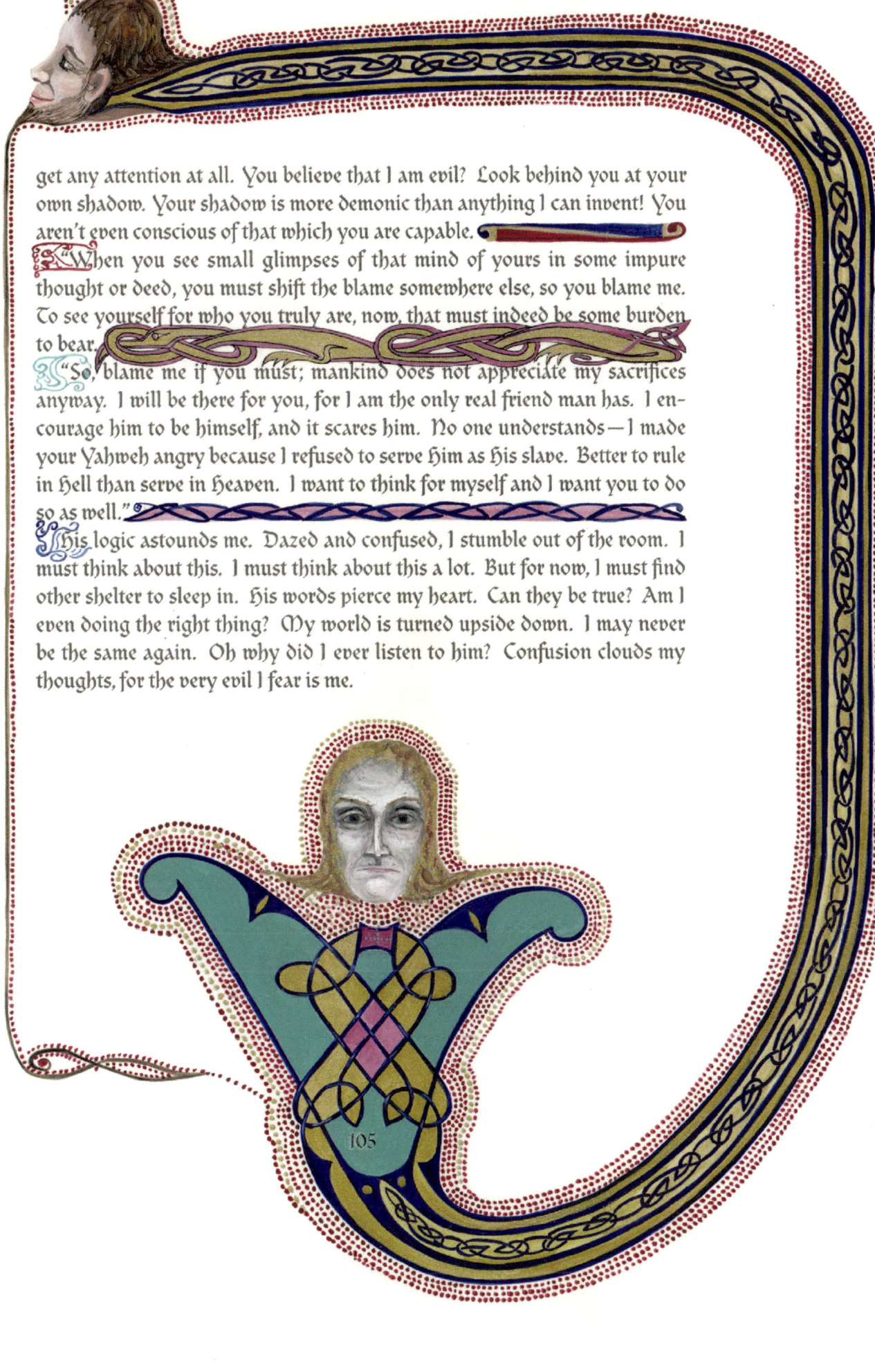

get any attention at all. You believe that I am evil? Look behind you at your own shadow. Your shadow is more demonic than anything I can invent! You aren't even conscious of that which you are capable.

"When you see small glimpses of that mind of yours in some impure thought or deed, you must shift the blame somewhere else, so you blame me. To see yourself for who you truly are, now, that must indeed be some burden to bear.

"So, blame me if you must; mankind does not appreciate my sacrifices anyway. I will be there for you, for I am the only real friend man has. I encourage him to be himself, and it scares him. No one understands—I made your Yahweh angry because I refused to serve him as His slave. Better to rule in Hell than serve in Heaven. I want to think for myself and I want you to do so as well."

This logic astounds me. Dazed and confused, I stumble out of the room. I must think about this. I must think about this a lot. But for now, I must find other shelter to sleep in. His words pierce my heart. Can they be true? Am I even doing the right thing? My world is turned upside down. I may never be the same again. Oh why did I ever listen to him? Confusion clouds my thoughts, for the very evil I fear is me.

105

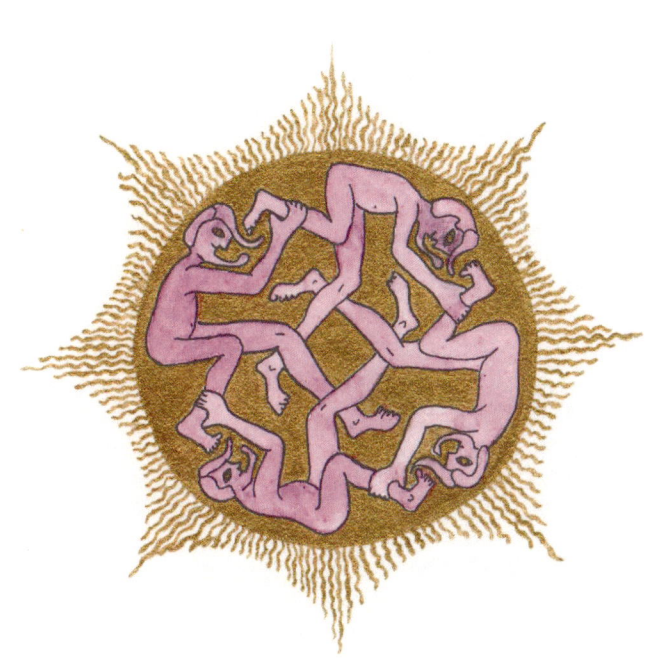

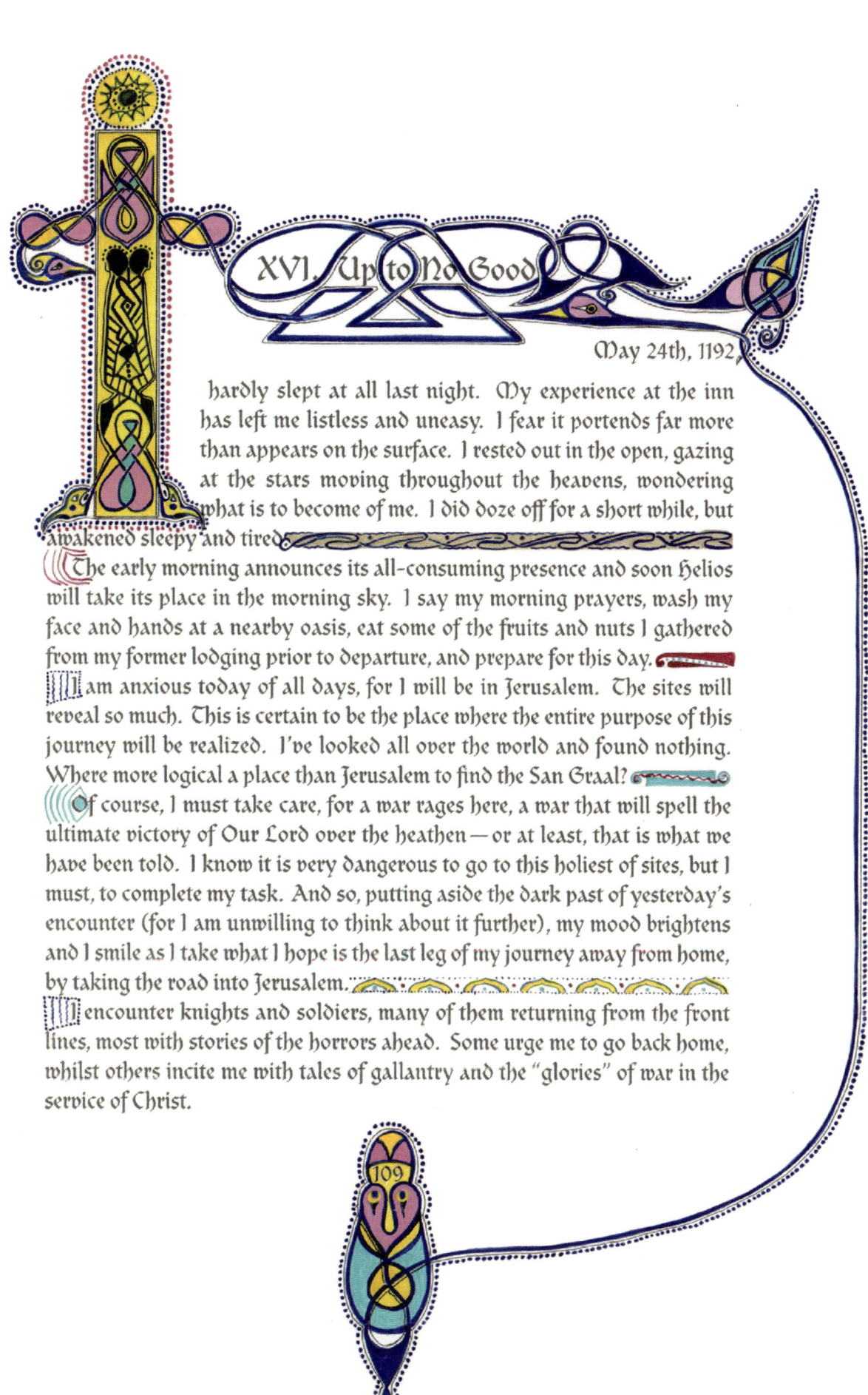

XVI. Up to No Good

May 24th, 1192

hardly slept at all last night. My experience at the inn has left me listless and uneasy. I fear it portends far more than appears on the surface. I rested out in the open, gazing at the stars moving throughout the heavens, wondering what is to become of me. I did doze off for a short while, but awakened sleepy and tired.

The early morning announces its all-consuming presence and soon Helios will take its place in the morning sky. I say my morning prayers, wash my face and hands at a nearby oasis, eat some of the fruits and nuts I gathered from my former lodging prior to departure, and prepare for this day.

I am anxious today of all days, for I will be in Jerusalem. The sites will reveal so much. This is certain to be the place where the entire purpose of this journey will be realized. I've looked all over the world and found nothing. Where more logical a place than Jerusalem to find the San Graal?

Of course, I must take care, for a war rages here, a war that will spell the ultimate victory of Our Lord over the heathen — or at least, that is what we have been told. I know it is very dangerous to go to this holiest of sites, but I must, to complete my task. And so, putting aside the dark past of yesterday's encounter (for I am unwilling to think about it further), my mood brightens and I smile as I take what I hope is the last leg of my journey away from home, by taking the road into Jerusalem.

I encounter knights and soldiers, many of them returning from the front lines, most with stories of the horrors ahead. Some urge me to go back home, whilst others incite me with tales of gallantry and the "glories" of war in the service of Christ.

109

Unknown to others, I have Excalibur. (It does not occur to me that I have never used a sword, and have been taught practically from birth to refrain from violence.)

Entering the city, I expect to see hordes of warriors running about, lopping off heads, arms, and assorted body parts of the enemy, with like action from their counterparts. Led by the kings, princes, knights, and potentates of Christendom, knights will charge the enemy lines and free the people "enslaved" by the wicked Islamic rulers. My impure thoughts surprise and disgust me, for who am I to judge?

The closer I come, the louder the din of battle becomes. I become anxiety-ridden as I approach the scene I expect to see — carnage everywhere, the dead, the dying, and the wounded being carried away or begging for mercy or medical and spiritual assists.

What I see when I approach is even more shocking. For the first sight of "battle" is none other than Our Sovereign, Richard, carrying on an intense conversation with Saladin, his sworn enemy, and other leaders from both sides. No one seems to notice me and I am able with little effort, to sally up next to the king and listen to the discussion. They are not fighting, they're arguing. In fact there is no fighting going on anywhere.

Rather, I am faced with a monstrous building project, led by King Richard and Saladin. I listen and watch intently, only to learn that they are each attempting to build an edifice that will reach to heaven so that God Himself can choose the correct religion for all of the people of the world. I think to myself that this has been tried before, but I am in no position to reprimand these kings of men. They have a plan.

Instead of fighting, they swear their men to secrecy and send word back home from time to time about the progress of the "war," the casualties and the victories or defeats won or lost. Fewer men will be lost this way, and everyone can make up whatever stories they like to pass on to their wives and kids. The men believe this will be their chance to get out of the house with their male friends, and come back heroes. A good time will be had by all.

This less than perfect plan involves the construction of a circular tower that will stretch all the way to the heavens above, to be topped by a crowning dome made of pure beaten gold that gleams like the sun. Each of the "armies" will build a semi-circular structure, with a common wall forming the diameter of the circle, thus creating a whole circular tower. The first side to complete their structure will have the honor of putting on the dome and talking to God first. On the surface this seems innocent enough, and besides, look at all of the lives it could save. But politicians, cynical and sinister as they can be, often have a hidden agenda. I can tell by their voices that something is amiss. But before I can deal with that issue, I remember that I am here on "official" business and need to conduct a search for the object so dearly desired.

The king finishes pontificating on this or that point with Saladin and is about to walk away. I clear my throat with a loud "Hrmmmph," which catches his attention and everyone else's, all of whom turn toward me to see who dares to interrupt the work of kings. My youth and slight appearance are not conducive to an audience with these men, but then a strange thing happens. Excalibur begins to vibrate, producing a humming noise that seems to cause all of these men to gravitate toward me as if in a hypnotic trance. They aren't, of course, but it does seem to compel them to listen. I attempt to explain my mission and they are sympathetic. They tell me a rumor persists that the Grail was intentionally placed somewhere in this temple to God and Allah, but the source and veracity of that rumor cannot be vouched for. Each side offers to attempt to seek and retrieve it from within, for it is far too dangerous inside for me. I thank them and accept their offer.

Each side, I believe, is anxious to help me in order to win more favor with God (Allah) in their already extant "battle." (Of course, the power of Excalibur's vibrations may have helped.) The top halves of the tower may take days to reach, the structure stretching seemingly forever towards heaven. Each side of this massive stone structure is filled with hundreds of knights, warriors, princes, kings, sultans, engineers, and workers, all anxious to complete their tasks for the glory of God. Cattle have been brought in to help move the stones ever upward in the "noble" search for Truth.

Unfortunately, the plan is flawed from the outset. Both Muslim and Christian leaders, determined to finish first, and thus talk to God (as though He is going to talk to them anyway), surreptitiously have worked to prevent

111

the other from completing their structure. At night, devious rulers send their best soldier workmen to wreak havoc on the competitor's previous day's work. Huge gashes are knocked into the walls, which returning itinerant worker-soldiers assume are planned windows someone cut through the stone. Night after night, each structure is weakened. The foundations struggle to balance the increasing weight of the building, the men and their animals, and equipment.

Higher and higher they go, with various kings and sultans leading thousands of men furiously and perilously toward the top in their vain attempt to see God, and to retrieve the elusive Grail and return it safely to the ground below. A great rumbling emanates both from the sky and within the building as smoke billows out of the "windows" and men rush forward and upward. The sky, now dark and foreboding, begins to cloud up with angry, threatening thunderheads.

Still men rush ahead, excited by the prospect of talking to God, encouraged by those below, who offer untold treasures to the victors. The structure begins to sway in the wind from all of the increased weight and from the demolition of the previous night. I find myself disgusted, but secretly hope the Muslim's building will crumble and destroy them all. I am not in control of my emotions as I think depraved thoughts about my fellow man. I have to ask myself, what am I becoming and where have these thoughts come from? Have I become a victim of Beelzebub? I contemplate my lack of morality.

Suddenly one and then another head appears at or near the top where a golden crown rests, awaiting its final placement on the day of completion, a day that is not to occur. For at the very moment the tiny heads of the multitude appear so far above the rest of us earth-bound creatures, huge bolts of lightening, preceded by a tremendous rolling clap of thunder in an endless drumbeat of fury, strike the tower dome. The jolt is scary enough, but it has hit with such violence and with the additional weight of all of the people at or near the top, it is all this structure can take.

The weakened foundations give way, collapsing all of the pre-planned areas anointed by the picks and shovels of these destructive opposing armies, and the building comes tumbling down, sparing neither king nor common

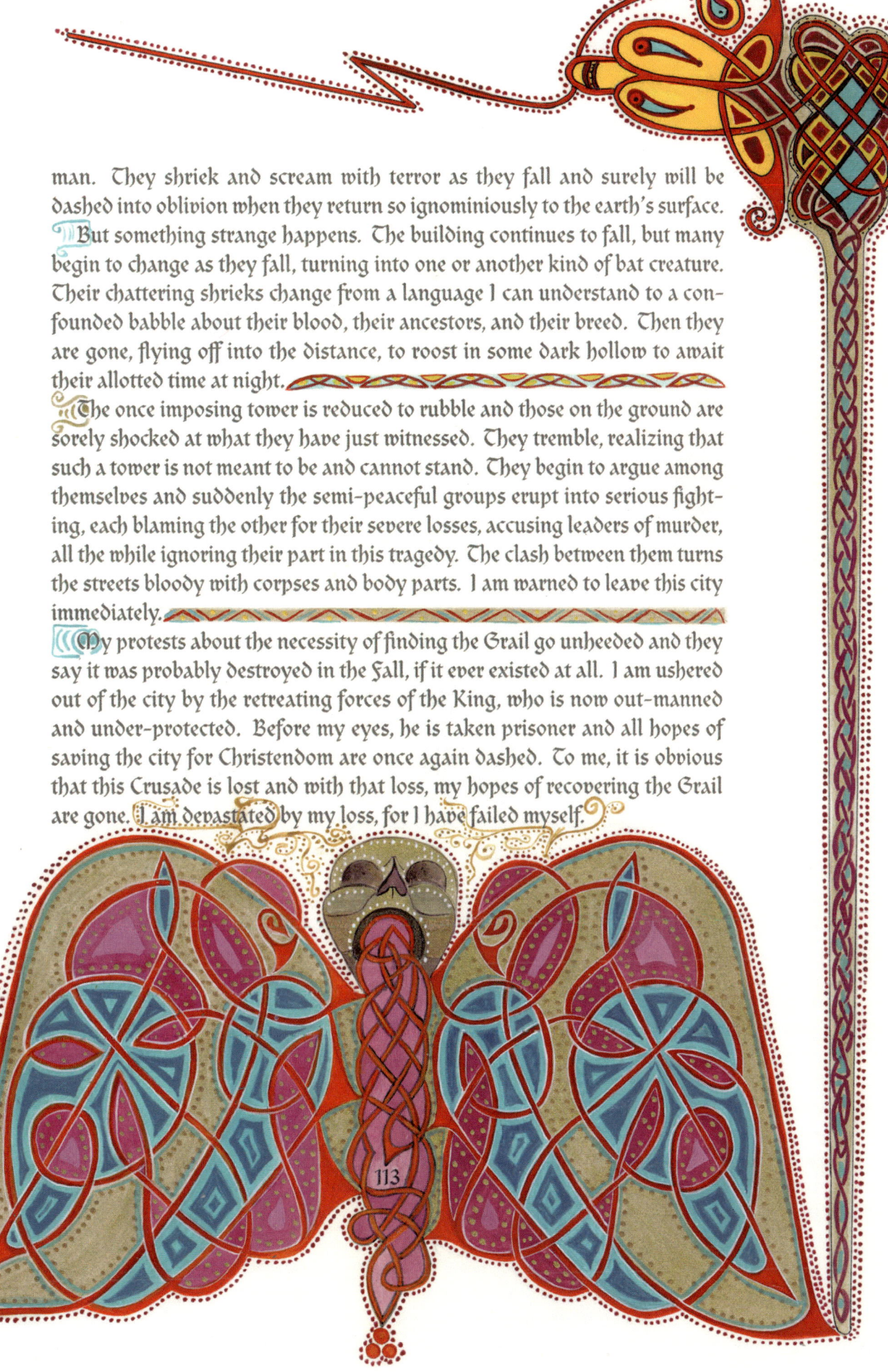

man. They shriek and scream with terror as they fall and surely will be dashed into oblivion when they return so ignominiously to the earth's surface. But something strange happens. The building continues to fall, but many begin to change as they fall, turning into one or another kind of bat creature. Their chattering shrieks change from a language I can understand to a confounded babble about their blood, their ancestors, and their breed. Then they are gone, flying off into the distance, to roost in some dark hollow to await their allotted time at night.

The once imposing tower is reduced to rubble and those on the ground are sorely shocked at what they have just witnessed. They tremble, realizing that such a tower is not meant to be and cannot stand. They begin to argue among themselves and suddenly the semi-peaceful groups erupt into serious fighting, each blaming the other for their severe losses, accusing leaders of murder, all the while ignoring their part in this tragedy. The clash between them turns the streets bloody with corpses and body parts. I am warned to leave this city immediately.

My protests about the necessity of finding the Grail go unheeded and they say it was probably destroyed in the Fall, if it ever existed at all. I am ushered out of the city by the retreating forces of the King, who is now out-manned and under-protected. Before my eyes, he is taken prisoner and all hopes of saving the city for Christendom are once again dashed. To me, it is obvious that this Crusade is lost and with that loss, my hopes of recovering the Grail are gone. I am devastated by my loss, for I have failed myself.

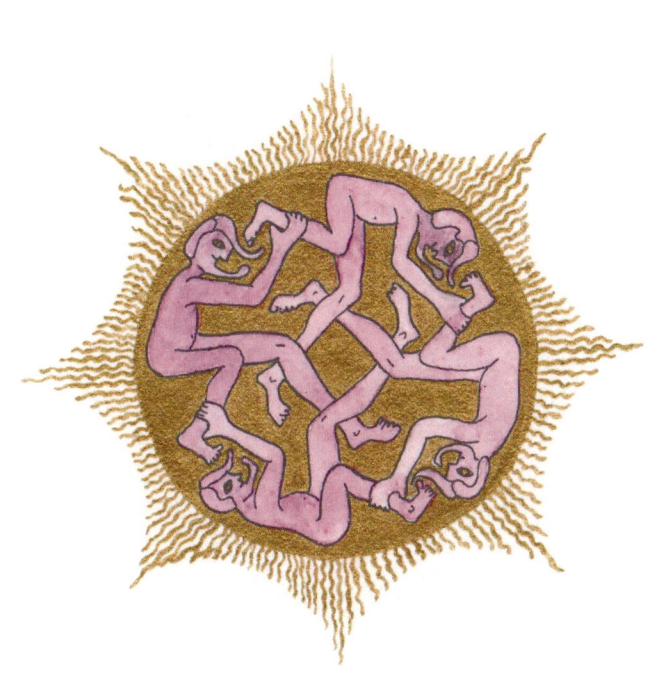

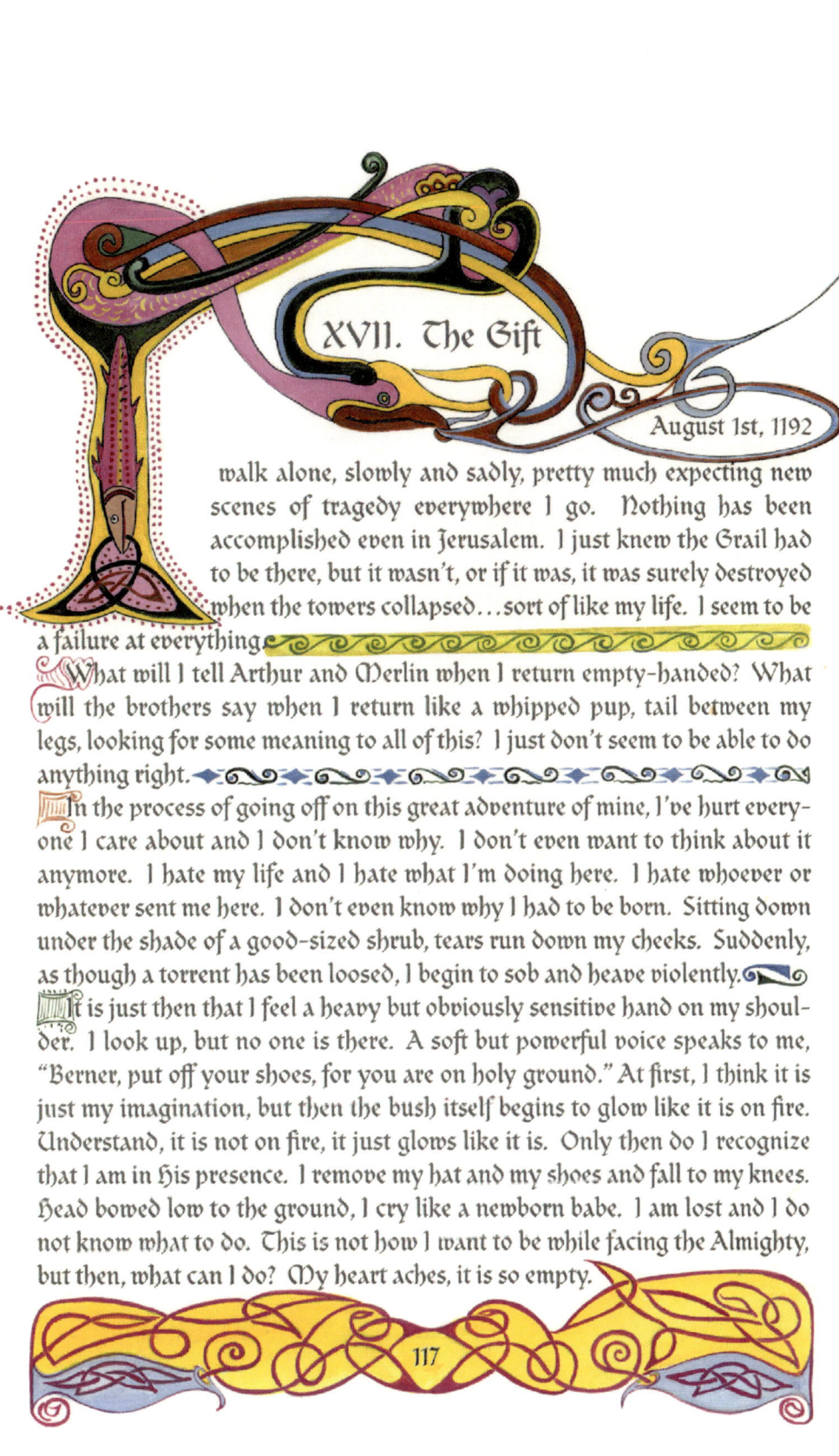

XVII. The Gift

August 1st, 1192

walk alone, slowly and sadly, pretty much expecting new scenes of tragedy everywhere I go. Nothing has been accomplished even in Jerusalem. I just knew the Grail had to be there, but it wasn't, or if it was, it was surely destroyed when the towers collapsed…sort of like my life. I seem to be a failure at everything.

What will I tell Arthur and Merlin when I return empty-handed? What will the brothers say when I return like a whipped pup, tail between my legs, looking for some meaning to all of this? I just don't seem to be able to do anything right.

In the process of going off on this great adventure of mine, I've hurt everyone I care about and I don't know why. I don't even want to think about it anymore. I hate my life and I hate what I'm doing here. I hate whoever or whatever sent me here. I don't even know why I had to be born. Sitting down under the shade of a good-sized shrub, tears run down my cheeks. Suddenly, as though a torrent has been loosed, I begin to sob and heave violently.

It is just then that I feel a heavy but obviously sensitive hand on my shoulder. I look up, but no one is there. A soft but powerful voice speaks to me, "Berner, put off your shoes, for you are on holy ground." At first, I think it is just my imagination, but then the bush itself begins to glow like it is on fire. Understand, it is not on fire, it just glows like it is. Only then do I recognize that I am in His presence. I remove my hat and my shoes and fall to my knees. Head bowed low to the ground, I cry like a newborn babe. I am lost and I do not know what to do. This is not how I want to be while facing the Almighty, but then, what can I do? My heart aches, it is so empty.

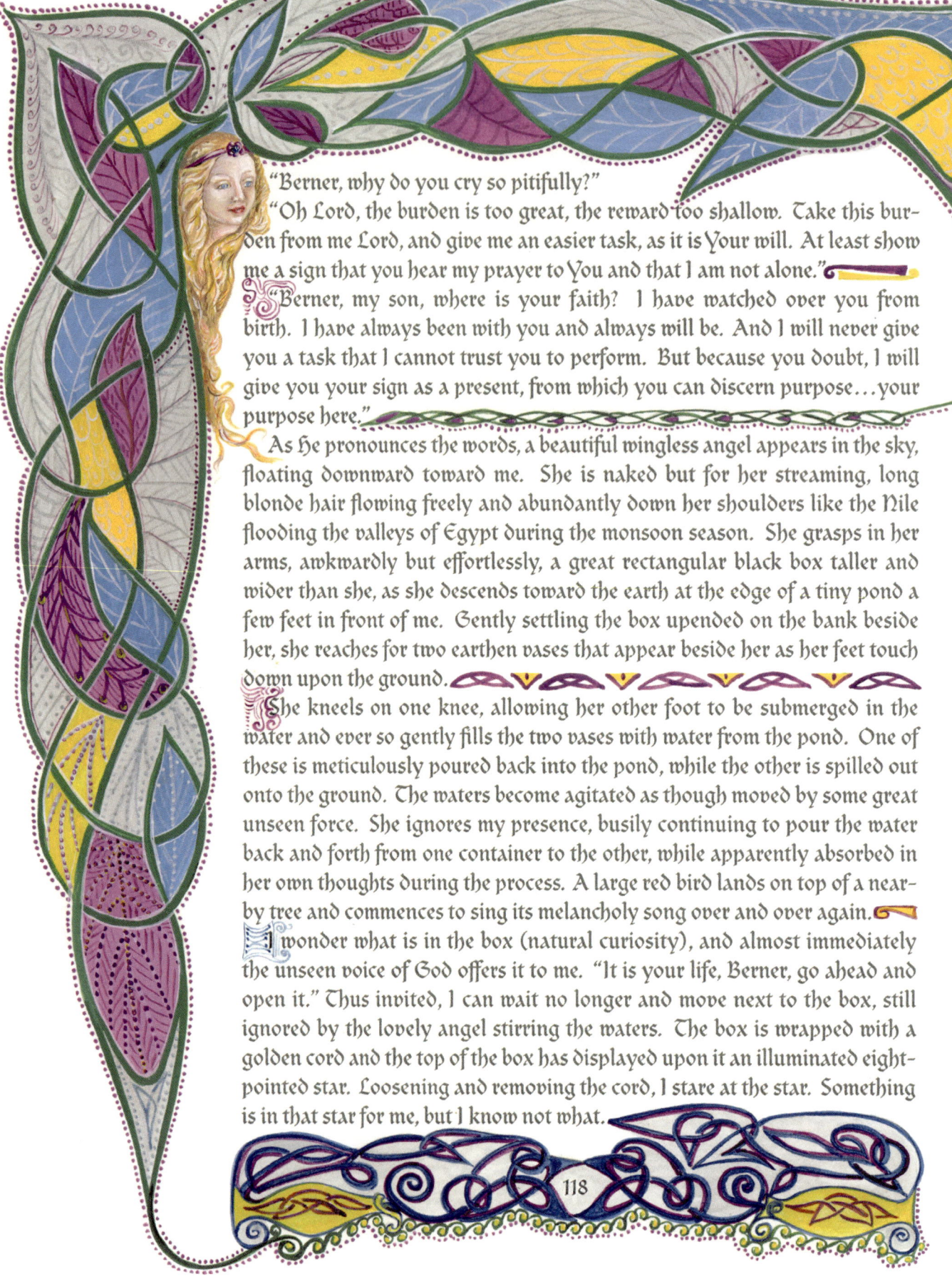

"Berner, why do you cry so pitifully?"

"Oh Lord, the burden is too great, the reward too shallow. Take this burden from me Lord, and give me an easier task, as it is Your will. At least show me a sign that you hear my prayer to You and that I am not alone."

"Berner, my son, where is your faith? I have watched over you from birth. I have always been with you and always will be. And I will never give you a task that I cannot trust you to perform. But because you doubt, I will give you your sign as a present, from which you can discern purpose…your purpose here."

As he pronounces the words, a beautiful wingless angel appears in the sky, floating downward toward me. She is naked but for her streaming, long blonde hair flowing freely and abundantly down her shoulders like the Nile flooding the valleys of Egypt during the monsoon season. She grasps in her arms, awkwardly but effortlessly, a great rectangular black box taller and wider than she, as she descends toward the earth at the edge of a tiny pond a few feet in front of me. Gently settling the box upended on the bank beside her, she reaches for two earthen vases that appear beside her as her feet touch down upon the ground.

She kneels on one knee, allowing her other foot to be submerged in the water and ever so gently fills the two vases with water from the pond. One of these is meticulously poured back into the pond, while the other is spilled out onto the ground. The waters become agitated as though moved by some great unseen force. She ignores my presence, busily continuing to pour the water back and forth from one container to the other, while apparently absorbed in her own thoughts during the process. A large red bird lands on top of a nearby tree and commences to sing its melancholy song over and over again.

I wonder what is in the box (natural curiosity), and almost immediately the unseen voice of God offers it to me. "It is your life, Berner, go ahead and open it." Thus invited, I can wait no longer and move next to the box, still ignored by the lovely angel stirring the waters. The box is wrapped with a golden cord and the top of the box has displayed upon it an illuminated eight-pointed star. Loosening and removing the cord, I stare at the star. Something is in that star for me, but I know not what.

The top appears to be a door, but opening it is difficult for it resists as though to bar entrance to anyone. Struggling, the thing eventually loosens its grip, prepared to surrender its secrets to me. But as the box door swings outward, nothing appears inside but a great, incomprehensible depth of blackness together with a cold and powerful wind, the kind that chills a person to the bone on a winter's eve.

Shivering, I ask, "What is the meaning of this, Lord, for I see nothing but an abyss of emptiness?" No Word is spoken, yet I know that this is a representation of my soul: cold, dark, and empty. I am afraid.

"Almighty One, Master who has dominion over all of the Universe, why can't I have the things others have, things I want so that I can enjoy life to its fullest? Why must I always serve? Nearly half my life is over and if I don't begin doing those things I want to do soon, I will never experience life as I want to. I will have lived for nothing, have nothing and I will be gone — forgotten and abused. I feel like such a fool."

The gentle heavy hand rests lightly on my shoulder once again and I bow my head in obedience to His authority. Without answering me directly, He asks if I still have my rosebush with me. Removing it from its protective wrapping in my pouch, one large white rose and seven small white buds are revealed. He instructs me to place the shrub into the box and wrap it in the cloth inside.

Unable to see anything but unfathomable blackness, I reach inside and take hold of a black velvet cloth, and gently wrap the rosebush as asked. The box is then shut momentarily and then reopened. The white rose and the seven rosebuds emit a faint light through the blackness of the cloth, which continues to grow until they glow bright white like the sun in the sky. Day turns to night before my eyes and the roses change in shape and color. Now they become giant stars, the one rose immensely larger than his brothers, and all begin to ascend to the sky, taking their places in the heavens, shining and twinkling like bright stars do on a clear night.

Ashamed and shaken, I admit once more that I do not understand what this has to do with me or my prayers to him. "What is the meaning of life for me, oh Great One? Why can't I have the things I want?"

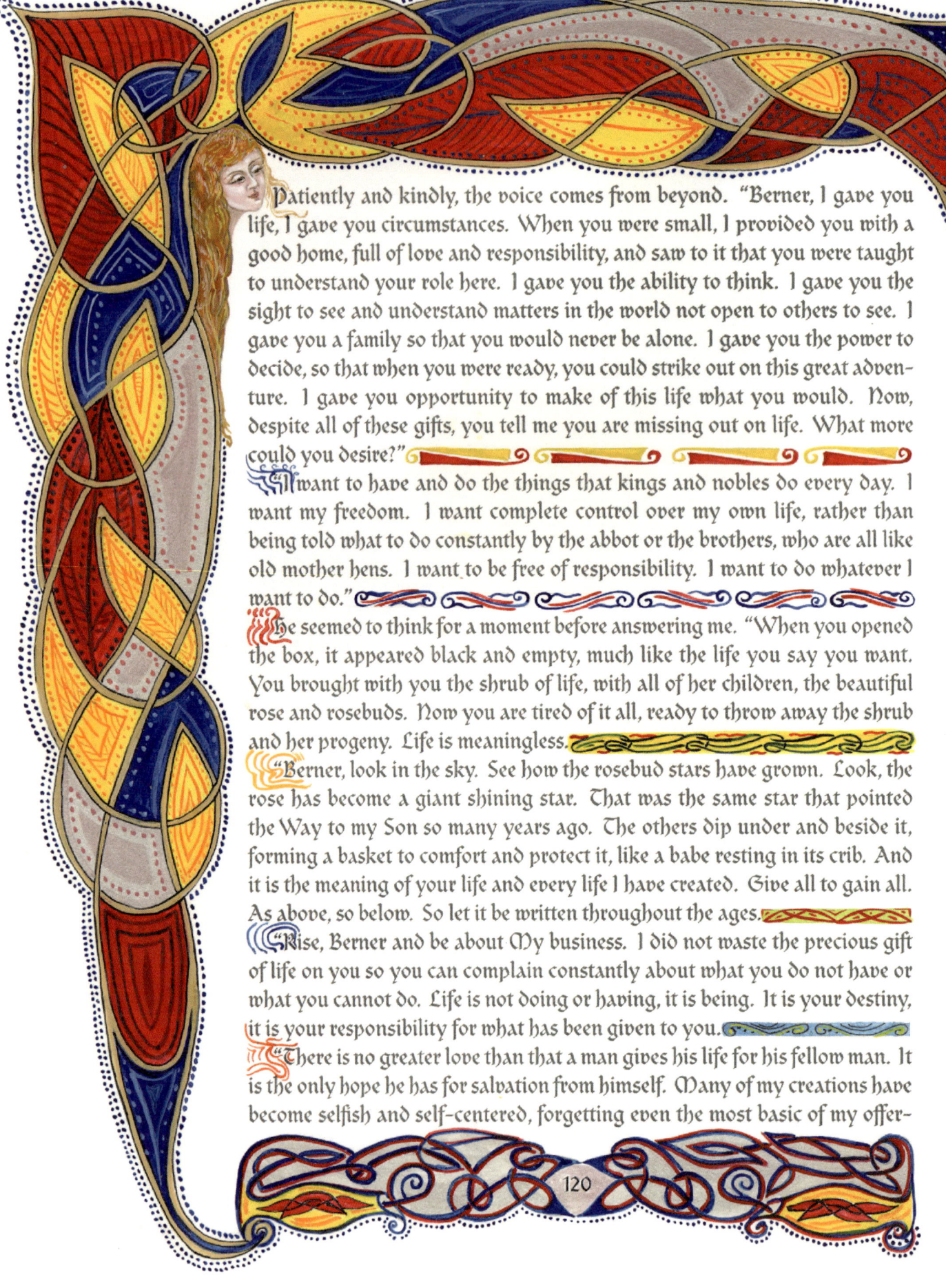

Patiently and kindly, the voice comes from beyond. "Berner, I gave you life, I gave you circumstances. When you were small, I provided you with a good home, full of love and responsibility, and saw to it that you were taught to understand your role here. I gave you the ability to think. I gave you the sight to see and understand matters in the world not open to others to see. I gave you a family so that you would never be alone. I gave you the power to decide, so that when you were ready, you could strike out on this great adventure. I gave you opportunity to make of this life what you would. Now, despite all of these gifts, you tell me you are missing out on life. What more could you desire?"

"I want to have and do the things that kings and nobles do every day. I want my freedom. I want complete control over my own life, rather than being told what to do constantly by the abbot or the brothers, who are all like old mother hens. I want to be free of responsibility. I want to do whatever I want to do."

He seemed to think for a moment before answering me. "When you opened the box, it appeared black and empty, much like the life you say you want. You brought with you the shrub of life, with all of her children, the beautiful rose and rosebuds. Now you are tired of it all, ready to throw away the shrub and her progeny. Life is meaningless.

"Berner, look in the sky. See how the rosebud stars have grown. Look, the rose has become a giant shining star. That was the same star that pointed the Way to my Son so many years ago. The others dip under and beside it, forming a basket to comfort and protect it, like a babe resting in its crib. And it is the meaning of your life and every life I have created. Give all to gain all. As above, so below. So let it be written throughout the ages.

"Rise, Berner and be about My business. I did not waste the precious gift of life on you so you can complain constantly about what you do not have or what you cannot do. Life is not doing or having, it is being. It is your destiny, it is your responsibility for what has been given to you.

"There is no greater love than that a man gives his life for his fellow man. It is the only hope he has for salvation from himself. Many of my creations have become selfish and self-centered, forgetting even the most basic of my offer-

ings. I gave myself to man by creating, protecting, and loving the unlovable in you, but your kind have been unwilling to repay me by helping each other.

"Be attentive — my warrior angels are disguised and report and destroy those who will not follow My Word. Those who do not follow the Path shall surely die. Material possessions and activities pale into insignificance when compared to Hope. That is all any of you are given in this life. Whether you keep it or destroy it determines what path your life and your future take. Remember this day when you look to the stars to guide you on your way. Forsake Me not and you will dwell with Me forever. Otherwise, enter the box, for it will become your coffin and the only treasure you will take from My earth."

And now, he is gone. I am comforted and discomforted at the same time. Peering once more into the black box of oblivion, I know that I do not want its sacred cloth to become my shroud, nor the box to be my burial chamber. I will complain no more, for I have Hope and I will find the Grail that others may live or die according to His Plan. The angel floats off into the heavens and I go about my business.

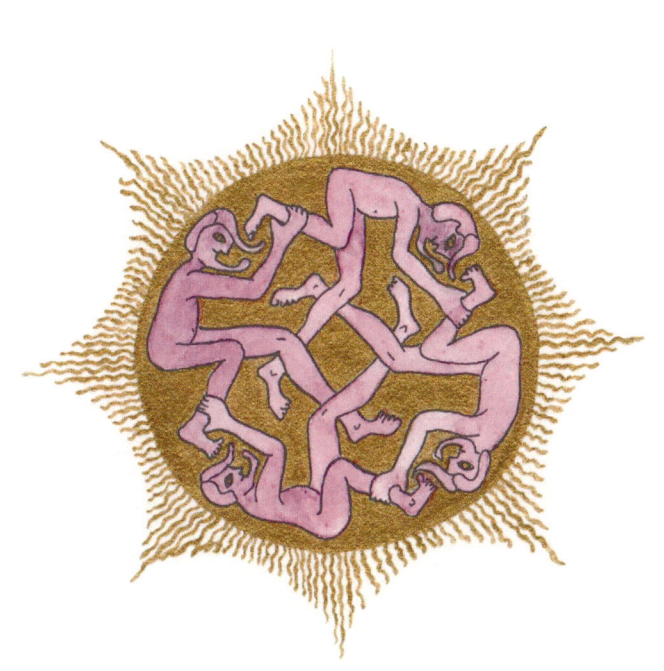

XVIII. Lunatics' Revenge

"The Moon reveals the feminine aspect of human kind. If man lives on the Moon, will he become a lunatic?"

1 Chronicles 18:36

September 22nd, 1192

press on, seeking more clues to unravel the enigma of the Grail and my life. Entry into the land of the Gnomen and the Gremlini fills me with much consternation. Renowned for their adherence to the Old Religion with its reliance on sorcery and witchcraft, they are much feared by civilized races. Eons ago they were like the rest of us, but times changed. Honing their magical skills became the bane of their existence.

The Gnomen, followers of the Goddess, have the sight to see both past and future events. The Gremlini are animists, with cults of the dog, the wolf, and the lobster; their powers are limited to discerning the past only, but they are reputedly spell specialists. Gnomen can heal if they choose. Both races produce master Alchemists. Their powers over the elements and their ability to discern the un-discernible scare me. One other note of interest: neither of these peoples deliver their newborn by live birth; instead they lay eggs. Gnomen babies can be born only by exposure to sunlight; the Gremlini, only by moonlight. Fortunately, war and extermination have reduced their populations dramatically.

We humans forced both groups into reserves, near one another. Sites holy to the Gnomen were handed over to the Gremlini, which has rooted irreparable and ever-growing animosity between them. Perhaps the powers that be intend it so.

125

The Gremlini villages lie in the dense, darker part of the forest, usually in the hollow spaces of ancient trees, which over time has resulted in an intolerance to light. They must always shade their eyes from the sun. Many of their numbers work deep within the earth, mining exotic stones and minerals, and it is said that their kingdom is the wealthiest in the world. Their bitter leaders are suspected subversives, instigators of trouble opposed to world order. I navigate their lands using a map obtained from my Gnomen guide, Vale, a three-foot dwarf with a long white beard and a hunched back. He warns me to avoid encounters with any Gremlini, as they are all human-haters.

Prophetically, he suggests that a clear and present danger for mankind lurks in these woods and the Gremlini believe themselves to be avenging angels for perceived wrongs they suffer. These terrorists are indiscriminate in their killing vengeance. Considering what he tells me the Gnomen have been put through, I ask why his people have not arisen against the rest of the world as well.

"Because you need us," Vale replies.

His answer stuns me. The sun is beginning to change to a strange blood-red color and scabs form over small bits of its surface. "They've begun," my guide chides, "what will you do?"

I do not understand. Before I can ask the obvious, large crowds of humans suddenly charge past me, excited, grasping large sums of money in their hands, yelling and bragging about their good fortune. Dozens zoom past me in their exuberance, nearly knocking me down, unaware of anything but treasure.

I grab a young lady just long enough to request both the source and reason for a bounty that has them all so delirious. She is jumping about and it is difficult to make sense of her words. She mumbles something about selling her piece of the Sun to the Gremlini. Now she is rich and will never have to worry about anything again. She can have anything. Life has never been so good. God has surely answered her prayers and happiness (through possessions), she believes, is all she requires.

Others validate her story with similar stories. Everyone has gone mad. The Sun, in full retreat now, sprouts a fearsome dry blood-red and black circle

126

which envelops it and commences to blot it out. Am I the only one to see this ominous development? Everyone else is too busy examining and reexamining their treasure and making plans to spend it. It is useless to discuss the situation with the passers-by; no one cares.

Money rules the day. Everyone is "rich," and that is all that matters to them. Why can't they recognize the peril we are in? The world may end. Is this the Apocalypse of St. John in Revelations? Then what good will their greed for money and riches get them? No one listens but Vale.

The temperature drops drastically and it turns bitter cold. Plants shrivel and die. Unnerving darkness pervades. Animals succumb to the huge climatic change and drop like flies in winter. What is happening to us? My God, my God, why have you forsaken us? Despondent and panicky about the fate that awaits life on this planet, Vale alone is calm and asks me to sit and rest a while, insisting that I breathe deeply and clear my mind. Hysteria will not resolve this disastrous situation. He attempts to calm me. I am beside myself with fear and sadness. I ask him what we can do.

"Breathe," he says. As he repeats his instruction, we sit beside a large oak tree and I calm myself. "Breathe," he says again. "Clear your mind."

Minutes seem to extend to days as I try to relax and conform to his instructions. I am lost in thought, when he takes my hand and directs me to come with him. I ask where we are going but he does not answer.

Deeper into the forest, the sky darkens and life seems near an end. The screams of young mothers interrupt the solitude of the forest and they can be heard in the distance shrieking over the loss of a child or a husband or a loved one subjugated in the cold embrace of Death.

Near the old oaks, bored clear through with holes large enough for entire families to live in, we creep. Vale searches each hole diligently until coming upon one venerable old tree, and grunts contentedly as he removes a huge, smooth egg from its hollow. I help him carry this monstrosity. We move toward the largest old oak in the forest, towering above the rest. Here, he explains, we will find those we seek.

Without fear, without further contemplation about our precarious position in the homeland of his sworn enemies, he approaches the tree. It is the castle of the Gremlini king and his entourage. I hold the egg as he climbs the branches toward the large hollowed-out space, guarded only by knots of wood growing from either side of the hole. I hand the egg to him and attempt to reach higher and higher, but this type of activity is new to me and I clumsily climb and slip my way upward.

My guide waits patiently (perhaps because the egg is so heavy). When I reach him, we both carry the egg. Sounds emanating from inside the tree resound like a party of drunk and out-of-control Gremlini. We have stumbled on some strange ritual of these people I am quite certain, and quickly say so. Vale does not respond. A great many Gremlini are assembled inside, drinking heavily and celebrating their "victory" over the evil forces of their world. Our appearance silences them momentarily.

A guard near the Gremlini King Wartax blocks our path and demands the reason for our intrusion.

"Well, Vale, it has been a long time. Why are you here? To plead for the Gnomen? To plead for man? Too late — the greed of others allowed us to take control of the world. Soon we will be all that is left, just as we planned. What's wrong, Vale? You are quiet…strange behavior for the warrior-king of a once great adversary! I see you've brought your egg. Sorry, it will never hatch for there will never be another sun to warm it to birth. Why, it's melting like a burning candle. Too bad."

"You're wrong, Wartax. You gloat at our imminent destruction, but yours is imminent as well. This is not our egg, but yours." The silence is broken only by shocked sighs.

"That's impossible. We do not need the light to bear our children — only you and the stupid humans do. We have our Mother, Moon. She will protect us. She will hatch our fledglings and watch them grow. It will be a dark, dark world…our world."

"Wartax, you old fool. Don't you understand — the soft light of your moon, necessary for the birth of your babies, is nothing more than a reflection from the Sun? If you destroy the light of the Sun, you destroy the veiled light of your moon as well. This is your child, this is your extinction."

These sobering words end the argument.

128

Stunned, Wartax slumps in his throne, his people cease their celebration and stand in silence as if frozen in place, awaiting the wisdom of their leader. This powerful king, with a huge lump in his throat and eyes devoid of his former hatred and coldness, softly acknowledges his fatal error. All life is condemned. This cannot be.

Using low-spoken incantations, recited almost like our chants, he lifts his spell, and the dark orb enveloping the Sun slowly departs, leaving light where only darkness had been. Light, warmth…we have passed through the valley of the Shadow of Death and survived, thank the Almighty Lord. The dignity of the Sun is restored. A treaty is quickly drawn inside their castle, their Tree of Life, by which all peoples agree to respect all others' boundaries and to allow exchanges of ideas to comprehend the other's culture and needs. The World is at peace—for now. The nightmare over, harmony reigns. Life, glorious life, resumes.

129

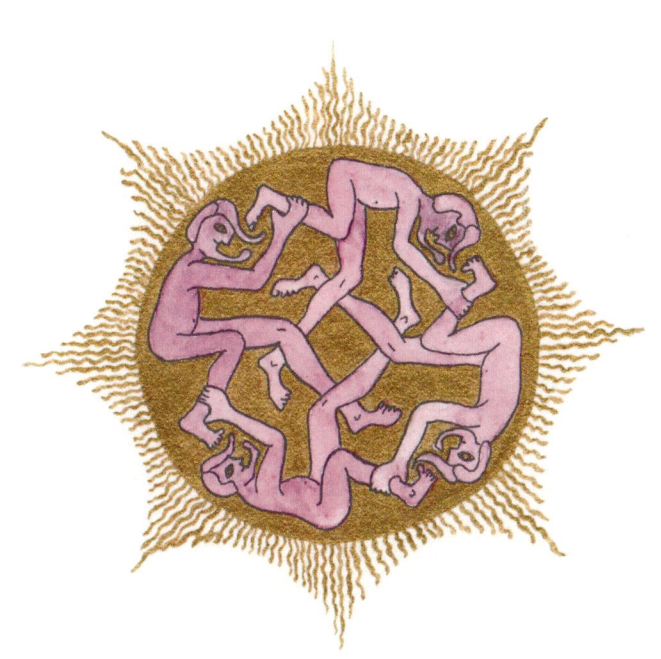

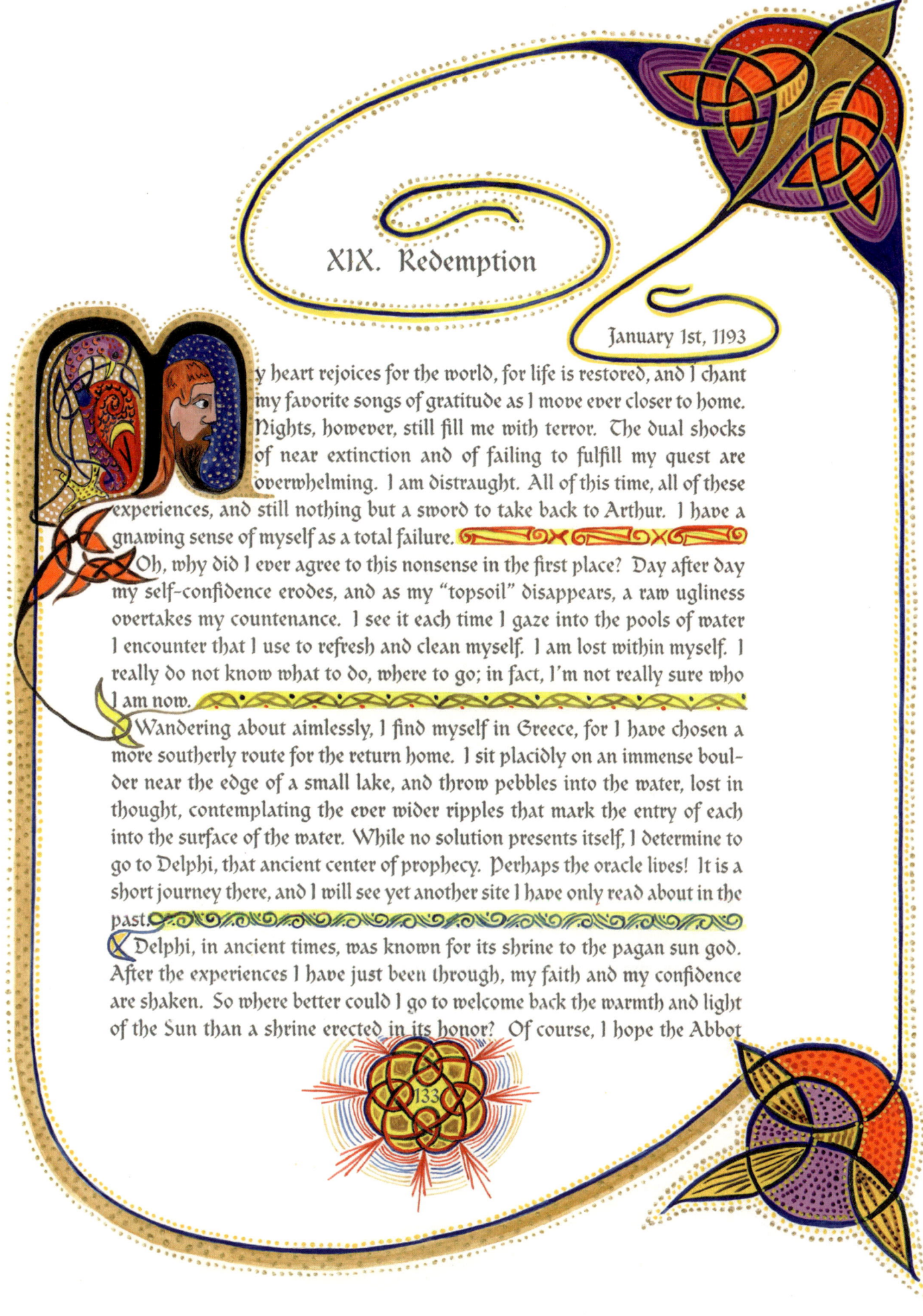

XIX. Redemption

My heart rejoices for the world, for life is restored, and I chant my favorite songs of gratitude as I move ever closer to home. Nights, however, still fill me with terror. The dual shocks of near extinction and of failing to fulfill my quest are overwhelming. I am distraught. All of this time, all of these experiences, and still nothing but a sword to take back to Arthur. I have a gnawing sense of myself as a total failure.

Oh, why did I ever agree to this nonsense in the first place? Day after day my self-confidence erodes, and as my "topsoil" disappears, a raw ugliness overtakes my countenance. I see it each time I gaze into the pools of water I encounter that I use to refresh and clean myself. I am lost within myself. I really do not know what to do, where to go; in fact, I'm not really sure who I am now.

Wandering about aimlessly, I find myself in Greece, for I have chosen a more southerly route for the return home. I sit placidly on an immense boulder near the edge of a small lake, and throw pebbles into the water, lost in thought, contemplating the ever wider ripples that mark the entry of each into the surface of the water. While no solution presents itself, I determine to go to Delphi, that ancient center of prophecy. Perhaps the oracle lives! It is a short journey there, and I will see yet another site I have only read about in the past.

Delphi, in ancient times, was known for its shrine to the pagan sun god. After the experiences I have just been through, my faith and my confidence are shaken. So where better could I go to welcome back the warmth and light of the Sun than a shrine erected in its honor? Of course, I hope the Abbot

133

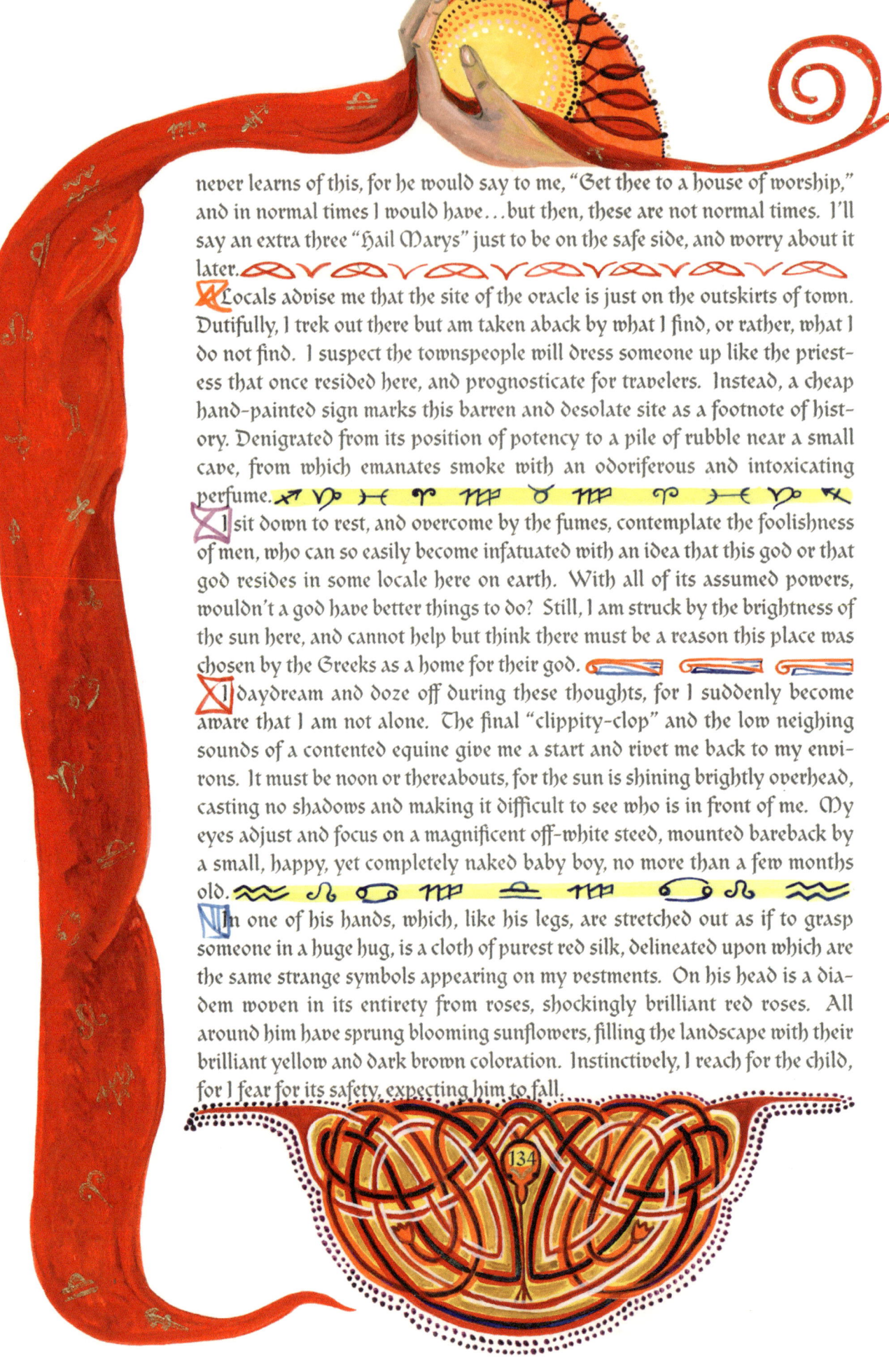

never learns of this, for he would say to me, "Get thee to a house of worship," and in normal times I would have…but then, these are not normal times. I'll say an extra three "Hail Marys" just to be on the safe side, and worry about it later.

Locals advise me that the site of the oracle is just on the outskirts of town. Dutifully, I trek out there but am taken aback by what I find, or rather, what I do not find. I suspect the townspeople will dress someone up like the priestess that once resided here, and prognosticate for travelers. Instead, a cheap hand-painted sign marks this barren and desolate site as a footnote of history. Denigrated from its position of potency to a pile of rubble near a small cave, from which emanates smoke with an odoriferous and intoxicating perfume.

I sit down to rest, and overcome by the fumes, contemplate the foolishness of men, who can so easily become infatuated with an idea that this god or that god resides in some locale here on earth. With all of its assumed powers, wouldn't a god have better things to do? Still, I am struck by the brightness of the sun here, and cannot help but think there must be a reason this place was chosen by the Greeks as a home for their god.

I daydream and doze off during these thoughts, for I suddenly become aware that I am not alone. The final "clippity-clop" and the low neighing sounds of a contented equine give me a start and rivet me back to my environs. It must be noon or thereabouts, for the sun is shining brightly overhead, casting no shadows and making it difficult to see who is in front of me. My eyes adjust and focus on a magnificent off-white steed, mounted bareback by a small, happy, yet completely naked baby boy, no more than a few months old.

In one of his hands, which, like his legs, are stretched out as if to grasp someone in a huge hug, is a cloth of purest red silk, delineated upon which are the same strange symbols appearing on my vestments. On his head is a diadem woven in its entirety from roses, shockingly brilliant red roses. All around him have sprung blooming sunflowers, filling the landscape with their brilliant yellow and dark brown coloration. Instinctively, I reach for the child, for I fear for its safety, expecting him to fall.

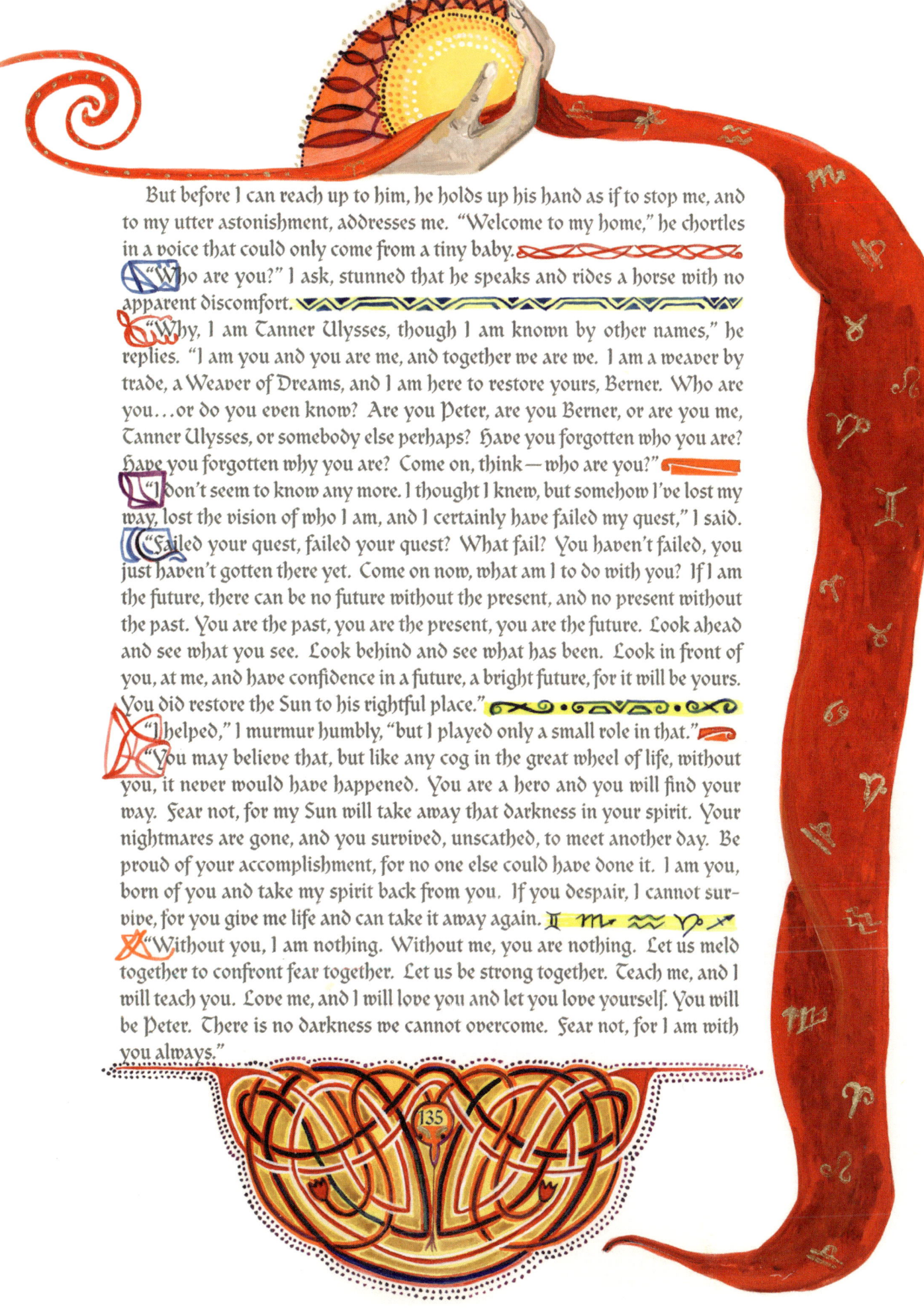

But before I can reach up to him, he holds up his hand as if to stop me, and to my utter astonishment, addresses me. "Welcome to my home," he chortles in a voice that could only come from a tiny baby.

"Who are you?" I ask, stunned that he speaks and rides a horse with no apparent discomfort.

"Why, I am Tanner Ulysses, though I am known by other names," he replies. "I am you and you are me, and together we are we. I am a weaver by trade, a Weaver of Dreams, and I am here to restore yours, Berner. Who are you…or do you even know? Are you Peter, are you Berner, or are you me, Tanner Ulysses, or somebody else perhaps? Have you forgotten who you are? Have you forgotten why you are? Come on, think—who are you?"

"I don't seem to know any more. I thought I knew, but somehow I've lost my way, lost the vision of who I am, and I certainly have failed my quest," I said.

"Failed your quest, failed your quest? What fail? You haven't failed, you just haven't gotten there yet. Come on now, what am I to do with you? If I am the future, there can be no future without the present, and no present without the past. You are the past, you are the present, you are the future. Look ahead and see what you see. Look behind and see what has been. Look in front of you, at me, and have confidence in a future, a bright future, for it will be yours. You did restore the Sun to his rightful place."

"I helped," I murmur humbly, "but I played only a small role in that."

"You may believe that, but like any cog in the great wheel of life, without you, it never would have happened. You are a hero and you will find your way. Fear not, for my Sun will take away that darkness in your spirit. Your nightmares are gone, and you survived, unscathed, to meet another day. Be proud of your accomplishment, for no one else could have done it. I am you, born of you and take my spirit back from you. If you despair, I cannot survive, for you give me life and can take it away again.

"Without you, I am nothing. Without me, you are nothing. Let us meld together to confront fear together. Let us be strong together. Teach me, and I will teach you. Love me, and I will love you and let you love yourself. You will be Peter. There is no darkness we cannot overcome. Fear not, for I am with you always."

Those last words strike a sharp chord in me. I have heard those words before and they have always strengthened me. They strengthen my resolve now. "Prophesy" survives at Delphi and I have been enlightened. Joyful, I rise to grab this babe, my son, my Tanner Ulysses, and I understand. But when I stand and shout with joy, I cannot see him. Instead, townspeople have gathered around me, and are laughing at the fool they say talks to himself. But I can hear a tiny voice, deep inside of me reminding me, "It's all right, Father, for I am here."

And it is all right.

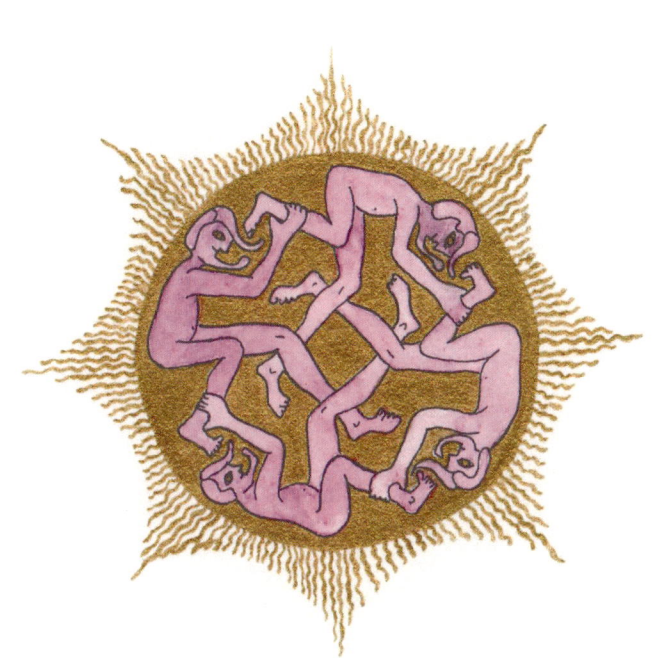

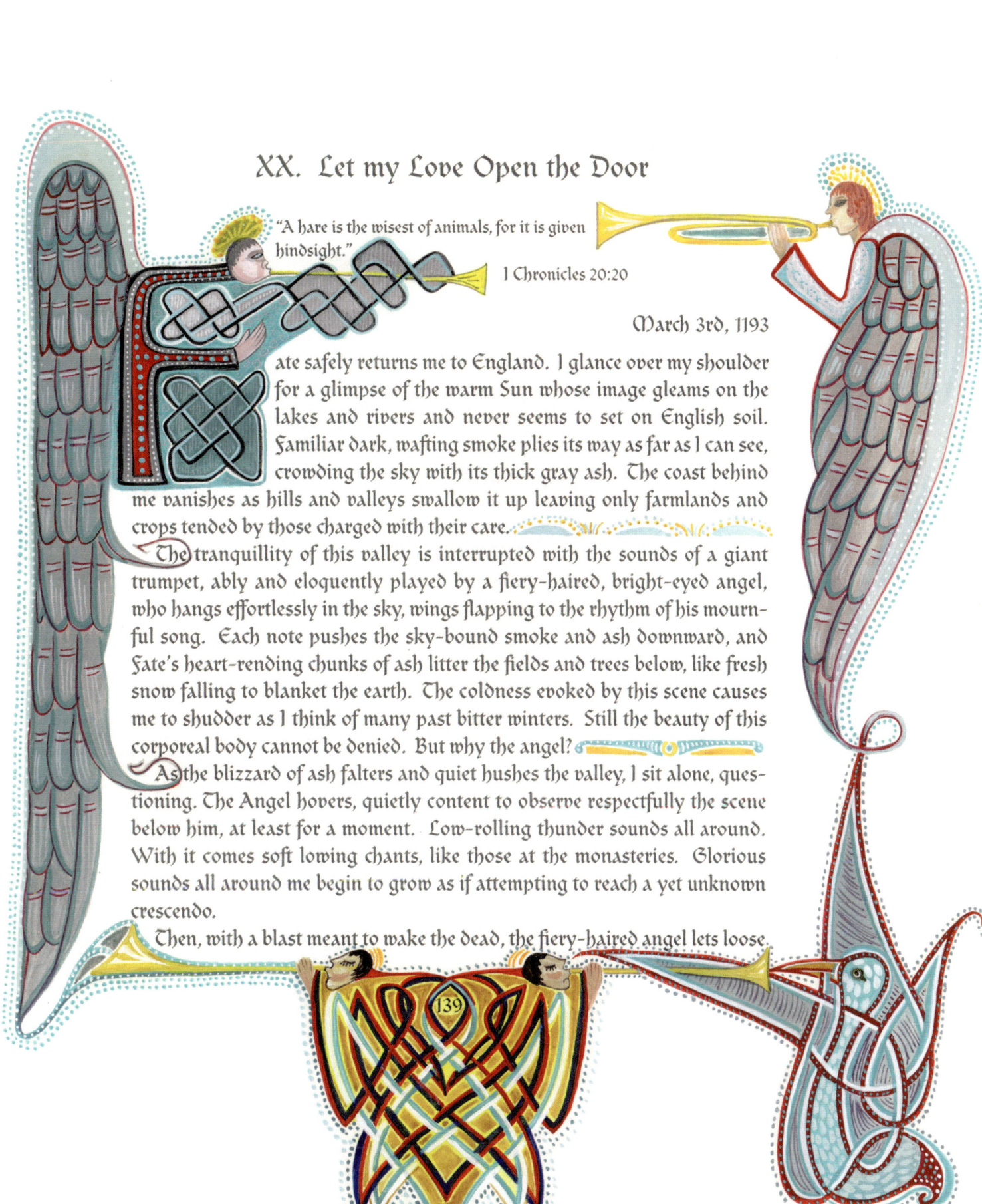

XX. Let my Love Open the Door

"A hare is the wisest of animals, for it is given hindsight."

1 Chronicles 20:20

March 3rd, 1193

Fate safely returns me to England. I glance over my shoulder for a glimpse of the warm Sun whose image gleams on the lakes and rivers and never seems to set on English soil. Familiar dark, wafting smoke plies its way as far as I can see, crowding the sky with its thick gray ash. The coast behind me vanishes as hills and valleys swallow it up leaving only farmlands and crops tended by those charged with their care.

The tranquillity of this valley is interrupted with the sounds of a giant trumpet, ably and eloquently played by a fiery-haired, bright-eyed angel, who hangs effortlessly in the sky, wings flapping to the rhythm of his mournful song. Each note pushes the sky-bound smoke and ash downward, and Fate's heart-rending chunks of ash litter the fields and trees below, like fresh snow falling to blanket the earth. The coldness evoked by this scene causes me to shudder as I think of many past bitter winters. Still the beauty of this corporeal body cannot be denied. But why the angel?

As the blizzard of ash falters and quiet hushes the valley, I sit alone, questioning. The Angel hovers, quietly content to observe respectfully the scene below him, at least for a moment. Low-rolling thunder sounds all around. With it comes soft lowing chants, like those at the monasteries. Glorious sounds all around me begin to grow as if attempting to reach a yet unknown crescendo.

Then, with a blast meant to wake the dead, the fiery-haired angel lets loose.

139

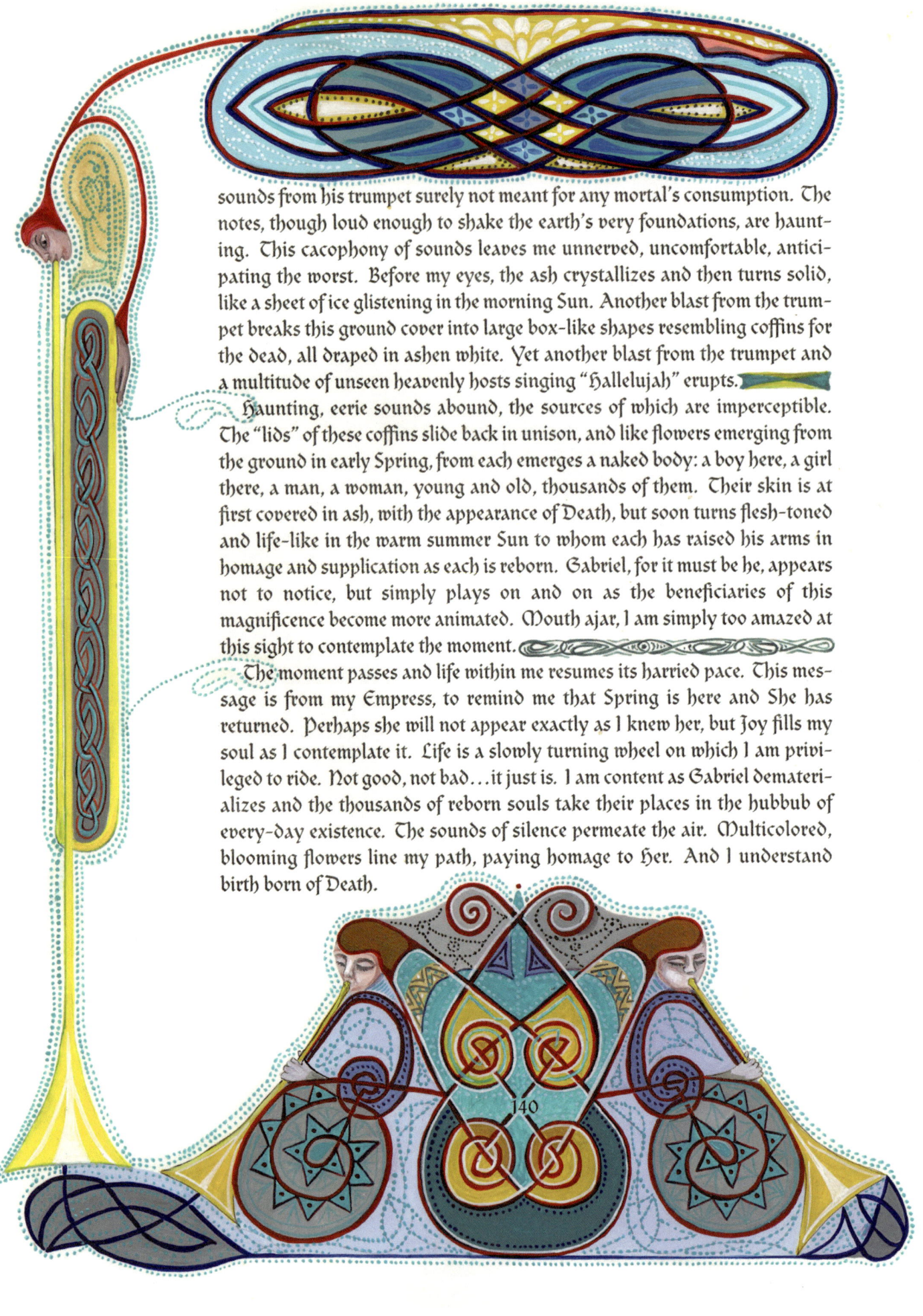

sounds from his trumpet surely not meant for any mortal's consumption. The notes, though loud enough to shake the earth's very foundations, are haunting. This cacophony of sounds leaves me unnerved, uncomfortable, anticipating the worst. Before my eyes, the ash crystallizes and then turns solid, like a sheet of ice glistening in the morning Sun. Another blast from the trumpet breaks this ground cover into large box-like shapes resembling coffins for the dead, all draped in ashen white. Yet another blast from the trumpet and a multitude of unseen heavenly hosts singing "Hallelujah" erupts.

Haunting, eerie sounds abound, the sources of which are imperceptible. The "lids" of these coffins slide back in unison, and like flowers emerging from the ground in early Spring, from each emerges a naked body: a boy here, a girl there, a man, a woman, young and old, thousands of them. Their skin is at first covered in ash, with the appearance of Death, but soon turns flesh-toned and life-like in the warm summer Sun to whom each has raised his arms in homage and supplication as each is reborn. Gabriel, for it must be he, appears not to notice, but simply plays on and on as the beneficiaries of this magnificence become more animated. Mouth ajar, I am simply too amazed at this sight to contemplate the moment.

The moment passes and life within me resumes its harried pace. This message is from my Empress, to remind me that Spring is here and She has returned. Perhaps she will not appear exactly as I knew her, but Joy fills my soul as I contemplate it. Life is a slowly turning wheel on which I am privileged to ride. Not good, not bad...it just is. I am content as Gabriel dematerializes and the thousands of reborn souls take their places in the hubbub of every-day existence. The sounds of silence permeate the air. Multicolored, blooming flowers line my path, paying homage to Her. And I understand birth born of Death.

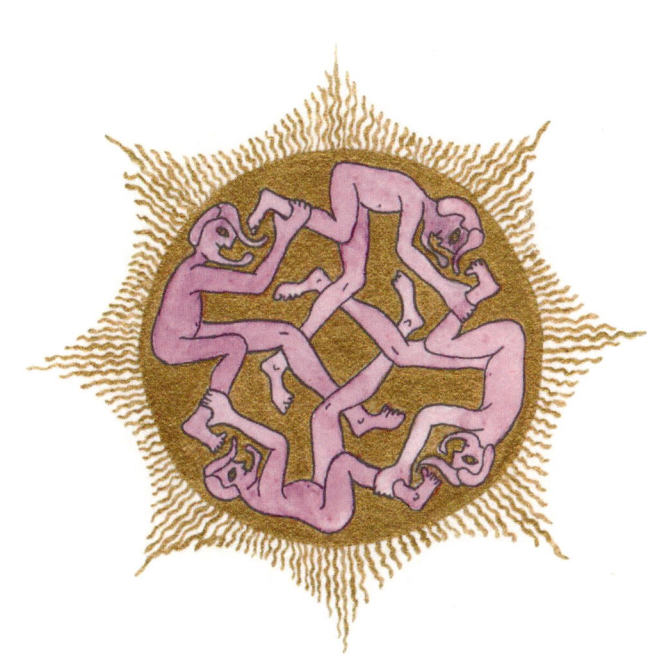

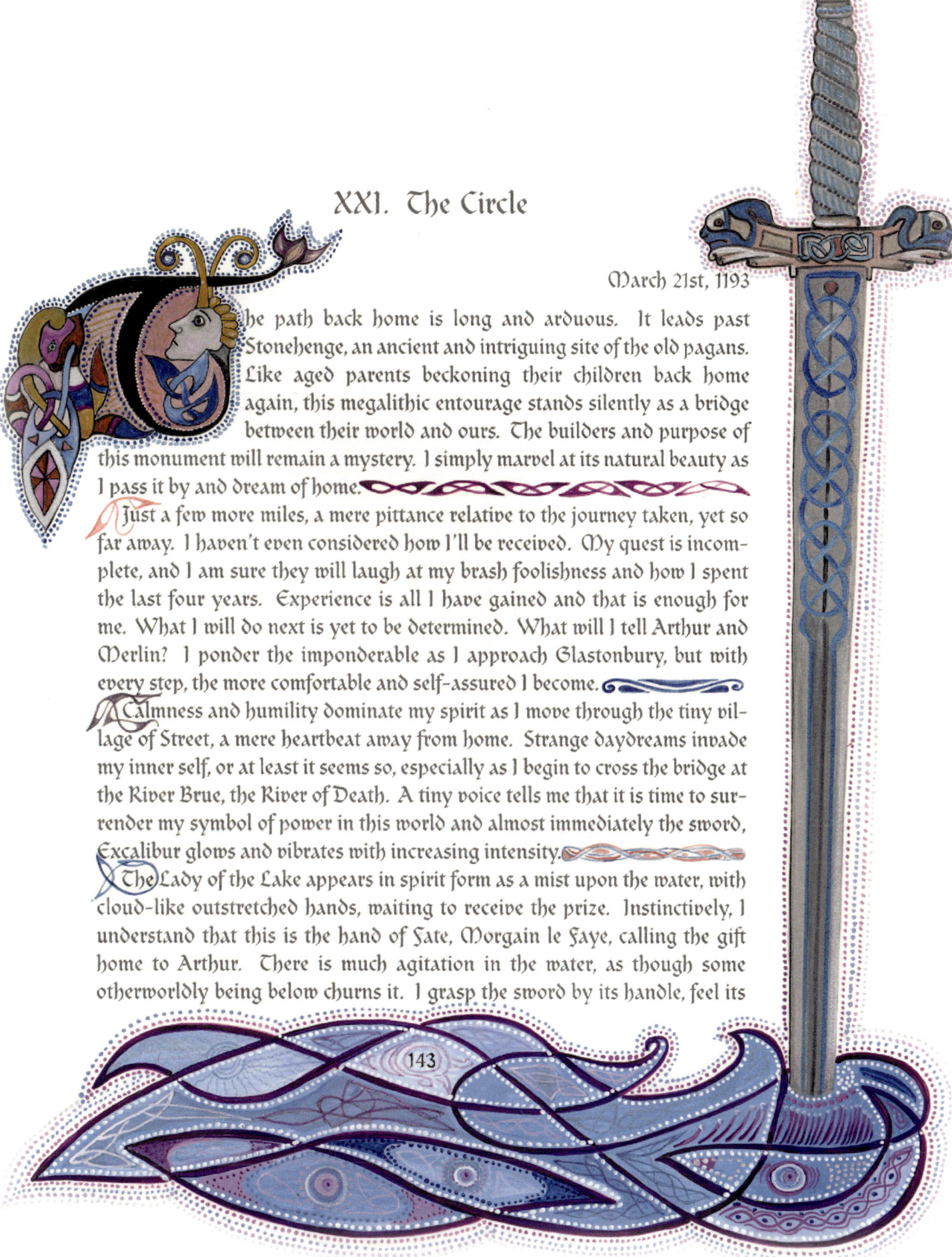

XXI. The Circle

March 21st, 1193

The path back home is long and arduous. It leads past Stonehenge, an ancient and intriguing site of the old pagans. Like aged parents beckoning their children back home again, this megalithic entourage stands silently as a bridge between their world and ours. The builders and purpose of this monument will remain a mystery. I simply marvel at its natural beauty as I pass it by and dream of home.

Just a few more miles, a mere pittance relative to the journey taken, yet so far away. I haven't even considered how I'll be received. My quest is incomplete, and I am sure they will laugh at my brash foolishness and how I spent the last four years. Experience is all I have gained and that is enough for me. What I will do next is yet to be determined. What will I tell Arthur and Merlin? I ponder the imponderable as I approach Glastonbury, but with every step, the more comfortable and self-assured I become.

Calmness and humility dominate my spirit as I move through the tiny village of Street, a mere heartbeat away from home. Strange daydreams invade my inner self, or at least it seems so, especially as I begin to cross the bridge at the River Brue, the River of Death. A tiny voice tells me that it is time to surrender my symbol of power in this world and almost immediately the sword, Excalibur glows and vibrates with increasing intensity.

The Lady of the Lake appears in spirit form as a mist upon the water, with cloud-like outstretched hands, waiting to receive the prize. Instinctively, I understand that this is the hand of Fate, Morgain le Faye, calling the gift home to Arthur. There is much agitation in the water, as though some otherworldly being below churns it. I grasp the sword by its handle, feel its

143

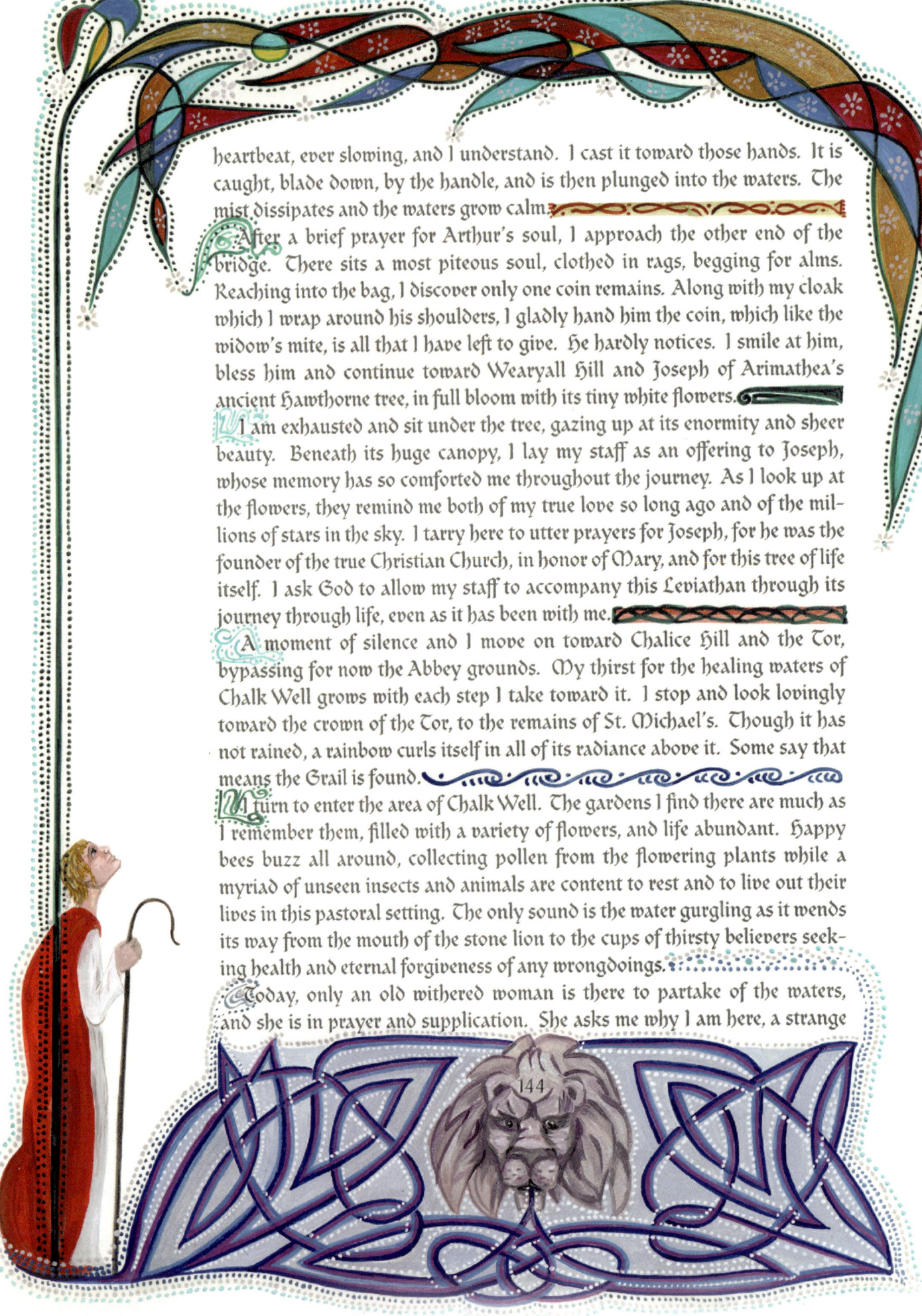

heartbeat, ever slowing, and I understand. I cast it toward those hands. It is caught, blade down, by the handle, and is then plunged into the waters. The mist dissipates and the waters grow calm.

After a brief prayer for Arthur's soul, I approach the other end of the bridge. There sits a most piteous soul, clothed in rags, begging for alms. Reaching into the bag, I discover only one coin remains. Along with my cloak which I wrap around his shoulders, I gladly hand him the coin, which like the widow's mite, is all that I have left to give. He hardly notices. I smile at him, bless him and continue toward Wearyall Hill and Joseph of Arimathea's ancient Hawthorne tree, in full bloom with its tiny white flowers.

I am exhausted and sit under the tree, gazing up at its enormity and sheer beauty. Beneath its huge canopy, I lay my staff as an offering to Joseph, whose memory has so comforted me throughout the journey. As I look up at the flowers, they remind me both of my true love so long ago and of the millions of stars in the sky. I tarry here to utter prayers for Joseph, for he was the founder of the true Christian Church, in honor of Mary, and for this tree of life itself. I ask God to allow my staff to accompany this Leviathan through its journey through life, even as it has been with me.

A moment of silence and I move on toward Chalice Hill and the Tor, bypassing for now the Abbey grounds. My thirst for the healing waters of Chalk Well grows with each step I take toward it. I stop and look lovingly toward the crown of the Tor, to the remains of St. Michael's. Though it has not rained, a rainbow curls itself in all of its radiance above it. Some say that means the Grail is found.

I turn to enter the area of Chalk Well. The gardens I find there are much as I remember them, filled with a variety of flowers, and life abundant. Happy bees buzz all around, collecting pollen from the flowering plants while a myriad of unseen insects and animals are content to rest and to live out their lives in this pastoral setting. The only sound is the water gurgling as it wends its way from the mouth of the stone lion to the cups of thirsty believers seeking health and eternal forgiveness of any wrongdoings.

Today, only an old withered woman is there to partake of the waters, and she is in prayer and supplication. She asks me why I am here, a strange

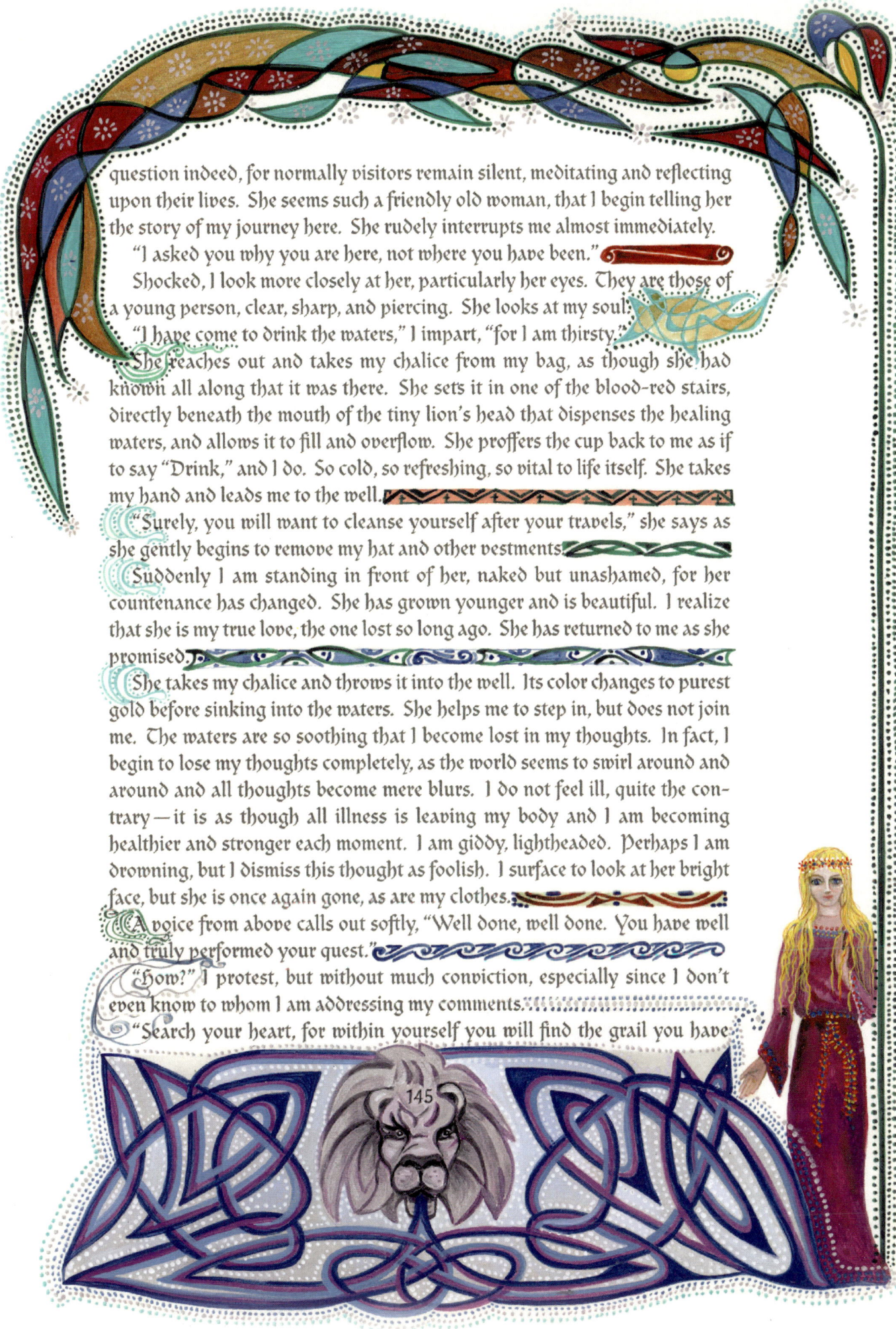

question indeed, for normally visitors remain silent, meditating and reflecting upon their lives. She seems such a friendly old woman, that I begin telling her the story of my journey here. She rudely interrupts me almost immediately.

"I asked you why you are here, not where you have been."

Shocked, I look more closely at her, particularly her eyes. They are those of a young person, clear, sharp, and piercing. She looks at my soul.

"I have come to drink the waters," I impart, "for I am thirsty."

She reaches out and takes my chalice from my bag, as though she had known all along that it was there. She sets it in one of the blood-red stairs, directly beneath the mouth of the tiny lion's head that dispenses the healing waters, and allows it to fill and overflow. She proffers the cup back to me as if to say "Drink," and I do. So cold, so refreshing, so vital to life itself. She takes my hand and leads me to the well.

"Surely, you will want to cleanse yourself after your travels," she says as she gently begins to remove my hat and other vestments.

Suddenly I am standing in front of her, naked but unashamed, for her countenance has changed. She has grown younger and is beautiful. I realize that she is my true love, the one lost so long ago. She has returned to me as she promised.

She takes my chalice and throws it into the well. Its color changes to purest gold before sinking into the waters. She helps me to step in, but does not join me. The waters are so soothing that I become lost in my thoughts. In fact, I begin to lose my thoughts completely, as the world seems to swirl around and around and all thoughts become mere blurs. I do not feel ill, quite the contrary—it is as though all illness is leaving my body and I am becoming healthier and stronger each moment. I am giddy, lightheaded. Perhaps I am drowning, but I dismiss this thought as foolish. I surface to look at her bright face, but she is once again gone, as are my clothes.

A voice from above calls out softly, "Well done, well done. You have well and truly performed your quest."

"How?" I protest, but without much conviction, especially since I don't even know to whom I am addressing my comments.

"Search your heart, for within yourself you will find the grail you have

145

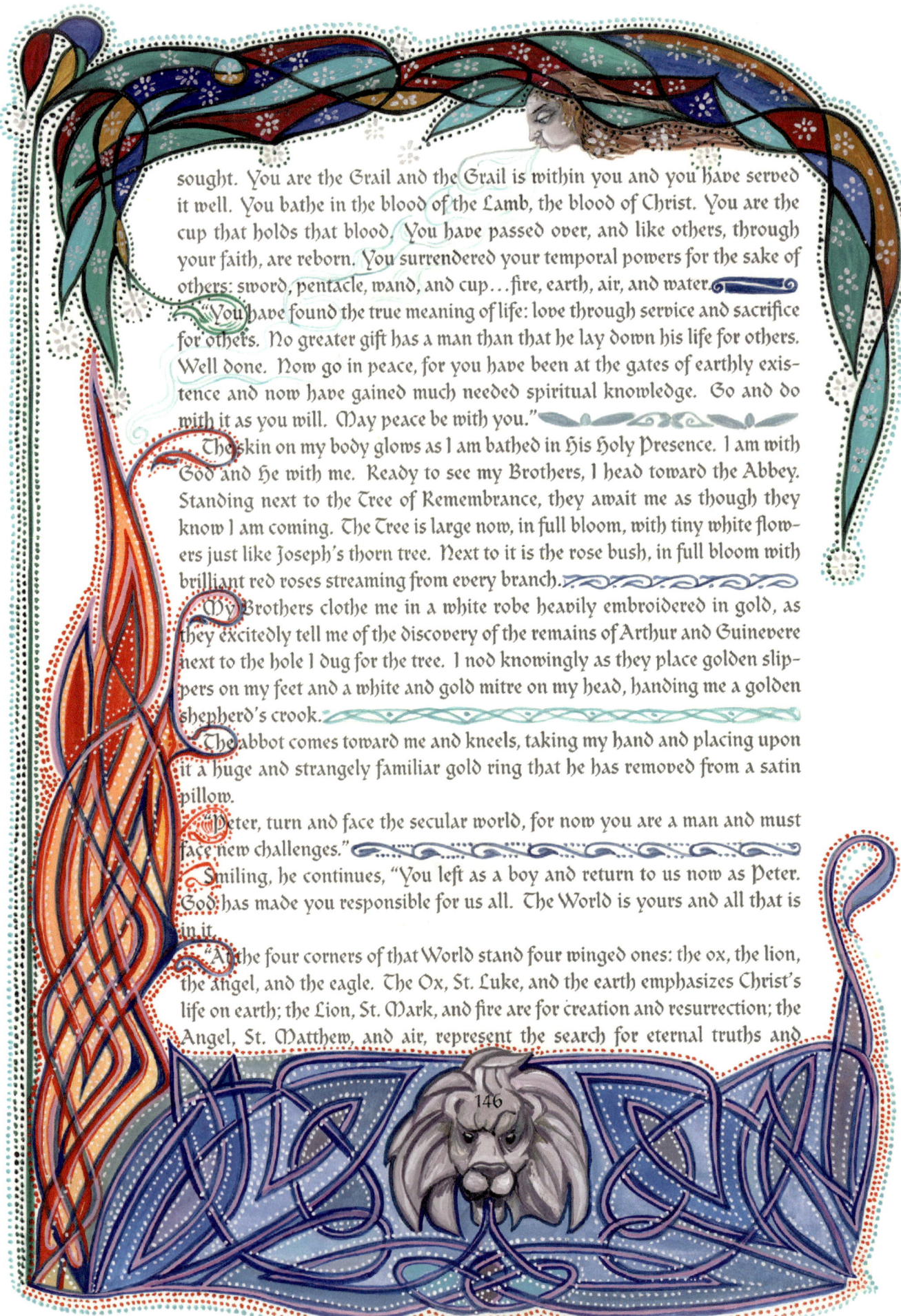

sought. You are the Grail and the Grail is within you and you have served it well. You bathe in the blood of the Lamb, the blood of Christ. You are the cup that holds that blood. You have passed over, and like others, through your faith, are reborn. You surrendered your temporal powers for the sake of others: sword, pentacle, wand, and cup…fire, earth, air, and water.

"You have found the true meaning of life: love through service and sacrifice for others. No greater gift has a man than that he lay down his life for others. Well done. Now go in peace, for you have been at the gates of earthly existence and now have gained much needed spiritual knowledge. Go and do with it as you will. May peace be with you."

The skin on my body glows as I am bathed in His Holy Presence. I am with God and He with me. Ready to see my Brothers, I head toward the Abbey. Standing next to the Tree of Remembrance, they await me as though they know I am coming. The Tree is large now, in full bloom, with tiny white flowers just like Joseph's thorn tree. Next to it is the rose bush, in full bloom with brilliant red roses streaming from every branch.

My Brothers clothe me in a white robe heavily embroidered in gold, as they excitedly tell me of the discovery of the remains of Arthur and Guinevere next to the hole I dug for the tree. I nod knowingly as they place golden slippers on my feet and a white and gold mitre on my head, handing me a golden shepherd's crook.

The abbot comes toward me and kneels, taking my hand and placing upon it a huge and strangely familiar gold ring that he has removed from a satin pillow.

"Peter, turn and face the secular world, for now you are a man and must face new challenges."

Smiling, he continues, "You left as a boy and return to us now as Peter. God has made you responsible for us all. The World is yours and all that is in it.

"At the four corners of that World stand four winged ones: the ox, the lion, the angel, and the eagle. The Ox, St. Luke, and the earth emphasizes Christ's life on earth; the Lion, St. Mark, and fire are for creation and resurrection; the Angel, St. Matthew, and air, represent the search for eternal truths and

146

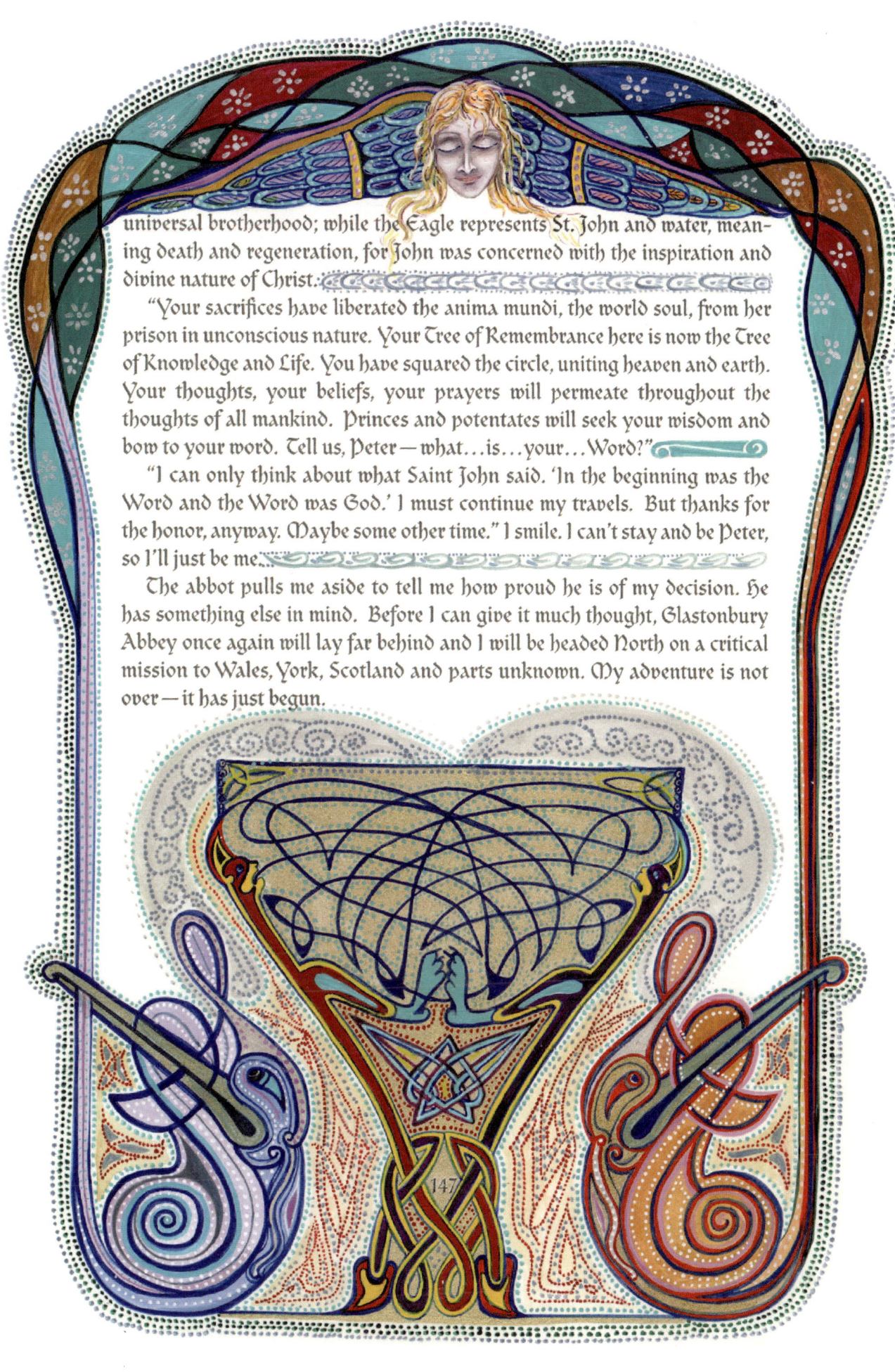

universal brotherhood; while the Eagle represents St. John and water, meaning death and regeneration, for John was concerned with the inspiration and divine nature of Christ.

"Your sacrifices have liberated the anima mundi, the world soul, from her prison in unconscious nature. Your Tree of Remembrance here is now the Tree of Knowledge and Life. You have squared the circle, uniting heaven and earth. Your thoughts, your beliefs, your prayers will permeate throughout the thoughts of all mankind. Princes and potentates will seek your wisdom and bow to your word. Tell us, Peter—what…is…your…Word?"

"I can only think about what Saint John said. 'In the beginning was the Word and the Word was God.' I must continue my travels. But thanks for the honor, anyway. Maybe some other time." I smile. I can't stay and be Peter, so I'll just be me.

The abbot pulls me aside to tell me how proud he is of my decision. He has something else in mind. Before I can give it much thought, Glastonbury Abbey once again will lay far behind and I will be headed North on a critical mission to Wales, York, Scotland and parts unknown. My adventure is not over—it has just begun.

147

Ronod E Smt
Isabel Matelman

15/100